THE LIFE OF THE BUDDHA AND THE EARLY HISTORY OF HIS ORDER

THE LIFE OF THE BUDDHA AND THE EARLY HISTORY OF HIS ORDER:

DERIVED

FROM TIBETAN WORKS IN THE BKAH-HGYUR AND BSTAN-HGYUR

FOLLOWED BY NOTICES ON THE EARLY HISTORY OF TIBET AND KHOTEN

TRANSLATED

W.WOODVILLE ROCKHILL

GYAN

Published by

Gyan Publishing House
5, Ansari Road
Daryaganj, New Delhi-110002
Phone: 011-47034999, 9811692060
E-mail: books@gyanbooks.com

Distribution Network
gyanbooks.com
India, USA, Canada, UK, Australia

ISBN: 978-93-6920-118-1 (HB)

First Published, 1884

2nd Impression 2025

Printed at: Gyan Press, Delhi.

THE LIFE OF THE BUDDHA AND THE EARLY HISTORY OF HIS ORDER

Translated: W.WOODVILLE ROCKHILL

TRÜBNER'S
ORIENTAL SERIES.

THE LIFE OF THE BUDDHA AND THE EARLY HISTORY OF HIS ORDER.

DERIVED FROM

TIBETAN WORKS IN THE BKAH-HGYUR AND BSTAN-HGYUR.

FOLLOWED BY NOTICES ON THE EARLY HISTORY OF TIBET AND KHOTEN.

TRANSLATED BY

W. WOODVILLE ROCKHILL,

SECOND SECRETARY U. S. LEGATION IN CHINA.

LONDON:

TRÜBNER & CO., LUDGATE HILL.

1884.

INTRODUCTION.

Any one who has glanced at the analysis of the Tibetan Bkah-hgyur by Alexander Csoma de Körös, published in the 20th volume of the "Asiatic Researches," must have been struck with the wonderful patience and perseverance of this extraordinary scholar. Some idea of the extent of the researches which are embodied in his analysis of the Dulva, about the tenth part of the whole Bkah-hgyur, may be had when it is known that it occupies more than 4000 leaves of seven lines to the page, each line averaging twenty-two syllables. But notwithstanding all that Csoma did to make known to Europe the vast Buddhist literature of Tibet, his work is hardly more than an index of the Tibetan Tripiṭaka. Moreover, when he wrote it, Buddhist studies were in their infancy, and many important subjects on which the Bkah-hgyur furnishes answers, which, if not always acceptable, are still plausible and interesting, had not been investigated by scholars, and their importance was as yet ignored.

Csoma's premature death prevented him examining as fully as we could have desired the Tibetan Bstan-hgyur, in which may be found many important works which help to elucidate the difficulties which so frequently beset the canonical works in the Bkah-hgyur.

From what has been said we may safely assert that it is not impossible to extend the analysis of the Bkah-hgyur far beyond the limits reached by Csoma. So numerous, however, are the materials which are supplied us, that it is beyond the power of any one scholar to examine them in their entirety, and he must necessarily confine himself to one special subject or branch of research.

In the first part of this work we have endeavoured to give a substantial and connected analysis, and frequently literal translations, of the greater part of the historical or legendary texts contained in the Tibetan Dulva or Vinaya-piṭaka, which is unquestionably the most trustworthy, and probably the oldest portion of the Bkah-hgyur.

By frequent reference to the pages of the original (the East India Office copy of the Bkah-hgyur), we hope we will have facilitated researches in the cumbrous Tibetan volumes, to which no indices are attached.

Some of the passages of this volume have been analysed by Anton Schiefner in his Tibetische Libensbescriebung Çakyamuni (St. Petersburg, 1849), but as the work from which he translated them was composed by a Tibetan lama of the seventeenth century, it could hardly be considered as authoritative, and it has been thought advisable not to omit these documents in their original Tibetan form.

The Tibetan Vinaya (Dulva) is not solely devoted to recording the rules and regulations of the Buddhist order, as is the Pâli work of this name, but it contains jâtakas,[1] avadanas, vyakaranas, sûtras, and udânas, and in that it resembles the Sanskrit Vinaya, which Burnouf tells us presents the same peculiarity. A few of these texts have been introduced in this work, because they appeared of sufficient interest to justify their presence in a volume

[1] The third volume of the Dulva contains 13 jâtakas, and the fourth volume 39, some of which I have not met with in the Pâli jâtaka.

which is intended to give an idea of the Tibetan Vinaya literature.

By comparing the following notes on the life of the Buddha with other works on the same subject, but derived from different sources, it will be seen that two periods of the life of Gautama are narrated by all Buddhist authors in about the same terms (probably because they all drew from the same source their information), the history of his life down to his visit to Kapilavastu in the early part of his ministry, and that of the last year of his life. All the events which occurred between these two periods are with difficulty assigned to any particular year of his life, and we have been obliged to avail ourselves of any incidental remarks in the texts for arranging our narrative in even a semi-chronological order. Thus the oft-recurring phrase that Adjatasatru was king of Magadha when such and such an event took place, suggested the idea of taking the commencement of his reign (five or eight years before the Buddha's death) as a dividing-point in the Buddha's life, and of putting in the same chapter all the texts which are prefaced with this remark.

The histories of the councils of Râjagriha and of Vaisali, contained in the eleventh volume of the Dulva, are here translated for the first time, and they differ in many respects from the versions of these events previously translated from Pâli or Chinese.

The authenticity of the council of Râjagriha has been doubted on insufficient grounds, and, without examining the merits of the case, we cannot help thinking that it was much more rational that a compilation or collation of the utterances of the Master and of the rules of the order should have been made shortly after his death, than that his followers, however united they may have been, should have allowed a century to elapse before fixing in any definite shape the sacred words and ordinances. Moreover, both Pâli and Tibetan works only credit the council of Vaisali with having settled some unimportant questions of discipline, and do not mention any revision of the sacred works performed by this synod.

In the sixth chapter will be found a literal translation of the greater part of a work on the Buddhist schools of the Hinayâna by Bhavya, an Indian Buddhist of great renown. His work is especially interesting, as it differs materially from that of Vasumitra on the same subject, which has been translated by Professor Wassilief. Both of these works, unfortunately, are far from being satisfactory, and though Bhavya often appears to quote Vasumitra, he has not made use (at least in the Tibetan translation) of terms which might enable us to better understand the frequently enigmatical explanations of Vasumitra.

A few words are necessary to explain the presence in a volume of translations from the Tibetan sacred writings of a chapter on the early history of Tibet. What little information we possess of the early history of this secluded country is scattered about in a number of works not always accessible, and frequently unsatisfactory on account of the defective transcription of Tibetan words. It was thought that an abstract of the greater and more reliable part of the works bearing on this question might prove acceptable to those who may desire to have some knowledge on this subject, but who are unwilling to look over all the different documents which treat of it. We have endeavoured to supplement the researches of our predecessors in this field with what new facts we have been able to derive from a somewhat hurried examination of the Tibetan Bstan-hgyur and some other books which have come under our notice.

The extracts incorporated in chapter viii. are quite new, and it is believed that no scholar has heretofore called attention to them. The texts from which they have been taken, with the exception of one, belong to a class of Buddhist works called Vyakarana or Prophecies. In them the Buddha predicts to his disciples the events which will occur in days to come in such a country or to such an individual. In this case these Predictions are all corroborated by the statements of the Li-yul-lo-rgyus-pa or Annals of Li-yul, the most important of the works on this subject which I have met with.

This last-named work seems to have been compiled from documents unknown to Northern Buddhist writers in general, and from the particular form in which certain proper names have been transcribed (such as *Yâço* instead of *Yâças* or *Yasheska,* which is always met with in Northern texts), we think its author had access to some Southern documents on the early history of Buddhism. This supposition is still more strengthened by the fact that this work does not confound the two Açokas, as do all Northern Buddhist ones, but gives about the same date for his reign as the Dipawansa and Mahâwansa. Still it is strange, if it was inspired from these Pâli documents, that it does not give exactly the same dates as they do. These extracts are interesting, moreover, in that they show with what care and precision the great Chinese traveller Hiuen Thsang recorded the traditions of the different countries he visited.

My most sincere thanks are due to Dr. Ernst Leumann and to Mr. Bunyiu Nanjio for the notes they have kindly furnished me, and which are reproduced in the

Appendix. Dr. Leumann's translation from the Bhagavatī will prove of great assistance in elucidating the very obscure passage of the Samana-phala Sûtra relative to Gosala's theories, and Mr. Bunyiu Nanjio's parallel translations of two Chinese versions of the Samana-phala Sûtra tend to prove the existence at an early date of several distinct versions of this very interesting sûtra.

One of the most embarrassing parts of reading Tibetan Buddhist works is the habit of those who did these works into Tibetan of translating all the proper names which were susceptible of being translated. It is hoped that the special index of Tibetan words with their Sanskrit equivalents at the end of this volume will prove of assistance to those who may wish to study Tibetan Buddhism in the original works.

Throughout this volume no attempt has been made to criticise the texts which have been studied; they are only intended as materials for those who hereafter may undertake to write a history of the Buddha founded on the comparative study of works extant in the different countries in which his doctrines flourished; and if our labours facilitate this, we will feel fully compensated for all our pains.

LAUSANNE, *June* 6, 1884.

CONTENTS.

THE LIFE OF THE BUDDHA.

CHAPTER I.

HISTORY OF THE WORLD FROM THE TIME OF ITS RENOVATION TO THE REIGN OF ÇUDDHODANA, FATHER OF THE BUDDHA.

THE following history of the world's renovation and of the origin of castes is taken from the fifth volume of the 'Dulva, fol. 155–166. It also occurs in the third volume of the same work, fol. 421–430, but several interesting passages are there omitted, although the rest of the text is exactly the same as that of vol. v. In the third volume it is Maudgalyayana who, at the Buddha's request, tells to the Çakyas the story of the world's regeneration, and of the ancient peoples who inhabited it. The Buddha feared that if he himself told the story the tirthikas would accuse him of unduly extolling his own clan (D. iii. 420ᵇ). In the fifth volume the story is told to the bhikshus by the Buddha, to teach them how sin first made its appearance in the world.

"At the time when the world was destroyed, many of its inhabitants were born in the region of the Â'bhâsvara devas, and there they had ethereal bodies, free from every impurity; their faculties were unimpaired, they were perfect in all their principal and secondary parts, of goodly appearance and of a pleasing colour. Light proceeded from their persons; they moved through space and fed on joy, and they lived in this state to great ages for a long period.

In the meanwhile this great earth was mingled up with the waters and with the mighty deep. Then on the face of the great earth, of the water and of the ocean that were mingled together, there blew a wind,[1] which solidified and concentrated the rich surface (lit. the cream); as when the wind blowing over the surface of boiled milk which is cooling, solidifies and concentrates the cream, so likewise did this wind blowing over the surface of the earth, the water and the ocean which were mixed together, solidify and coagulate it.

This rime (lit. essence of the earth, *prithivîrasa*) was of exquisite colour, of delicious taste, of delightful (f. 156[b]) fragrance, in colour like unto butter, its taste like that of uncooked honey.

At this period when the world was formed, some of the beings in the region of the Âbhâsvara devas had accomplished their allotted time, the merit of their good works being exhausted; so they departed that life and became men, but with attributes similar to those they previously had.[2]

At that period there was neither sun nor moon in the world; there were no stars in the world, neither was there night or day, minutes, seconds, or fractions of seconds; there were no months, half months, no periods of time, no years: neither were there males or females; there were only animated beings.

Then it happened that a being of an inquisitive nature tasted the rime with the tip of his finger, and thus he conceived a liking (f. 157[a]) for it, and he commenced eating pieces of it as food.[3]

Other beings saw this being tasting the rime [so they

[1] Cf. Gen. i. 2, and Ps. xxxiii. 6, "And the Spirit of God moved upon the face of the water." See B. H. Hodgson, Essays, i. p. 43, and p. 55, note 3.

[2] The first beings were devas, in the Vedic sense of "bright ones."

[3] In Scandinavian mythology the renovated human race is fed on dew. So likewise the cow Audhumbla lived on salt that came from the rime produced by the ice-cold streams. See Anderson, Norse Mythol., p. 194.

followed his example], and commenced eating pieces of it as food.

From these beings eating the rime as food their bodies became coarse and gross; they lost their brilliancy and their goodly appearance, and darkness was upon the face of the earth.

For these reasons the sun and moon were created; stars also (f. 157b) came into existence, as did night and day, minutes, seconds, fractions of seconds, months and half months, divisions of time and years. The beings feeding on this rime lived to great ages for a long space of time.

The complexion of those who ate but little of this food was clear, whereas that of those who ate much of it was dark. Then those whose complexion was clear said to the others, "Why, I have a fine complexion, whereas you are dark!" and thus were established distinctions. They whose complexion was clear were proud of it, and became sinful and iniquitous, and then the rime vanished.

(f. 158a.) When the rime had vanished from these beings, there appeared a fatty substance (*prithivîparvataka*) of exquisite colour and savour, of delicious fragrance, in colour as a dongka flower, in flavour like uncooked honey; and they took this as their food, and they lived to great ages for a long while.

[This fatty substance vanished after a while, for the same reason as had brought about the disappearance of the rime.]

When the fatty substance had vanished from mankind, there appeared bunches of reeds (*vanalatâ*) of exquisite colour and savour, of delicious fragrance, in colour like a kadambuka flower (f. 159a), in flavour like uncooked honey. Then they took this as their food, and on it they lived to great ages for a long while.

[This food also vanished after a while, for the same reasons as above.]

(f. 159b.) When the bunches of reeds had vanished from mankind, there appeared a spontaneously growing rice, not coarse, without pellicule, clean, four fingers in length. There was never any lack of it; for if it was cut down in the evening, it was grown up again in the morning; if it was cut down in the morning, it was grown ere evening; what was cut down grew up afresh, so that it was not missed.

Then they took this as their food, and on it they lived to great ages for a long time.

From eating this rice their different organs were developed; some had those of males and others those of females. Then they saw each other, and conceived love for each other, and, burning with lust, they came to commit fornication.

Other beings (f. 160[a]) saw what they were doing, so they threw at them earth, stones, gravel, pebbles, and potsherds, saying unto them, "Thou doest wrongly! thou doest that which is wrong!" But those who had acted wrongly, who had done that which was wrong, exclaimed, "Why do you thus insult us?"

As nowadays when a man takes unto himself a wife, they sprinkle her over with dust, perfumes, flowers, and parched rice, with cries of "Good luck, sister!" so those beings, seeing the wickedness of those other beings, sprinkled them with earth, threw at them stones and gravel, pebbles and potsherds, crying after that, "Thou doest wrongly! thou doest that which is not right!" But they who had done wrong, who had done that which was wrong, exclaimed, "Why do you thus insult us?"

And thus it was that what was formerly considered unlawful has become lawful nowadays; what was not tolerated in former times has become tolerated nowadays; what was looked down (f. 160[b]) on in former days has become praiseworthy now.

Now, when they had done wrong one, two, three, even unto seven days, these sinful beings were so possessed by the ways of wickedness that they commenced building houses. "Here," they said, "we may do what is not allowed;" and from this expression originated the word "house."[1]

Now this is the first appearance in the world of divisions by houses, and this (division) is lawful or not lawful according to the king's decision, and he is the lord of the law.

If these beings wanted rice to eat in the evening or in the morning, they would go and get what was requisite; but it happened that one being who was of an indolent disposition took at one time enough rice for evening and morning. Now another being said to him, "Come, let us go for rice." Then he answered him, "Look after your own rice; I have taken enough at one time to last me morning and evening" (f. 161[a]). Then the other thought, "Good, capital! I will take enough rice for two, three, seven days;" and he did accordingly.

Then it happened that some one said to this person, "Come, let us go for rice;" but he answered him, "Look after your own rice; I have taken enough at one time to last me two, three, seven days."

"Good, capital!" thought the other, "I will take enough rice for a fortnight, for a month;" and he did accordingly.

And because these beings took to laying up provisions of this spontaneously growing rice, it became coarse; a husk enveloped the grain, and when it had been cut down it grew not up again, but remained as it had been left.

Then these beings (f. 161[b]) assembled together in sorrow, grief, and lamentation, and said, "Sirs, formerly we had ethereal bodies, free from every impurity, with faculties unimpaired, &c., &c. . . . .[2] Let us now draw lines of demarcation and establish boundaries between each one's

[1] *Khyim* is probably derived from *hyims-pa*, "to encircle," in accordance with this supposition, which derives the Sanskrit *griha*, "house," from *grah*, "to embrace, to contain." This leads us to suppose that the word *khyim*, like a very large class of other words in Tibetan, was not used with this signification until after the introduction of Buddhism into Tibet.

[2] Here follows a recapitulation of all the preceding history.

property." So they drew lines of demarcation and set up bounds—"This is thine—this is mine" (they said).

Now, this is the first appearance in the world of a system of boundary lines, and this (boundary) is right or not right according to the king's decision, and he is the lord of the law.

After this it happened that one person took another's rice without his consent, as if it was his own, and when other persons saw him, they said to him, "Why do you take the rice of another without his consent, as if it was your own? You must not do this again." But he went a second and a third time, and took the rice of another without his consent, as if it was his own. When the other persons saw this (f. 163[b]) they said to him, "Why do you thus take the rice of another without his consent, as though it was your own?" So they laid hold of him and led him into their midst.

"Sirs," they said, "this person has been guilty of taking the rice of another without his consent, as though it was his own." Then they said unto him, "Why have you taken the rice of another without his consent, as though it was your own? Go, and do wrong no more." But he who had stolen said to them, "Sirs, I have been badly treated in that I have been laid hold of by these persons on account of some rice and brought into this assembly."

Then they said to those who had brought him thither, and who had spoken about the rice, "Why did you bring this man here to whom you had spoken about the rice? In bringing him here into our midst you have done him a wrong; go, and do not so again" (f. 164[a]). Then they thought, "Let us, in view of what has just happened, assemble together, and choose from out our midst those who are the finest-looking, the largest, the handsomest, the strongest, and let us make them lords over our fields, and they shall punish those of us who do what is punishable, and they shall recompense those of us who do what is praiseworthy, and from the produce of our fields and of the fruits we gather we will give them a portion."

So they gathered together [and did as they had decided upon], and they made him lord over their fields with these words: "Henceforth thou shalt punish those of us who deserve punishment, and thou shalt recompense those of us who deserve recompense, and we will give thee a portion of the produce of our fields (f. 164ᵇ) and of the fruits we gather."

From his receiving the homages of many he was called "Honoured by many, or Mahâsammata;" and as he was lord over the fields and kept them from harm, he received the name of "Protector of the fields," or Kshatriya; and as he was a righteous man and wise, and one who brought happiness to mankind with the law, he was called "King," or Râjâ.

Some beings who were afflicted with diseases, ulcerations, pains, and misery, left their villages for the wilds; they made themselves huts with boughs and leaves, and they dwelt therein. Each evening when they (f. 165ᵇ) wanted food, they would go into the villages to gather alms, and in the morning when they required food they would do likewise; and the people gave to them with willing hearts, for they thought, "These learned men are afflicted by disease, ulcerations [the rest as above down to], morning and evening they come into the village to beg alms."

Then it happened that some persons not having been able to find perfection in meditation and perfect seclusion, went to a certain place, where they made huts with boughs and leaves. "Here," they said, "we will compose mantras, we will compile the vedas." And they did as they had said.

Now some others of their number not having been able to (f. 165ᵇ) find perfection in either meditation and perfect seclusion, or in composing mantras and in compiling the vedas, left the wilds and went back to their villages.

"Here," they said, "we will distribute alms and do good works. All those who come and sit down at our board shall have all they may wish, either food or drink." And so they gave alms [and did as they had said they would do].

Those who lived "away" from villages were called "detached minds," or Brahmans, and from the fact that (some) were not given to contemplation, but did read, they were called "readers" or Pâthaka. Those who lived away from the forests and in villages were called "Villagers."

Some beings (f. 166[a]) applying themselves to different handicrafts and occupations in their homes, made "different kinds" of things (which they did sell), and they were therefore called "merchants," or Vaisyas.[1]

Thus were created in the world these three castes. There was also a fourth one created, that of the Çramaṇas.

Members of kshatriya families cut off their hair and beard, and putting on saffron-coloured gowns, they left their homes for a homeless state, and completely retired from the world (*pravradjita*); and to them the kshatriya spoke with respect; they arose in their presence and bowed reverentially to them. The brahmans and vaisyas [treated them with like respect].

Members of (f. 166[b]) brahman and vaisya families cut off their hair and beard, and putting on saffron-coloured gowns, they left their homes for a homeless state, and completely retired from the world; and to them the kshatriyas spoke with respect; they arose in their presence and bowed reverentially to them. The brahmans and vaisyas [treated them with like respect].

Then it was that when a person first took rice from another, as if it had been his own, by this transgression stealing first showed itself in the world, in which there had been no trace of it until then. By this act, by

[1] *Rjeu-rigs.* Both Csoma and Jaschke derive this word from *rje-bo*, "lord," whereas it is evidently derived from *rje-ba*, "to barter." In our text, vaisya is derived from *vis*, *vi* = *so-so*, "different (kinds of things").

stealing, sin now exists in the world, in which there was no trace of it in the first place.

The history of the succeeding events is taken from the third volume of the Dulva, fol. 420[a] *et seq.*

King Mahâsammata's son was Rokha (*Od mdjes*), whose son was Kalyana (*Dge-ba*), whose son was Varakalyana (*Dge-mtchog*), whose son was Utposhadha (*Gso-sbyong-hphags*) (f. 430[a]). From King Utposhadha's head was born a son whose name was Mandhatar (*Nga-las nu*) (f. 430[b]). These six kings are called the six incommensurables, for exceeding long were their lives.

From a tumour on King Mandhatar's right shoulder (?) was born a son whose name was Kâru (*Mdjes-pa*), and great were his magical powers. He ruled over the four continents. From his left shoulder was born a son whose name was Upakâru (*Nye-mdjes-pa*), and he ruled over three continents (f. 431).

From a fleshy excrescence on his left foot was born a son whose name was Kârumant (*Mdjes-ldan*). He ruled over two continents (f. 431[b]).

From this one's right foot was born a son whose name was Upakârumant (*Nye-mdjes-ldan*), and he ruled over one continent.

[Then followed a long succession of kings, whose descendants ruled in Varaṇasi (f. 432[b]), in Kamapala (? do.), in Hastipura, in Takshaçila, in Kanyakubdja, &c.; but as they are not immediately connected with the Çakyas, it is useless to lose time with them.]

(F. 433[b]) Mahesvarasena (*Dbang-phyug tchen-poi sde*) of Varaṇasi had many descendants, who reigned in Kuçinagara and also in Potala (*Gru-hdjin*); one of these was King Karnika (*Rna-ba-chan*), who had two sons, Gautama and Baradvadja (f. 435[a]); the former was a virtuous man, whereas the latter was wicked. Gautama, though the elder, begged his father to allow him to become a recluse, for he dreaded the responsibility of a sovereign ruler. Having obtained the necessary consent, he became the disciple of a rishi called Krichnavarna (*Mdog-nag*). After a while, King Karnika died, and Baradvadja became king (f. 436^{a}).

Following his master's advice, Gautama built a hut within the precincts of Potala, and there he dwelt. It happened once that a courtesan of Potala called Bhadrâ was killed by her crafty lover near the recluse's hut[1] (f. 437^{a}), into which the murderer threw his bloody sword.

The people of the town finding the murdered woman and the sword in the hermit's hut, thought him the murderer, and he was condemned to death. He was marched through the city with a wreath of karapira (*sic*) flowers around his neck and dressed in rags; then they took him outside the southern gate and impaled him (f. 437^{b}).

While yet alive, his master, the rishi Krichnavarna saw him, and questioned him as to his guilt. "If I am innocent," Gautama replied, "may you from black become golden-coloured!" and straightway the rishi became golden-coloured, and was from that time known as Kanakavarna (? *Gser-gyi-mdog*). Gautama also told the rishi that he was greatly worried at the thought that the throne of Potala would become vacant, for his brother had no children (f. 438^{b}); so the rishi caused a great rain to fall on Gautama, and a mighty wind to arise which soothed his pains and revived his senses, and two drops of semen mingled with blood fell from him.

After a little while these two drops became eggs, and the heat of the rising sun caused them to open, and from out them came two children, who went into a sugar-cane plantation near by. The heat of the sun went on increasing, so that the rishi Gautama dried up and died.

Now the rishi Kanakavarna perceived that these children must be Gautama's, so he took them home with

[1] See Dulva, iii. f. 1 *et seq.*

him and provided for them. Having been born as the sun arose, and having been brought forth by its rays, they were called "of the sun family" or Suryavansa. They were, moreover, called Gautama, being the children of Gautama, and as they were "born from his loins," they were, in the third place, called Angirasas (*Yan-lag skyes*). Having been found in a "sugar-cane plantation," they were called Ikshvaku (*Bu-ram shing-pa*) (f. 439).

Baradvadja died without issue, and the ministers consulted the rishi to know if Gautama had left children (f. 439[b]). He told them the strange story, and they took the children and made the elder one king. He died, however, without issue, and the younger became king under the name of Ikshvaku. One hundred of his descendants reigned in Potala, the last of which was Ikshvaku Virudhaka (*Hphags-skyes-po*) (f. 440).

He had four sons, Ulkâmukha (*Skar-mdah gdong*), Karakarna (*Lag rna*), Hastinâjaka (*Glang-po tche hdul*), and Nûpura (*Rkang-gdub-chan*). He married, however, a second time, on condition that if his wife bore a son, he should be king.

After a while she had a son whose name was Râjyananda (?) (*Rgyal-srid dgah*)[1] (f. 441[b]).

When this last child had grown up, King Virudhaka, on the representation of his wife's father, was obliged to declare his youngest son his successor and to exile his four other sons.

The princes set out, accompanied by their sisters and a great many people. They travelled toward the Himalaya mountains, and coming to the hermitage of the rishi Kapila, on the bank of the Bhagirathi (*Skal-ldan shing rta*), they built huts of leaves, and fed on the produce of their hunting (f. 443).

[1] Spence Hardy, Man. of Budh., p. 133, calls this prince Janta, so also Beal, Romantic Legend, p. 20. Cf. Bigandet, Leg. of the Burmese Buddha, 3d edition, p. 11. Cf. the first part of the story of Mahaushada and Visakha in Schiefner's Tib. Tales, p. 128, where mention is made of a prince called Râjyâbhinanda. See also Turnour's Mahawanso, p. xxxv.

Following the rishi's advice, they took as their wives sisters who were not of the same mother as themselves, and in this way they had many children.[1]

The rishi showed them where to build a town, and he marked it out with golden sand mixed with water, and they built it according to his directions (f. 444). The rishi Kapila having given the soil (*vastu*) of the place, they called the town "the soil of Kapila" or Kapilavastu.

When they had become very numerous, a deva pointed out another spot, on which they built a town, which they called "shown by a deva" or Devadaha.[2]

They made a law in a general assembly of the clan that they should only marry one wife, and that she must be of their own clan (f. 444[b]).

King Virudhaka thought one day of his comely sons, so he asked his courtiers what had become of them; then they told him their adventures. "The daring young men! the daring young men!" he exclaimed; and from this they became known as "Çakyas" (f. 444[b]).

King Virudhaka died, and his youngest son succeeded him (f. 445); but dying without issue, Ulkâmukha became king of Potala; but he also left no issue, and was succeeded by Karakarna, and he by Hastinâjaka. Neither of these left children, so Nûpura became king.

His son was Vasishta (*Gnas-hjog*), and his successors, 55,000 in number, reigned in Kapilavastu. The last of these was Dhanvadurga (? *Gdju-brtan*), who had two sons,

[1] All this legend of Ikshvaku Virudhaka's children is to be found also in Dulva xi. fol. 292[b] *et seq.*, although abridged.

[2] This is the town known in the Southern tradition as Koli. Beal, Romantic Legend, p. 23, calls it Devadaho, and Foucaux, Rgya-tcher rol-pa, p. 83, "Dêvadarcita?" See Rhys Davids, Buddhism, p. 52, where Devadaha occurs as the name of the Raja of Koli, father of Suprabuddha. Also Spence Hardy, *loc. cit.*, p. 140. Bigandet, *op. cit.*, p. 12, gives a different account; he calls the town Kaulya. But p. 13, he speaks also of the town of Dewaha near a lake "somewhat distant from the city" (of Kapilavastu). See also Bigandet's note, p. 34, and Rhys Davids, Buddh. Birth Stories, p. 65, where the town is also called Devadaha.

Sinhahanu (*Seng-ge hgram*) and Sinhanada (*Seng-gei sgra*) (f. 445[a]). Sinhahanu had four sons, Çuddhodana (*Zas-gtsang*), Çuklodana (*Zas-dkar*), Dronodana (*Bre-bo zas*), and Amritodana (*Ts'ad-med zas*). He had also four daughters, Çuddhâ (*Gtsang-ma*), Çuklâ (*Dkar-mo*), Dronâ (*Bre-bo-ma*), and Amritâ (*Ts'ad-med ma*).

Çuddhodana had two sons, "the Blessed One" and the ayuchmat Nanda[1] (*Dgah-bo*).

Çuklodana had two sons, the ayuchmat Djina (? *Rgyal*) and the Çakyarâjâ Bhadra (or Bhallika, *Bzang-ldan*).

Dronodana had two sons, Mahânâman (*Ming-tchen*) and the ayuchmat Aniruddha (*Ma-hgags-pa*).

Amritodana had two sons, the ayuchmat Ananda (*Kun-dgah-bo*) and Devadatta[2] (*Lhas-sbyin*).

Çuddhâ's son was Suprabuddha (or Suprabodha, *Legs-par rab-sad*).

Çuklâ's son (or daughter) was Mallika (*Phreng-ba-chan*).

Dronâ's son was Sulabha (? *Bzang-len*).

Amritâ's son was Kalyanavardana[3] (? *Dge-hphel*).

The Blessed One's son was Râhula (*Sgra-gchan zin*) (f. 445[b]).

[1] He is also called Sundarananda or "Nanda the fair" (*Mdjes dgah-bo*). See Foucaux, Rgya-tcher rol-pa, translation, p. 137; according to Fausböll, Dhammapada, p. 313, and Rhys Davids, Buddhism, p. 52, there were three sons of Çuddhodana, two by Mâyâ (or Prajâpatî), Nanda and Rûpanandâ and Siddhârtha. Rûpanandâ was the same as Sundarananda, I think, and these names are most likely different ones for Nanda, for he is the only one by this name (at least among the Çakya princes), who is mentioned in the texts. Cf. Beal, *loc. cit.*, p. 64.

[2] According to Spence Hardy, Manual, p. 326, Devadatta was son of Suprabuddha, his mother being a sister of Çuddhodana; Amrita according to Rhys Davids, *loc. cit.*, p. 52. The similarity of the two names has occasioned the confusion. Huen Thsang, B. vi. p. 301, says that he was son of Dronodana.

[3] According to Beal, *loc. cit.*, p. 64, Amritachittra's (or Amrita's) son was Tishya, which would be *Od-ldan* or *Skar-rgyal* in Tibetan.

CHAPTER II.

FROM THE REIGN OF ÇUDDHODANA UNTIL THE COMMENCEMENT OF THE BUDDHA'S MINISTRY.

(Dulva iii. f. 446[a].) DURING King Sinhahanu's reign the country of Kapilavastu enjoyed peace and prosperity, as did also the country of Devadaha, over which Suprabuddha was reigning. This latter married a woman by the name of Lumbini,[1] who was exceedingly fair; and in her company he was in the habit of visiting a beautiful grove near the city, which belonged to a wealthy citizen.

The queen took such a fancy to the place, that she begged the king to give it to her. He told her he was not able to do so; but he had her one made more beautiful still, and it was called Lumbini's grove (f. 447[a]).

After a while Lumbini brought forth a child of such extraordinary and supernatural beauty that they called her Mâyâ.[2] Some time after a second daughter was born, and she they called Mahâmâyâ. Suprabuddha offered the hands of his daughters to Sinhahanu for his son Çuddhodana (f. 448[a]). He took Mahâmâyâ, for it had been predicted that she would bear a son with all the characteristics

[1] Rhys Davids, Buddh., p. 52, says that Suprabuddha's wife was Amritâ, and Beal, Romantic Legend, p. 42, note, has "the Lumbini garden was so called after the name of the wife of the chief minister of Suprabuddha." See also Bigandet, *op. cit.*, p. 13.

[2] Mâyâ is better known as Mahâpradjapati Gautami, the foster-mother of the Buddha, the mother of Nanda, and the head of the order of female mendicants. She is called by this name, Dulva iii. f. 368, note, and wherever she is mentioned, after she had become a bhikshuni, as in Dulva x. and xi. It is remarkable that our text does not mention Mahâmâyâ's death seven days after the birth of Siddhartha. According to Bigandet, *loc. cit.*, p. 14 and 27, the Buddha's mother was called Mâyâ, and her sister Pradjapati.

of a chakravartin monarch; but he was obliged, for the time being, to refuse the elder sister, on account of the çakya law allowing a man only one wife.

At that time the hillmen of the Paṇḍava tribe (*Skya-bseng-kyi-bu*) were raiding the Çakya country (f. 449[a]), and the people begged the king to send his son Çuddhodana to subdue them. The king consented, and the young prince vanquished them. Sinhahanu requested that, as a recompense, they would allow his son to have two wives. The people allowed him this privilege, and Çuddhodana married Mâyâ.

After a while Sinhahanu died, and Çuddhodana reigned in his stead; and he knew Mahâmâyâ his wife; but she bore him no children (f. 449[b]).

Now the future Buddha was in the Tushita heaven, and knowing that his time had come, he made the five preliminary examinations—1° of the proper family (in which to be born), 2° of the country, 3° of the time, 4° of the race, 5° of the woman; and having decided that Mahâmâyâ was the right mother, in the midnight watch he entered her womb under the appearance of an elephant[1] (f. 452[a]). Then the queen had four dreams. (1°) She saw a six-tusked white elephant enter her womb; (2°) she moved in space above; (3°) she ascended a great rocky mountain; (4°) a great multitude bowed down to her.

The soothsayers predicted that she would bring forth a son with the thirty-two signs of the great man. "If he stays at home, he will become a universal monarch; but if he shaves his hair and beard, and, putting on an orange-coloured robe, leaves his home for a homeless state and renounces the world, he will become a Tathâgata, arhat, a perfectly enlightened Buddha."

While visiting the Lumbini garden (f. 457[b]) the pains

[1] The dream of the queen has evidently occasioned the legend of the Bodhisattva's incarnation under the form of an elephant. Cf. on this point and on the queen's dreams Spence Hardy, Manual, p. 144. The Lalita Vistara, p. 63, does not agree with the Southern version as well as our text. See also Bigandet, p. 28, and Rhys Davids, Buddh. Birth Stories, p. 63.

of childbirth came upon her, and she seized hold of a wide-spreading açoka tree. Then Çataketu (Indra) caused a violent rain to fall and a wind to blow, which dispersed all the crowd (of her attendants). Assuming the appearance of an old woman, he went to receive the new-born child in his lap.

The Bodhisattva, however, ordered him back, and then took seven steps in the direction of each of the cardinal points.

Looking to the east he said, "I will reach the highest nirvana."

To the south, "I will be the first of all creatures."

To the west, "This will be my last birth."

To the north, "I will cross the ocean of existence!"[1] (f. 458).

In accordance with what happens at the birth of every Buddha, there fell on his head a stream of cold water and one of warm, which washed him, and at the spot where he had been born there appeared a spring in which his mother bathed.

At the same time as the Buddha was born a son was born to Bing Aranemi Brahmadatta of Çravasti; from the whole country being illuminated at the time of his birth he was called Prasenadjit[2] (f. 458[b]).

In Râjâgriha, King Mahâpadma had a son born to him, who, being the son of (queen) Bimbî, and being also brilliant as the rising sun of the world, was called Bimbisara.[3]

The king of Kauçâmbi, Çatanika (*Dmag-brgya-ba*), had a son born to him at the same time, and as the world was

[1] Cf. the Lalita Vistara, chap. vii. p. 89, where he takes seven steps in the direction of the east, and seven toward the west. Also Bigandet, p. 37; and Rhys Davids, *op cit.*, p. 67; Huen Thsang, B. vi. p. 323; and Fah Hian (Beal's trans.), p. 85 *et seq.*

[2] Cf. Dulva xi. f. 99[a].

[3] He received the surname of "the expert," Çrênika or Çrênya, on account of his adroitness in all arts. See Dulva i. f. 5. It is also said that he was called Vimbasâra, because at his birth the world was lit up as when the disk (*vimba*) of the sun appears. See Foucaux, Lal. Vist., p. 229, note 2; and Dulva xi. f. 99.

illuminated at his birth as with the sun, he was called Udayana.[1]

At Udjayani there was born a son to King Anantanemi (*Mu-khyud mthah-yas*), and from the fact that the world was illuminated as if by a lamp at the time of his birth, he was called Pradyota (*Rab-snang*)[2] (f. 459[a]).

On the same day as that on which the future Buddha was born many blessings of different kinds were granted his father, so the child was called Sarvârthasiddha (All fulfilled, *Thams-chad-grub-pa*) (f. 460[a]).

It was the habit of the Çakyas to make all new-born children bow down at the feet of a statue of the yaksha Çakyavardana (*Çâkya-hphel* or *spel*); so the king took the young child to the temple, but the yaksha bowed down at his feet[3] (f. 460[b]).

On the way to the temple every one was struck with the infant's bold appearance, so he received the second name of "The mighty one of the Çakyas or Çakyamuni;" and when the king saw the yaksha bow at the child's feet he exclaimed, "He is the god of gods!" and the child was therefore called Devatideva[4] (f. 461[a]).

Now at that time there lived on the Sarvadhâra (*Kun-*

[1] In the texts of the Bkah-hygur where his name occurs he is called Udayana, Râjâ of Vadsala. See Mdo xvii. f. 339, and Dulva xi. f. 99.

[2] He was afterwards surnamed "the cruel" Tchaṇḍa. The instructive legends concerning him given in Dulva xi. have been translated by Schiefner in his "Mahâkâtyâyana und König Tshaṇḍa-Pradjota," St. Petersburg, 1875, in 4to. As the St. Petersburg edition of the Bkah-hgyur differs from that of Paris and London (India Office), the following concordance may be of use to those who may desire to consult the original of these legends. In the Paris and London edition, Schiefner's ch. i. commences on fol. 99 of Dulva xi.; ch. ii., fol. 106; ch. iii., fol. 114; ch. iv., fol. 118; ch. v., fol. 128; ch. vi., fol. 137; ch. vii., fol. 139; ch. viii., fol. 147; ch. ix., fol. 151; ch. x., fol. 154; ch. xi., fol. 156; ch. xii., fol. 158; ch. xiii., fol. 162; ch. xiv., fol. 163; ch. xv., fol. 165; ch. xvi., fol. 173; ch. xvii., fol. 178; ch. xviii., fol. 183; ch. xix. fol. 185; ch. xx., fol. 194–210. See, for another explanation of the name, Rhys Davids, Buddhism, p. 27. We learn, moreover, that on the same day on which the Buddha was born were also born Yaçodhâra, Tchandaka, Kâludâyi, the horse Kanthaka, &c. See Bigandet, p. 39; Rhys Davids, Buddhist Birth Stories, p. 68; Lalita Vistara (Foucaux's trans.), p. 96, &c. See also Dulva vi. f. 93 *et seq.*

[3] Cf. Lalita Vistara, chap. viii.; and Beal, *op. cit.*, p. 52.

[4] Cf. Huen Thsang, B. vi. p. 321.

hdsin) mountain[1] a rishi called Akleça (*Kun-mongs-med* =Asita), a mighty seer, and with him was Nalada (*Mis-byin*), his nephew. These two came to see the child (f. 464[b]), and Asita took him in his arms, and asked what had been prophesied about him. He predicted that he would leave his home at twenty-nine, that he would be an ascetic for six years, and that then he would find the drink of the cessation of death (amrita).

Shortly after, feeling his end approaching (f. 467[b]), he begged Nalada to enter the order of the young Çakya as soon as he should have found the truth, and then he died.

Nalada went to Varaṇasi, where he entered into a company of five hundred mantra-studying brahmans; and as he was of the family of Katya, he became known as Katyayana (f. 467[b]). Later on, having been converted by the Buddha, he was called "the great member of Katya's family," or Mahâkatyayana.[2]

While the Bodhisattva was still in his nurse's arms, she wanted to give him a golden bowl in which was rice and meat, but she was unable to move it from its place. She called the king, the ministers, all the town's people; but they were all unable to move it. Neither could five hundred elephants; but the Bodhisattva took hold of the

[1] Schiefner, Mém. de l'Acad. de St. Peters., xxii. No. 7, p. 1, also Dulva xi. f. 99, calls the mountain Kishkindha. The Lalita Vistara, chap. vii. p. 103, does not mention the name of the mountain; nor does Beal, *loc. cit.*, p. 56. In the Lalita Vistara, *loc. cit.*, the rishi is called Asita (or Kala, *Nag-po*), which agrees with the name given him in the Southern legend, Kâladêvalo. Schiefner, *loc. cit.*, calls the nephew Narada, as does Beal, p. 39. The Tibetan *Mis-byin*, "given by a man," is in Sanskrit, Narada or Naradatta. See Foucaux, Rgya-tcher rol-pa, p. lii. According to Spence Hardy, Manual, p. 149, Kâladewala (Asita) had been chief counsellor of King Sinhahanu. The nephew he calls Naraka (p. 151). Bigandet, p. 42, calls him Nalaka. Rhys Davids, Buddh. Birth Stories, p. 69, agrees with Spence Hardy in saying that Asita had been a samâpatti of the king. He also calls the nephew Nâlaka, p. 71.

[2] With this, however, Rhys Davids, *loc. cit.*, p. 71, and Bigandet, p. 44, do not agree. They say that Nâlaka became a disciple of the Buddha shortly after his enlightenment; that he then went back to the Himâlayas, reached arhatship, and died after seven months. Cf. with the present version Dulva xi. 99[b] *et seq.*, where we find another epitome of the Buddha's early life, substantially the same as that of our text.

bowl with one finger and pulled it out. On account of this exploit he was called "As mighty as a thousand elephants" (f. 468).

Together with five hundred Çakya children he went to be taught his letters by Kauçika (? *Sprin-bu go-tcha* = Viçvamitra), but he knew everything he could teach (f. 469ᵃ).[1]

After that his uncle Sulabha taught him how to manage elephants, and Sahadeva (*Lhar-bchas*) taught him archery (f. 469ᵇ).

When he was yet hardly grown up, the Licchavis of Vaisâli offered him an elephant of exceptional beauty, for they had heard that he would be a chakravartin monarch. So having covered it with jewels, they led it to Kapilavastu, but when they were near the town, Devadatta noticed it, and, filled with envy, he killed it with a blow of his fist (f. 470). Nanda coming that way, saw the carcass lying in the road, so he threw it to one side; but the Bodhisattva seeing it there, took it by the tail, and threw it over seven fences and ditches, and it dug a great ditch in falling, which became known as "the elephant ditch, or Hastigarta" (f. 470), and on that spot the believing brahmans and householders built a stupa, and it is reverenced to the present day by the bhikshus.

And here it is said—

"Devadatta killed the mighty elephant,
Nanda carried it seven paces,
The Bodhisattva through space with his hand
Did cast it as a stone far away."

After this the young Çakyas tried their skill at archery. The arrow of the Bodhisattva, after having pierced all the targets, went so far into the ground that it caused a spring to rush forth, and there also the believing brahmans and householders built a stupa, &c. (f. 471ᵇ).

When this last event happened, the Bodhisattva was

[1] Cf. Lalita Vistara, chap. x., where the master is called Viçvamitra. I have followed Schiefner, Tib. Lebens, p. 236, in translating *Sprin-bu go-tcha*, "manner of a worm," by Kauçika.

seventeen,[1] for we are told that when the young Çakyas, riding their chariots, re-entered the city, the soothsayers, seeing the Bodhisattva, exclaimed, "If twelve years hence he does not give up the world, he will become a universal monarch" (f. 471[b]).

Çuddhodana decided that his son must marry; so he had all the maidens of the clan assembled for him to choose, and he took Yaçôdhâra (*Grags hdsin-ma*), daughter of the Çakya Daṇḍapâni (*Lag-na dbyug-chan*)[2] (f. 472[b]).

On the day of the Buddha's birth there had appeared a tree called "essence of virtue" (Kalyanagarbha, *Dgebai snying-po*), which had grown exceedingly big, and when the Bodhisattva was twenty, undermined by the waters of the Rohita, it had been overthrown by the wind and had made a dam between Kapilavastu and Devadaha, so that the latter place was deprived of water, whereas the former was flooded. All the people were unable to move the tree, so Suprabuddha asked Çuddhodana to request his son to do it, but the father did not like to disturb him (f. 473). Tchandaka (*Hdun-pa*), the prince's charioteer,[3] thought he could induce the prince to come without asking him. Now, on the banks of the Rohita there were gardens

[1] Spence Hardy, Manual, p. 155, has it that the prince was first married when he was sixteen, and that he showed his dexterity with the bow *after* his marriage, not before, as the Lalita Vistara, chap. xii., has it.

[2] Cf. Spence Hardy, *loc. cit.*, p. 140, where he makes Daṇḍapani brother of Suprabuddha, and consequently Siddhartha's maternal uncle. Rhys Davids, Buddh, p. 52, says Yaçôdhâra was daughter of Suprabuddha and Amritâ, aunt of the Bodhisattva. The Lalita Vistara, p. 152, Foucaux's trans., says that Daṇḍapani's daughter was Gôpâ; Beal, *loc. cit.*, p. 80, makes her daughter of Mahânâman. The Tibetan version of the Abhinishkramana Sûtra, fol. 32, agrees with the Dulva. See Foucaux, *loc. cit.*; Beal, Rom. Leg., p. 96, says Daṇḍapani's daughter was called Gôtamî (Gôpâ?). See also his note on this subject, same page. Bigandet, p. 52, agrees with Rhys Davids. Dulva x. 105[b] only mentions two wives of the Bodhisattva, "Mrigadjâ, Yacôdhâra, and 60,000 women."

[3] Tchandaka is here introduced for the first time, as if he was a personage with whom the reader was well acquainted. This and many more important omissions in the text seem to indicate that the present version is but a summary derived from older texts at present lost. This obliges us not to attach any undue importance to the chronological order in which the stories are given, at least in the first part of this work.

belonging to the young Çakyas, and there Tchandaka went with the young nobles, knowing that the Bodhisattva was there. On a sudden the Bodhisattva heard shouts, and asking Tchandaka what was the matter, he learnt that the people were unable to move the tree, so he at once offered to go and do it.

While they were still in the gardens, Devadatta saw a goose flying overhead, so he shot it, and it fell in the Bodhisattva's garden, who took it, and, having extracted the arrow, bound up its wound. Devadatta sent a messenger to claim the bird, but the Bodhisattva would not give it up, saying that it belonged not to him who had attempted to take its life, but to him who had saved it. And this was the first quarrel between these two (f. 474).

As they were going to assist the people, a viper ran out before the Bodhisattva, but Udayi (*Htchar-ka*) struck it down, not, however, before it had bitten him, so that his skin became black, and he was henceforth called "Udayi the black," or Kalûdayi[1] (f. 474).

None of the young Çakyas could any more than move the fallen tree, but the Bodhisattva threw it into the air, and it broke in two, a piece falling on either bank of the Rohita. Now this happened when the prince was in his twenty-second year (f. 474[b]).

The Çakya Kinkinisvara[2] (*Dril-bu sgra*) had a daughter called Gôpâ (*Sa-hts'o-ma*), and as the Bodhisattva was riding home (from removing the tree?) she saw him from

[1] According to Beal, *op. cit.*, p. 123, Udayi was son of Mahânâman and brother of Yaçôdhâra.

[2] Schiefner calls him Gantâcabda, *loc. cit.*, p. 238. He also says that his daughter was Guptâ, and on p. 236 he tells us that Gôpâ was another name for Yaçôdhâra. The Dulva, however, distinctly speaks of three different wives, Yaçôdhâra, Gôpâ, and Mrigadjâ. It is also to be noticed that our text does not connect the different tests of skill and dexterity on the part of Siddhârtha with his marriage to Yaçôdhâra. See Bigandet, p. 52. I have not seen mentioned in the Dulva that Utpalavarnâ was wife of Siddhartha. She is mentioned as being a Çakya in Dulva iv. f. 448. There was another bhikshuni of the same name, but from Takshasilâ. See Schiefner, *Tib. Tales*, p. 206 *et seq.*, and Schmidt, *Dsang Blun.*, p. 208 *et seq.*

the terrace of her house, and he also noticing her, stopped his chariot to look at her. The people saw that they were fascinated with each other, so they told the king, and he took Gôpâ and made her his son's wife.

One day the prince told Tchandaka that he wanted to go drive in the park, and while there he saw an old man, and the charioteer explained what old age was and how all were subject to it (f. 476). Deeply impressed, the prince turned back and went home.

A short time after, while out driving, he met a dropsical man (*rbab rbab-po*), emaciated, weak, with faculties impaired (f. 477), and Tchandaka told him what disease was (D. iv. f. 1–2), and again he turned back.

Another time he came across a procession bearing along on a litter, with burning torches, something wrapped in many-coloured stuffs, the women accompanying it had dishevelled hair and were crying piteously. It was a corpse, Tchandaka told him, and to this state all must come (f. 6[a]).

And yet on another occasion he met a deva of the pure abode who had assumed the appearance of a shaved and shorn mendicant, bearing an alms-bowl and going from door to door. The charioteer told him that he was one who has forsaken the world, a righteous, virtuous man, who wandered here and there begging wherewith to satisfy his wants (f. 7[b]). So the Bodhisattva drove up to him and questioned him about himself, and received the same answer. Then pensively he drove back to the palace.

Çuddhodana heard from his son of what appeared to trouble so much his mind (f. 9[a]), so to divert him he sent him to a village to look at the ploughmen.[1] But there he

[1] This is evidently a reminiscence of the legend of the ploughing festival, which in the Southern legend (Spence Hardy, Manual, p. 153; Rhys Davids, Buddh. Birth Stories, p. 74), and also in the generality of Northern works (Lalita Vistara, ch. xi.; Beal, Romantic Legend, p. 73), occurred at a much earlier date. Bigandet (p. 55), however, mentions an excursion of the Bodhisattva to his garden after having met the bhikshu, and our legend seems to agree with what Rhys Davids, *loc. cit.*, p. 78, gives as the version of "the repeaters of the Dîgha Nikâya."

saw the labourers with hair erect, uncovered hands and feet, their bodies dirty and running with sweat, and the work-oxen pricked with iron goads, their backs and rumps streaming with blood, hungry and thirsty, panting with fast-beating hearts, burdened with a yoke which they had to drag great distances, flies and insects biting them, with bleeding and suppurating wounds, the ploughshare wounding them, running at the mouth and nose, covered with gadflies and mosquitoes (*sbrang-bu mtchu rings*) (f. 9[b]). His tender heart was touched with compassion. "To whom do you belong?" he asked the labourers. "We are the king's property," they answered. "From to-day you are no longer slaves; you shall be no longer servants; go where ere you please and live in joy." He freed also the oxen and said to them, "Go; from to-day eat the sweetest grass and drink the purest water, and may the breezes of the four quarters visit you" (f. 10[a]). Then, seeing a shady jambu-tree on one side, he sat down at its foot and gave himself to earnest meditation; and there his father found him, and lo! the shade had not moved from where he was.

Shortly after he went into the cemetery of Râjagriha and saw the dead and decaying bodies, and a great grief filled his heart, and there his father found him (f. 11[a]).

As he was going back to the city Mrigadjâ (*Ri-dags skyes*), the daughter of the Çakya Kâlika (*Dus-legs*) saw him from her window.[1] Then she sang—

> "Ah! happy is his mother;
> His father also, happy is he.
> Ah! she whose husband he shall be,
> That woman has gone beyond sorrow!"

The Bodhisattva threw her a necklace to pay her for her pretty words. Now the people saw all this, and they

[1] Cf. the story as told by Rhys Davids (Buddhism, p. 31) where the girl's name is not given. She thought young Siddhârtha was falling in love with her, but, after having sent her the necklace, "he took no further notice of her and passed on." According to the same

told Çuddhodana, so he took Mrigadjâ and made her the Bodhisattva's wife. So at that time the Bodhisattva's wives were Gôpâ, Mrigadjâ,[1] &c., and 60,000 attendant women (f. 11[b]). Mrigadjâ thus became the Bodhisattva's wife seven days before he left his home (f. 11[a]).

The prediction of the soothsayers, so often repeated, was ever in King Çuddhodana's ears; so the same day as that on which the last events had taken place he had troops stationed outside the city and guards placed at the gates. At the southern gate watched Dronodana; at the western one, Çuklodana; at the northern one, Amritodana; and at the eastern one, Çuddhodana; in the centre of the city was Mahânâman with a detachment of troops, and from there he patrolled the city (f. 12[a]).

In the meanwhile the Bodhisattva was in his palace in the midst of his harem, amusing himself with song and dance, and now it was that he knew Yaçôdhâra his wife (f. 13).

And so the king watched six days. On the night of the seventh the Bodhisattva noticed all his sleeping harem, and the women looked so like the dead in their sleep that he was filled with loathing (f. 14). On the same night Yaçôdhâra dreamt he was abandoning her, and she awoke and told her lord of her dream. "Oh, my lord, where e'er thou goest, there let me go to." And he, thinking of going to where there was no sorrow (*nirvâṇa*), replied, "So be it; wherever I go, there mayest thou go also" (f. 14[b]).

Çataketu (Indra) and the other gods, knowing the Bodhisattva's inclinations, came and exhorted him to flee the world. "Kauçika," he answered, "seest thou not all

authority, it was on the night of this same day that he left his home. Bigandet (p. 58) also mentions his rencontre with Keissa Gautami (= Mrigadjâ) after this occurrence, but he does not say that she became his wife.

[1] It is strange that Yaçodhâra is not mentioned. It is evidently an omission, for she is nowhere confounded with either Gôpâ or Mrigadjâ. It is also worthy of notice that several Chinese works say that the Bodhisattva left his home when he was nineteen. See Chin-i-tian, lxxvii. p. 28 *et seq.*, edited by Klaproth in Remusat's Foe-kone-ki, p. 231; also Kwo-hu-hien-tsai-yin-ko-king, kiuen ii., and Siu-hing-pen-ki-king, vi., cited by Beal, Sacred Books of the East, vol. xix. pp. xxvi. and xxi.

the armed men with horses and elephants that surround the city; how can I depart?" (f. 16[b]). Çataketu promised him his help; he went and aroused Tchandaka and told him to saddle his treasure-horse, Kanthaka (*Snags-ldan*).

The Bodhisattva patted the horse and quieted his fiery temper, and together with Tchandaka, Çataketu, with many other gods, he started out (f. 17[a]).[1] On leaving the palace, the devatas who inhabited it commenced to cry, so that their tears fell like rain (f. 18[a]). As he passed the eastern gate he perceived his sleeping father. "Father," he cried, "though I love thee, yet a fear possesses me and I may not stay. I must free myself from the fear of conquering time and death, of the horrors of age and death!" (f. 18[b]). Suddenly he came across Mahânâman patrolling the city; but though his cousin begged and cried aloud, telling him of all the sorrow he was bringing to those who loved him, yet he pursued his way and travelled that night twelve yojanas (f. 20).[2]

Then he stopped and told Tchandaka to return to the city with the horse and the jewels he had on his person; and though the faithful attendant begged to stay with his master to protect him against the wild beasts of the forest, he made him go so that he might tell his family what had become of him. So the charioteer and the horse turned back, and reached Kapilavastu after seven days.[3] Before Tchandaka left him the prince took his sword and cut off his hair, which he threw into the air, and Çataketu took it and carried it off to the Trayastrimcat heaven. On that spot the faithful brahmans and householders built

[1] Rhys Davids (*loc. cit.*, p. 84) says that the Bodhisattva left his home on the full-moon day of Asâḷhi, when the moon was in the Uttarâsâḷha mansion (*i.e.*, on the 1st July).

[2] Bigandet (*loc. cit.*, p. 64) says that he journeyed a distance of thirty yojanas, and arrived on the banks of the river Anauma, or Anamâ, as Rhys Davids (*loc. cit.*, p. 85) has it. The latter says that in that one night he passed through three kingdoms, &c.

[3] According to Bigandet (p. 67), the horse died on the spot where the Bodhisattva left him (also Rhys Davids, *op. cit.*, p. 87). Bigandet's version is an exact translation of the Pâli (Nidânakatha), as far as it goes.

the stupa of the taking of the hair and beard (*Tchuḍa-pratigraha*) (f. 21).

In former times a rich householder of Anupama (*Dpe-med*)[1] had ten sons, who all successively became Pratyeka Buddhas. They all had worn in succession the same cotton garment, and they gave it finally to an old woman, with instructions to give it after their death to the son of Çuddhodana-râjâ as soon as he should have become a Buddha, and that by so doing she would reap a great reward. On dying, the old woman left it to her daughter with similar instructions, and she, feeling her end approaching, committed it to the guard of a genii of a tree near by. Now Çataketu knew all this, so he went and took the robe; then assuming the appearance of an old decrepit hunter, with arrows in his hand and wearing this garment, he came and stood where the Bodhisattva could see him (f. 23). They exchanged clothes, and Çataketu carried off to the Trayastrimcat heaven the fine kaçi cotton garments of the prince. On this spot the faithful brahmans and householders built a stupa, &c. (as above).[2]

Thus attired, the prince went to the hermitage of the rishi, the son of Brigu (f. 23[b]),[3] of whom he inquired how far he was from Kapilavastu. "Twelve yojanas," he replied. "'Tis too near, Kapilavastu; I may be disturbed by the Çakyas. I will cross the Ganges and go to Râjagriha" (f. 24[a]). The Bodhisattva was expert in all handicrafts and occupations of men, so after having crossed the

[1] Lit. "unparalleled;" but may not this be a translation of Anoma, "high," "lofty"? the name of the river being given to a village on its bank.

[2] This legend is slightly different in Bigandet, p. 65.

[3] Bigandet, p. 65, says that he "spent seven days alone in a forest of mango trees. . . . This place is called Anupyia, in the country belonging to the Malla princes." "He then started for the country of Radjagriha, travelling on foot a distance of thirty yojanas." Rhys Davids, *op. cit.*, p. 87, has not the words "in the country of the Malla princes." I do not believe that the Bodhisattva's visit to Vaiçali, mentioned in the Lal. Vist., chap. xvi. p. 226, of Foucaux's trans., and by Rhys Davids, *loc. cit.*, took place at that time, but after he had been to Râjagriha; for a little farther on it says that Alara was at Vaiçali, and the Pâli text says he saw Alara after having been to Râjagriha.

Ganges he made an alms-bowl of karavira (*sic*) leaves and went into Râjagriha. The king of Magadha, Çrenika Bimbisara, noticed him from the terrace of his palace, and was struck with his noble bearing (f. 24^b), so he sent some one to fill his bowl, and another person to see where he went. The king then learned that he was stopping on the Paṇḍava (mountain),[1] and he went to visit him with his suite (f. 25^b), and offered him everything that makes life agreeable, women, riches, and pleasures.

"Râjâ," the Bodhisattva answered, "near the Himalaya, in a rich and prosperous country, Kosala it is named, there lives a tribe of Ishkvaku or Solar race, the Çakyas they are called. To this tribe I belong; I am of kshatriya caste. I care not for this world's treasures; they cannot bring contentment. 'Tis hard to cross the swamps of human passions; they are the root of fear, of sorrow, of despair. I seek to conquer, not to indulge desires; happy, free from sorrow, is he who has cast them far away. The treasure I am seeking is that wisdom which knoweth no superior" (f. 25^b). "When thou shalt have reached thy goal, ah! teach it then to me, that unsurpassable wisdom," said the king, and the Bodhisattva promised him that he would (f. 26^a).

After this interview the Bodhisattva went to the Vulture's Peak[2] (Gridrakuta parvata) near Râjagriha, and lived with the ascetics who dwelt there, surpassing them all in his mortifications, so that he became known as "the great ascetic or Mahâçramana" (f. 26^b). But he finally learned from them that the object they had in view was to become Çakra or Brahmâ, or even Mâra, and then he knew that they were not in the right way; so he left them and went to Arâta Kâlâma (*Rgyu-stsal shes-kyi-bu ring-du hphur*); but he taught that all depended on controlling the senses (f. 26^b), and with this he could not agree; so he left

[1] Or "under the shadow of the Paṇḍava rocks," as Rhys Davids, p. 88, has it.

[2] Bigandet, p. 70, says that he met Alara immediately after his interview with Bimbisara.

him and went to Rudraka Ramaputra (*Rangs-byed-kyi-bu lhag spyod*), who taught that there is neither consciousness or unconsciousness (f. 27[b]); but this also could not satisfy him, so he departed thence.

Now King Çuddhodana had heard through his messengers that his son was stopping with Rudraka Ramaputra, near Râjagriha, and that he had no attendant to minister to his wants; so he sent three hundred men, and Suprabuddha sent two hundred, to wait on him; but the Bodhisattva would only retain five of them as his attendants, and in their company he lived. Two of them were of the maternal tribe, and three of the paternal[1] (f. 29[a]). He went to the southern side of Mount Gâyâ, to the village of the school of Uruvilva Kâçyapa, and took up his abode at the foot of a tree near the bank of the lovely Nairanjana river, and there he continued his mortifications, gradually making them more and more severe.

The gods offered to feed him miraculously and unknown to mankind, but he refused (f. 33); so he went on fasting until he reduced his food to a single pea (*mâsha*) a day, and his body was emaciated, and of a blackish-red colour (f. 35[a]).

From the day on which his father heard that he was mortifying his body, he sent each day two hundred and

[1] Their names are given elsewhere. The two last probably came from Koli. Their names are always given in the following order—Kauṇḍiṇya, Açvadjit, Vâchpa, Mahâ-nâma, and Bhadrika. This Mahânâman can neither be the Buddha's uncle (for he was killed by Virudhaka), nor the minister of that name, for he was from Kapilavastu. Spence Hardy, p. 152, says that these five were sons of the Brahmans who had visited the Buddha shortly after his birth, and who had foretold his future greatness. Beal's account, p. 188, probably agrees with this latter version. The Lalita Vistara, p. 235, makes them out disciples of Rudraka Ramaputra, who left their master to follow the prince after having heard him discuss with Rudraka. Schiefner, Tibet. Lebens, p. 243, says that Kauṇḍiṇya, Açvadjit, and Vâchpa were disciples of Arâda Kâlâpa (Kâlâma), and Mahânâman and Bhadrika disciples of Rudraka; and though the first part of the paragraph in his work is evidently taken from our text, the latter part agrees with the general outline of the Lalita Vistara's version. Vâchpa is better known as Daçabala Kâçyapa (Schiefner, Tib. Lebens, p. 304). The Mahawansa, cited by Burnouf, Intr., p. 157, says that this Mahânâman was the elder son of Amritodana, and first cousin of Çâkya (the Buddha). With this our text does not agree.

fifty messengers (*bdog-pa*), as did also Suprabuddha, and they reported everything the Bodhisattva was doing. Then Çuddhodana, the prince's wives, and especially Yaçôdhâra, were greatly grieved, and the latter put away her flowers and jewels, and performed the same mortifications which her husband was practising;[1] but Çuddhodana, fearing for the child she bore, forbade any one to speak to her about the Bodhisattva (f. 37[b]).

Finally, the Bodhisattva saw that all this severe ascetism had not brought him nearer the truth; so he decided to take some food, but of a very unpalatable kind.[2]

After he had obtained and eaten it, he wandered into the cemetery, and lying down beside a corpse, he went to sleep. The village girls saw him, and thought he was a fiend (pisatcha) seeking human flesh to devour, and they threw dirt and stones at him (f. 38[a]).

Now, when the five attendants that were with him saw all this, they forsook him, thinking that he lacked the necessary perseverance to attain enlightenment, and they started out for Benares, and there they dwelt in the Mrigadava, where they became known as "the Five," or the Panchavarga (*Lnga-sde*).[3]

[1] Cf. Spence Hardy, Manual, p. 353.

[2] He takes the milk of a cow who had just calved, says our text. The Lal. Vist., chap. xviii., has a different, but more extraordinary, version of this part of the legend. The Lal. Vist., moreover, says that he made himself a robe out of the shroud of a girl who had been recently buried. It is generally recommended in Buddhist writings to make the robes of a bhikshu of similar materials; but that this practice did not long prevail, if it ever even became a common one, is evident from the following extract from Dulva xi. 32[b]:—"The bhikshu who wears the clothing of a corpse from the cemetery must not enter a vihara (*gtsug-lag*); he must not go to worship a chaitya; he must not go to bow to and circumambulate it; he shall not have the privilege of the house, nor shall he abide in the dormitory; he shall not abide among the bhikshus; he shall not teach the dharma to a number of brahmans and householders who have met together for that purpose; he must not enter the houses of brahmans and householders; if he goes to one, he must stop at the door; if he gets among the ariyas, he must say, 'I am a frequenter of burial-places' (*sosâniko*)." This low estimate in which these sosânikos were held explains what appeared strange to me in the eleventh paragraph of chap. xxvii. of the Udânavarga, p. 127, where the frequenters of burial-places are classed among those ascetics whose practices are not deemed justifiable.

[3] In Pâli, Fausböll's Jataka, i. p. 57, they are called *Pañcavaggiya*-

When the Bodhisattva forces had been restored, he went to the village of Senani (*Sde-chan*), the headman of which was Sena (*Sde*).[1] Now, this man had two daughters, Nandâ (*Dgah-mo*) and Nandâbalâ (*Dgah-stobs*), and they had heard about the Çakya prince of the Kapilavastu Çakyas who lived on the bank of the Bhagirathi, and that it had been prophesied of him that he would become an universal monarch or a Buddha; so they had prepared for him a milk-soup (f. 40[a]) (the story is told in about the same words as in chap. xviii. of the Lalita Vistara), and the Bodhisattva took it in a crystal vase adorned with jewels, which two devas of the Akanishta region had brought him.

Carrying the food with him, he went to the Nairanjana river and bathed, and when he had finished the devas bent down the branches of an arjuna tree,[2] which he seized to help him out of the water (f. 42[b]). Putting on his robes, he sat down on the bank and ate the honeyed soup, and having washed the bowl, he threw it into the river. The Nâgas took it, but Çakra,[3] assuming the form of a garuda (*Nam-mkah lding*), dashed into the river, and seizing the bowl, carried it off to the Trayastrimcat heaven, and there the gods built the stupa of the bowl (f. 41[b]).

When the two sisters made him their offering of food, he asked them what they sought by this gift. "The

therâ, or the company of the five elders.

[1] In the Lal. Vist., chap. xviii., the headman of the village is called Nandika, and only one daughter is mentioned, Sudjatâ by name. Beal, *op. cit.*, p. 191, calls him the brahman Senayana, and his daughters Nanda and Bala (= Nandâbalâ); as does also the Tibetan Abhinichkramana Sûtra. See, however, Beal, p. 193, where the text speaks of the two daughters of Sujata, the village lord; and p. 194, where he is called Nandika, and his daughter is called Sujata. Bigandet, p. 77, calls the villager Thena (Sena), and his daughter Thoodzata (Sujata). Rhys Davids, Buddh. Birth Stories, p. 91, calls the place "the village Senâni." Dulva xi. 106[a] also speaks of Nandâ and Nandabâlâ.

[2] The Lalita Vistara, p. 257, calls the tree a kakubha (*Pentaphera ardjuna*), which agrees with our text. Beal, p. 194, calls it pinjuna, which is most likely an incorrect transcription of arjuna. Cf. Bigandet, p. 83.

[3] The Lal. Vist., p. 260, says that it was Indra who retook the vase from the Nagas. Beal, p. 195, agrees with our text.

soothsayers," they replied, "have prophesied that you would become a chakravartin monarch; may this action, this seed of virtue, make you become our husband at that time." He explained to them that this could never be, then they said, "May you then quickly reach the highest wisdom and perfection" (f. 42[b]).

Then the Bodhisattva waded across the river, and many wondrous signs foretold that the hour of enlightenment was approaching.[1]

Çakra took the shape of the grass merchant, Svastika[2] (*Bkra-shis*), and from him the Bodhisattva obtained a handful of grass, out of which he made his seat at the foot of the Bodhi tree (f. 44[a]).

Then Mâra, the Evil one, went to him and said, "Devadatta has subdued Kapilavastu; he has seized the palace, and has crushed the Çakyas. Why stay you here?" He caused apparitions of Yaçôdhâra, of Mrigadjâ, and of Gôpâ, of Devadatta, and of the Çakyas who had escaped to appear before him, but the Bodhisattva remained unmoved (f. 44[b]). Then Mâra reasoned with him, saying that it was impossible for him to find enlightenment; but all to no purpose[3] (f. 45).

After that he called his three daughters, Desire, Pleasure, and Delight,[4] and they tried all their allurements, but in vain (f. 46); the Bodhisattva changed them into old hags.

All the Evil one's devices were unable to affect the Bodhisattva, and, seeing this, the devas of the pure abode

[1] Lotuses sprang up wherever he put down his foot, the four great oceans became lotus ponds, &c. Cf. on these signs the Lal. Vist., p. 262.

[2] Beal, p. 196, calls this man Kih-li (Santi?), "good luck" or "fortunate," which is also the meaning of Svastika. Bigandet, p. 84, speaks only of a young man returning with a grass load; but Rhys Davids, p. 95, calls the grass-cutter Sotthiya, which would agree with our text—*sotthi* = *svasti*.

[3] Cf. Beal, Romantic Legend, p. 207, where Mâra brings the Bodhisattva "a bundle of official notices, as if from all the Çakya princes."

[4] The Lalita Vistara, p. 353, calls Mâra's three daughters Ratî (pleasure), Aratî (displeasure), and Trichnâ (passion or desire). Spence Hardy, p. 183, names them Tanha, Rati, and Ranga; also Bigandet, p. 103. Cf. with the text Dulva xi. 106[a].

and all the gods showered down flowers on the conqueror (Djina), and sang songs of victory (f. 47).

Then reasoning within himself, the Bodhisattva saw the cause of existence, of age, of death, and the way to free oneself of all this trouble. The concatenation of causes and effects which bring about existence and its cessation (*i.e.*, the Nidanas) became known to him (f. 50), and he became enlightened, a Buddha.[1]

When all wisdom had been given him, Mâra's bow and his standard fell from his grasp (f. 51), and all his cohorts, a million and thirty-six thousand in number, fled, filled with dismay.

The rumour had reached Kapilavastu that the prince had died under the excess of his penances, and all the court was plunged in despair, and his wives fell fainting to the ground; but a little after came the news that he had attained enlightenment, and great was the rejoicing everywhere (f. 51). Just as the king was being told this news, they came and told him that Yaçôdhâra had brought forth a son, and also that Rahu had seized the moon (*i.e.*, that there was an eclipse).[2]

So they called the child Râhula (seized by Rahu), or Râhulabhadra. On the same day the wife of Amritodana brought forth a son, and as the city was rejoicing greatly that day, they called him All-joy or Ananda[3] (f. 51^{b}). Çuddhodana thought that Yaçôdhâra's child could not be Çakyamuni's, and great was the mother's distress on hearing his suspicions; so she took the child to a pond,

[1] Dulva xi. f. 106^{a} says that at that same time King Pradyota became sovereign of Udjayani. Edkins, Chinese Buddhism, p. 18, says that the prince became a Buddha at the age of thirty, and that "after this he lived forty-nine years."

[2] The Southern legend agrees tacitly with this one, for we are told by Spence Hardy, Manual, p. 211, that when the Buddha first visited Kapilavastu after commencing his ministry, Rahula was seven years old; and it is generally admitted that the Buddha visited his country twelve years after he had left it. Cf., however, the legend as told by Rhys Davids, Buddhism, p. 30, and Bigandet, p. 61.

[3] From p. 88 of Beal's Roman. Leg., we may infer that the Chinese Abhinichkram. Sûtra thinks that Ananda was about the same age as the Buddha, as does the Lalita Vistara, p. 145 (trans.)

put it on a stone,[1] and placed them together in the water with these words: "If the child be the Bodhisattva's, may it and the stone float; if it is not, may it sink!" And lo! the child floated on the stone as if it had been a ball of cotton. And the people saw this, and they rejoiced greatly, and went and took the young child out of the pond (f. 52[a]).

The two same devas of the Akanishta region who had previously offered the Bodhisattva a bowl in which he had eaten the food offered him by Sena's daughters, now came and sang his praises, and their voices recalled the Buddha from his abstraction, and he spoke these verses (f. 53[b]):—

"All the pleasures of worldly joys,
All those which are known among gods,
Compared with the joy of ending existence
Are not as its sixteenth part.

Sorry is he whose burden is heavy,
And happy he who has cast it down;
When once he has cast off his burden,
He will seek to be burthened no more.

When all existences are put away,
When all notions are at an end,
When all things are perfectly known,
Then no more will craving come back."[2]

So great was the joy he experienced in the newly discovered freedom, that he passed seven whole days without partaking of food.

[1] M. Foucaux in Rgya-tcher rol-pa, p. 389, note, translating this legend from the Abhinichkram, Sûtra, fol. 75, 76, says that the child was put on an ass which had formerly been the Bodhisattva's. This version is not as satisfactory as that of the Dulva. There is hardly any miracle remaining. Schiefner, Tib. Lebens, p. 246, agrees with our text.

[2] These are not the verses that the Buddha is generally supposed to have spoken on this occasion. The second stanza occurs in the Udânavarga, chap. xxx. 34 n. It is also remarkable that our text does not mention the famous udâna, "Through many different births," &c. See on this Udânavarga, p. 157; cf. also Beal, Rom. Leg., p. 225.

When the seven days were passed[1] there came along two merchants, Trapusha (*Ga-gon*) and Bhallika (*Bzang-po*), with five hundred waggons; and following the advice of a deva, they came to the Buddha and offered him food sweetened with honey and many other sweets. Each of the four great kings of the cardinal points brought him each a bowl in which to take the food; and not wishing to offend any of them, he took the four bowls and transformed them into one (f. 55^{b}).

Then the Buddha said to the merchants, "Merchants, go for a refuge to the Buddha, to the truth and to the church that will hereafter exist! Whatever wish you may have made when you made me this offering, it will be granted unto you." Then they bowed down before him and went on their way rejoicing (f. 55^{b}).

After their departure the Buddha sat down on the bank of the Nairanjana and ate the food which the merchants had given him, but the honey gave him colic. Then the Evil one, seeing the pain he was enduring, came to him and said, "Blessed One (Bhagavat), the time to die has come!"[2] But he answered him, "Mâra, as long as my disciples have not become wise and of quick understanding, as long as the bhikshus, the bhikshunis, and the lay disciples of either sex are not able to refute their adversaries according to the Dharma, as long as my moral teaching has not been spread far and wide among gods and men, so long will I not pass away" (f. 56^{b}).

Then Çakra, the lord of the devas, brought an arura (myrobolan *skyu-ru-ra*) fruit from a tree in Jambudvipa, and by it the Buddha was cured.

[1] Beal, *loc. cit.*, p. 236, agrees with this. See, however, Lal. Vist., p. 356, where the text has it that the offering was only made seven weeks after he had become Buddha. Bigandet, p. 107, agrees with the version of the Lal. Vist. At p. 108 he tells us that the two merchants were brothers.

[2] There seems to be a trace of this legend in Lal. Vist., p. 352, where Pâpiyân (Mâra) visits the Buddha four weeks after he had obtained enlightenment. See also Beal, p. 240. Bigandet, p. 107, speaking of the offering of fruit made by a deva, "to prepare his system to receive more substantial food," evidently alludes to this event.

After having remained under the Bo tree as long as pleased him, the Buddha went to where lived the nâga king Mutchilinda [1] (*Btang-bzung*); and he, wishing to protect him from the sun and rain, wrapped his body seven times around the Blessed One, and spread out his hood over his head, and there the Lord remained seven days in thought.

After having remained with Mutchilinda as long as pleased him, the Blessed One went to the Bodhimanda (*Byang-tchub-kyi-snying-po*),[2] and there he remained seven days seated on a grass mat studying the twelve branches of the theory of causes and effects (*pratityasamudpada*), and when that theory had become well fixed in his mind he spoke the udâna which is recorded in the last verses of the Udânavarga, commencing with "When to the earnest, meditative Brahmana," &c.[3]

The idea took possession of his mind that this doctrine of causes and effects was too deep for man's intellect, and he thought that he would not teach it; but Brahmâ, the lord of the world, came and begged him to have mercy on the erring world, for "the advent of a Buddha is as uncommon as is a flower on a fig tree."

Then the Lord reflected who would be a proper person for him to teach; he thought of Arata Kâlâma, but he found out that he had been dead seven days; Rudraka, son of Rama, had also died three days before (f. 6[b]), so he decided upon seeking the Five who were at Benares in the Mrigadava of Rishivadana.

Having stayed at Bodhimanda as long as pleased him, he started for Benares, the town of Kaçi, and on the way he met an adjivaka (*Kun-tu ht'so nyer-hgro*),[4] who questioned

[1] The Lalita Vistara, p. 354, says that the Buddha went to Mutchilinda's five weeks after he had been enlightened. Also Bigandet, p. 106.

[2] This is the same episode as that alluded to by Beal, *op. cit.*, p. 238, where the Buddha sat for seven days beneath a nyagrodha tree; and in Lal. Vist., p. 355, as the nyagrodha of the goatherd.

[3] Cf. Udânavarga, p. 199.

[4] Bigandet, p. 115, calls him "the heretic Rahan Upaka." P. 117 he says that Upaka went about inquiring for his friend Dzina (Djina).

him concerning himself and his master, and as to where he was going. When he heard his answers, he exclaimed, "Venerable Gautama, verily you are a conqueror (Djina)!" and then he went his way (f. 63[a]).

CHAPTER III.

LIFE OF THE BUDDHA FROM THE COMMENCEMENT OF HIS MINISTRY UNTIL THE REIGN OF ADJATASATRU.

JOURNEYING along from the Nairanjana river, the Buddha finally came to Benares, to the deer-park. When the Five saw him, they wanted to receive him coldly, nearly rudely, but they could not resist the grandeur of his transformed person, and, rising, they ministered to his wants (f. 63).

They questioned him as to his reason for giving up asceticism, and he answered them in the words that have been preserved in the *Dharma chakrapravartana Sûtra*, or "the sermon of the foundation of the kingdom of righteousness."[1] This work has been so frequently translated from different versions that it is useless to dwell on it here.

He imparted his doctrine to two of the Five in the morning, for the three others had gone to the city to beg, and in the evening he taught the latter while the other two went to collect alms (f. 64).[2]

Again he spoke to them about the four truths, and in addressing them he called them "*bhikshus*" or mendicants, a term which was very generally applied at that time to all ascetics.[3]

[1] There are at least six versions of this sûtra in the Tibetan canon. 1° Dulva, iv. 64–68; 2° Dulva, xi. 69–71; 3° Mdo, xxvi. 88–92 (Abhinichkramana Sûtra); 4° Mdo, xxvi. 425–431, Dharmachakra Sûtra; 5° Mdo, xxx. 427–431, Dharmachakra pravartana Sûtra; 6° Mdo, ii. chap. xxvi. of the Lalita Vistara.

[2] According to Bigandet, p. 118, he converted all five the same day; not so, however, in the Nidânakatha, Rhys Davids, Birth Stories, p. 113.

[3] Cf. G. Bühler, Sacred Laws of the Aryas, Gautama Dharmaçastra, iii. 2. The word *sanyasin*, generally used in the Dharmaçastra, conveys the same meaning.

When he had finished speaking, he turned to the oldest of the five, Kâundinya, and said, "Kâundinya, hast thou thoroughly understood the doctrine?" "Blessed One, I have thoroughly understood it." On this account he was called "Kâundinya, who knows all," or *Adjnata Kaundinya* (f. 66[b]).

Yet again he spoke to them about the four truths, and he converted the four other bhikshus. Now at that time there was one perfectly enlightened disciple (or *arhat*), Kâundinya. After that he preached to them about the impermanency of all created things, and the other four became arhats (f. 69[b]).

When he had thus converted the five, he went with them and stopped on the bank of the river of Benares, the Naçi[1] (? *Gnod-pa-chan*). There was a wealthy young man of Benares called Yaças[2] (*Grags-pa*), who came to the bank of the river by night, and seeing the Blessed One on the farther shore, he cried out to him, "Çramana, I am hurt; Çramana, I suffer!" Then he answered him, "Come hither and thou shalt suffer no more, nor be distressed." So he left his slippers on the river's bank and crossed over to where was the Blessed One, who talked to him of charity, of virtue, of heaven (*svarga*), of contentment, of the way to salvation, of the four truths, &c. (f. 71), and Yaças perceived the truth, he believed, and asked to become a lay follower (*upasaka*), (f. 71[b]). One of Yaças' slaves discovered, while it was yet night, that her master had left his home, so fearing an accident, she told his father, who started out to seek him. He came to the river, and seeing his son's slippers, he feared that he had been drowned or murdered. He crossed the stream and met the Blessed One, of whom he inquired concerning his son. The Buddha, before answering him, converted him (f. 73), and the same sermon made Yaças an arhat. It

[1] I have followed Schiefner, Tibet. Lebens, p. 247, in translating this name. Feer, Annales Musée Guimet, v. p. 21, translates it by Vâraṇa.

[2] He is called Ratha in Bigandet, p. 120. He does not mention the fact that he crossed a river.

was on this occasion that the Blessed One spoke the verse, "He who, though dressed in gorgeous apparel, walks in the way of truth," &c.[1] (f. 74).

Then Yaças and his father returned home, and when it was morning the Buddha went to his house, and, after having partaken of the food provided for him by the wife and mother of Yaças, he preached to them and converted them, and they became lay followers (*upasikas*), (f. 75[b]).

Now Yaças had four friends,[2] Purṇa (*Gang-po*), Vimala (*Dri-med*), Gavampati (*Ba-lang bdag*), and Subahu (*Lag-bzangs*), and when they had heard that Yaças had become a bhikshu, they also came and asked the Blessed One to admit them into his order. When he had finished preaching to them they became arhats. At that time there were ten arhats in the world, exclusive of the Buddha (f. 77[b]).

Fifty young men of the leading families of Benares,[3] on hearing of these conversions, entered the order (f. 78–79), and they also became arhats shortly after, so that there were sixty arhats in the world.

While still at the deer-park of Rishivadana he sent the sixty out two by two (f. 79[b]) to spread the doctrine that would help all creation, and he went towards the Senani village at Uruvilva.[4] Before he left, however, Mâra took the appearance of a young brahman and came and mocked at him for saying that he had found deliverance, whereas he was yet in Mâra's grasp. The Buddha recognised him, and with a few words put him to flight.[5] Then the Blessed One went towards the Senani

[1] See Udânavarga, chap. xxxiii. 1, p. 185; also Feer, *op. cit.*, p. 24.

[2] Bigandet (p. 126) says that they belonged "to the most illustrious families of Baranathu (Benares), and formerly connected with Ratha by the ties of friendship."

[3] "Who had been the companions of Ratha (Yaças) while in the world," adds Bigandet (p. 129).

[4] The text is "*Lteng-rgyas-kyi-grong-khyer-sde-chan*," which can only be translated by the Senani village of Uruvilva. See Feer, Etudes Bouddhiques, Le Sûtra de l'Enfant, p. 67, note. Bigandet (p. 132) says, "The village of Thena (Sena), situated in the vicinity of the solitude of Ooroowila (Uruvilva)." Also Rhys Davids, Sacred Books of the East, xiii. p. 113.

[5] Cf. Bigandet, p. 132; Feer, Annales de Musée Guimet, v. p. 31.

village, and entering a karvasika or cotton-tree forest[1] (*Ras-bal-chan*), he sat down at the foot of a tree. At that time there was a band of sixty young men who were called "the happy band" or *Bhadravarga*, who were in the habit of coming each day near Uruvilva to amuse themselves with women. One day one of the women ran away, and while looking for her the young men came across the Blessed One (f. 81[a]). They asked him if he had seen such and such a looking woman. Then he asked them, "What think ye? is it better to look for a woman or to look for oneself?" "Better to look for oneself," they replied. "Abide then with me a little and I will teach you the truth." So they sat down and he instructed them so that their hearts were opened; they believed and became lay followers (f. 82).

After this the Buddha converted a rich brahman of Kapilavastu called Deva, and also his wife. They had come to the Senani village and there they had heard of their countryman the Çakya prince (f. 82).

Then the Blessed One went into the village of Uruvilva and taught the two girls Nandâ and Nandâbala, and they also became lay disciples (f. 85[a]).[2]

Now the Buddha thought that the most important convert he could make in Magadha would be Uruvilva Kâçyapa, the jatila, then aged 120, a man greatly revered throughout the land, who was looked upon as an arhat, and who, with 500 disciples, was then stopping on the bank of the Nairanjana (f. 85). His two brothers, Nadi and Gâya Kâçyapa, each with 250 disciples, were also

[1] Cf. Rhys Davids, Birth Stories, Nidânakathâ, p. 114, where this forest is placed half-way between the Mrigadava and Uruvilva. He and also Bigandet (p. 134) say that, after sending out his disciples, he spent his first lent (*was*) in the solitude of Migadawon (Mrigadava), after which he went to Uruvilva. This would place the following events in the second year, according to the system here adopted of counting the years from the season of *was*. Rhys Davids (*loc. cit.*, p. 114) speaks of "the thirty young Baddha-vaggiyan nobles."

[2] Comp. Feer, *op. cit.* p. 42. M. Feer's translation is from the 6th volume of the Dulva, consequently our two translations complete each other and give an *ensemble* of all the Tibetan vinaya texts on the subject.

living on the bank of the same river, a little lower down the stream (f. 101). The Blessed One went to Uruvilva Kâçyapa's hermitage, entered into conversation with him, and finally asked his permission to pass the night in his fire-house, for he was a fire-worshipper (f. 86). Kâçyapa cautioned him about the terrible snake which belched forth fire and smoke, but the Buddha conquered it and put it in his alms-bowl (f. 87[b]). Notwithstanding this miracle, and many more which the Buddha performed (f. 88–100), Kâçyapa would not recognise his superiority, but at each new miracle he said to himself, "But I also am an arhat."

Finally (f. 100[a]), his pride was subdued, and he informed his disciples that he was going to adopt the rules of the order of the Mahâçramana. They told him that, as he was their master, they would follow him; so they threw into the river their skin couches, tree-bark, staffs, round bowls, and sacrificial spoons (f. 101), and then Kâçyapa begged admission into the order for himself and followers.

The two younger Kâçyapas, seeing all the implements of worship of their brother floating down the stream, feared that some misfortune coming from the king or robbers, from fire or water, had befallen him; so they and their disciples went to seek him, and they found him and his disciples listening to the Blessed One, and they also were converted (f. 102) and entered the order.

When the Blessed One had stayed at Uruvilva as long as pleased him, he and the thousand converts went to Gâyâ, and stopped at the tchaitya of Gâyâçirsha (f. 102[b]), and there he showed them many marvellous transformations by which he established their faith. He also preached to them the sermon on burning, or the *Aditta-pariyâya Sutta* of the Southern canon[1] (f. 103[b], 104[a]).

At this time the emissaries of Çrenika Bimbisara, king of Magadha, reported to him that there was a Buddha at

[1] Cf. Rhys Davids, Buddhism, p. 59, and Birth Stories, p. 114; and Feer, *op. cit.*, p. 131.

Gâyâçirsha with his disciples (f. 105). Now the king had made five wishes—1. That a Buddha might appear in his reign; 2. That he might see him; 3. That he might learn the truth from him; 4. That he might understand it; 5. That he might follow his commandments (f. 106). So, on hearing the happy tidings, he sent a messenger to the Blessed One to salute him, and to offer to him and his disciples his royal hospitality at the capital, Râjagriha (f. 107).

The Blessed One accepted the invitation and went to Râjagriha, and took up his abode with his thousand disciples in the grove of the consecrated (or the mighty) tchaitya of the people of Magadha,[1] and there the king sought him (f. 108^b). When the king and all the vast multitude which had come with him saw Kâçyapa the elder with the Buddha, they knew not what to think. Was he the Buddha's disciple, or was the Buddha his?

[1] This phrase is obscure, and my translation is subject to correction. The text is, "*Yul Magadha-pa-rnams-kyim tchod-rten legs-par rab-gnas ltang* (?) *bral-kyi ts'al.*" It is evidently the same place referred to by Feer, Etudes Bouddh., ii. p. 68, as "le jardin abondamment planté de l'est" (? *Shar pai ts'al gseb*). Schiefner, Tib. Lebens, p. 254, speaks of this place as the "Rohrhain des festen k'aitya." Spence Hardy, p. 196, calls it "the forest of Yashti, twelve miles from Râjagriha." Beal, Rom. Leg., p. 311, says that the Buddha "had arrived as far as the bamboo grove, and was resting for a time near a tower erected therein." According to another passage of the Dulva, ix. f. 53, King Bimbisara was converted in the Yashtivana, which would therefore be the same place as "the grove of the tchaitya" of our text. Feer, *loc. cit.*, agrees with this. The text of Dulva ix. says, however, that "from Venuvana the Blessed One betook himself at that time to Bahuputrachaitya," and there Mahâkâçyapa saw him under a tree, and was received into the order by him." This Kâçyapa was also called Nyagrodhaya, as "he had been obtained in consequence of a prayer addressed to a nyagrodha tree." See Schiefner, Tib. Tales, ch. ix. p. 186 *et seq.* The Nidâna-Katha, Rhys Davids, Birth Stories, p. 116, seems to allude to the place mentioned in our text, where it speaks of the Vannabhu, or place of praise, but it places Bimbisara's conversion at the Latthivana; Fausböll's text, p. 84, and Bigandet, p. 150, at the Tandivana, which he says is the same as the Latti grove. It is strange that notwithstanding this well-established version of Bimbisara's conversion, the Mdo (vol. xvi. f. 332–336) should have imagined another one in which the king, on hearing that the Buddha is coming, jealous of the homage the people are bestowing on him, makes a man throw a rock at the Buddha to kill him, but he hears a gatha and is converted. Cf. the conversion of Udayana, p. 74.

(f. 110). The Lord knew their thoughts, so he made Kâçyapa perform all kinds of miracles in their presence, and declare that the Buddha was his master (f. 111).

After that the Blessed One preached to the king and the people on form and its transitory nature, on upadana, sandjna, sanskara, &c. (f. 112), on the nidanas (f. 113–114), &c., so that the king and a great multitude of brahmans and householders were converted.

The king then invited the Blessed One to the city, and when he came there, he and his disciples stopped in the Yashtivana. The king came to see him, and after having heard the Buddha preach, he invited him to a feast on the morrow (f. 122[a]). When the feast was over, the king poured water over the Blessed One's hands, and said, "I give the Kalantakanivasa Bamboo grove to the Blessed One to dispose of as may please him" (f. 122). The Buddha accepted it, and this was the first vihara or permanent residence that the Buddhist order possessed.

The origin of the name of Kalantakanivasa Veluvana is this. Before Bimbisara had ascended the throne, he took a great fancy to a park belonging to a householder of Râjagriha. He asked the owner for it, but he would not give it up, so the prince made up his mind that as soon as he should become king he would confiscate it (f. 120). This he did, and the lawful owner became after death a venomous snake in his garden, and sought an occasion to bite the king. One day the king had gone into the park with his wives, and had fallen asleep while only one of the women was beside him. The snake was crawling near him, but some Kalantaka birds seized it and commenced crying, when the woman awoke and killed the snake.

To show his gratitude to the birds, the king had the place planted with bamboo groves, of which these birds were especially fond, so the park became known as the

Bamboo grove, the place of the Kalantaka birds (f. 121ᵇ).[1] In this grove the Buddha passed the rainy season of the first year of his ministry,[2] and there the sixty disciples whom he had previously sent out to preach joined him, as is shown by the following episode taken from Dulva i. f. 13–50.

There lived at Nâlanda, near Râjagriha, a brahman called Mâthara (*Gnas-len-kyi bu*), who had a son called Koshthila (*Stogs-rings*) (f. 13) and a daughter called Çarî. Koshthila went to Southern India to study the Lokayata system, and he received the surname of "the long-nailed," or Dirghanakha, because he had vowed not to cut his nails until he had learnt the çastras. Çarî married a brahman from Southern India called Tishya (*Skar-rgyal*). She bore him a son whom they called Upatishya[3] (*Nyer-rgyal*) after his father, Çariputra or son of Çarî, after his mother, and as they belonged to the Çâradvati family, he was also called Çâradvatiputra. He learnt all the sciences of the brahmans, and excelled in them at an early age (f. 21).

In a village near by, Modgal, the wife of the purohita of King Kaundinya Potâla bore a son, who was called Kolita, or "the lap-born," and as he greatly resembled his mother, he received the name of Modgalputra, or son of Modgal, and from the family to which he belonged he took the name of Maudgalyayana. He also became a master of all brahman lore at an early age.

These two youths met at school, and became fast friends, so when Maudgalyayana decided upon renouncing

[1] Bigandet, p. 157, speaks of this place as the Wiloowon (Veḷuvana), but it is only in the Northern legends that I have seen the term Kalantakanivasa (or nipata) joined to it. See Huen Thsang, B. ix. p. 29.

[2] See Schiefner, Tib. Lebens, p. 315.

[3] Cf. Bigandet, p. 158; Spence Hardy, Manual, p. 200; Feer, *op. cit.*, p. 4 *et seq.* Huen Thsang, B. ix. p. 54, says that Çariputra was born at Kâlapinâka, and (p. 51) that Maudgalyayana was born at Kulika. Fah Hian, p. 111, says that Nâlanda was Çariputra's birthplace.

the world, notwithstanding the opposition of his parents, his friend Çariputra resolved to follow him (f. 32).

Together they went to Râjagriha and became disciples of Sanjaya (*Yang-dag rgyal-ba-chan*), (f. 40). When their master died they each assumed the leadership of 250 disciples and took up their abode at Râjagriha. Before dying,[1] Sanjaya had spoken to them of the young Çakya, and had advised them to become his disciples (f. 41). One day Çariputra met Açvadjit while in Râjagriha begging his food. Struck with his appearance, he questioned him concerning himself and master.

Açvadjit replied that he was but a neophyte, and could not expound all the doctrine, but he repeated the verse, "*Ye dharma hetu prabhava*,"[2] &c., and this was enough to enable Çariputra to see the truth of the Buddha's doctrine. He inquired where the Buddha was, and learnt that he was at the Bamboo grove; so he went to Maudgalyayana, and repeated to him the verse he had heard, and he also perceived the truth; then together with 250 of their disciples they went to where the Buddha was, and entered the order.

A few days later Çariputra's uncle, Koshthila, came to the Bamboo grove, and was converted by the words of the Blessed One, which, at the same time, made Çariputra an arhat (f. 57). Çariputra and Maudgalyayana are known in Buddhist history as "the model pair;" the former was unsurpassable in wisdom, the latter in magical power.

It was at about this period of his ministry that the Buddha converted the nephew of the old rishi Asita, Nalada, who, under the name of Katyayana or Mahâkatyayana, played such a prominent rôle as a missionary.

[1] Bigandet, p. 161, says that Thindzi (Sanjaya) was not dead when they entered the Buddhist order, and that they each entered with 220 companions. Thindzi, enraged at being left alone, died, vomiting blood from his mouth. This Sanjaya must not be confounded with Sanjaya the son of Vairattî, one of the six heretical teachers. See p. 79.

[2] There is a good commentary on this verse by Nâgârjuna in the 72d vol. of the Mdo of the Bstan-hgyur, f. 244–245. The title is Dharmadhâtugarbha vivaraṇa.

His conversion is told as follows in Dulva xi. f. 118 *et seq.* While the Buddha was yet in the Tushita heaven he had spoken these two enigmatical verses:—

"To whom is lord and king (*i.e.*, the senses),
Under the rule of the passions, he is covered with dust (*raga*);
Free from passion (*raga*), he is free from dust (*raga*);
Who is it that thus speaks of passion here?

Wickedness, by it is sorrow produced;
Wisdom, by it is joy brought forth;
By being separated from the possession of what
Do we learn here what is perfection and bliss?"[1]

Before the Buddha's birth no one was even able to read these words, and after his birth they could be read, but not understood, as it required a Buddha to explain them. There lived at that time a nâga king called Suvarnaprabhasa (*Gser-od*), who saw in the palace of the nâga Vaiçravana (*Rnam-thos-kyi-bu*) a copy of these verses; he repeated them to Elapatra (*Elai-mdab*), another nâga who lived at Takshaçila, and who was very desirous of seeing a Buddha. Suvarnaprabhasa advised him to go everywhere offering a laksha of gold to any one who could explain these lines to him (f. 119). Elapatra followed his advice after having assumed the appearance of a young brahman. After a while he reached Benares, where was Nalada, who promised that he would bring him the desired explanation within seven days. Having found out that there was a Buddha in the world, and that he was stopping in the deer-park of Rishivadana, he went to him. He was as ravished with his appearance as would be a man who had been plunged in abstraction for twelve years, or as a childless man to whom a son is born, or as a poor man who sees a treasure; and as soon as the Buddha had preached to him, his eyes were opened, and he saw the truth. So having gone and fulfilled his promise

[1] These verses are very difficult to translate. Cf. Schiefner's transl. of them in his Mahâkatyayana und König Tshanda Pradyota, p. 11. See also Beal, Romantic Legend, p. 277.

to Elapatra, he came back and became a disciple (f. 126), and henceforth he was called Katyayana or Katyayana the Great (f. 128).

While stopping at the Çitavana of Râjagriha,[1] the Blessed One was invited to a feast by a householder of the city, at whose house was then stopping a rich merchant of Çravasti called Sudaṭṭa, better known on account of his generosity and charitableness as "the incomparable almsgiver," or Anathapiṇḍada. The night before the feast Sudaṭṭa heard the master of the house giving his orders; and having inquired the reason of these preparations, he heard of the Buddha and his disciples, and conceived great admiration for the Master. Early on the morrow he went to Çitavana, and finding the Buddha walking in front of the house, he was led by him into his room, and there the Blessed One talked to him of charity, morality, &c., so that he saw the truth, and became a lay follower.

Then the Blessed One questioned him as to his name, his country, &c., and Sudaṭṭa besought him to come to Çravasti in Kosala, and assured him that he would provide him and his disciples with all which they might require.

"Householder," the Buddha inquired, "is there any vihara at Çravasti?"

"There is none, Blessed One."

"If there was such a place, householder, bhikshus could go, come, and stay there."

"Only come, Blessed One, and I will provide a vihara also."

The Buddha promised him, and with that assurance Sudaṭṭa departed.

After a little while he came back and asked the Buddha

[1] Taken from Dulva iv. f. 123–139. This episode is also in Dulva iii. f. 317–341. The Nidanakatha, Rhys Davids, *op. cit.*, p. 130, places the donation of the Jetavana vihara after the journey to Kapilavastu, but the Tibetan texts do not agree with this, as it is said that he sent word to his father to build the vihara of the Banyan grove on the plan of the Jetavana. Prof. Rhys Davids, *loc. cit.*, translates Sîtavana by "grove of Sitâ." I cannot believe that this can be correct. Cf. Huen Thsang, B. vi. p. 296 *et seq.*

to send a bhikshu with him who could superintend the building of the vihara. The Buddha chose Çariputra, for well he knew that he would also work at the conversion of the people of Çravasti.

Sudaṭṭa sought to procure a suitable piece of ground for the vihara, and his choice fell upon a park belonging to Jeta[1] (*Rgyal-byed*), son of King Prasenadjit. He asked the prince for it; he at first refused, but finally agreed to sell it if Sudaṭṭa covered all the ground with gold pieces (f. 129). To this the householder consented. When he had nearly finished having the ground covered with gold, Jeta thought that it would be good for him to offer something to this Buddha for whose sake Sudaṭṭa was sacrificing so much, so he asked him to let him retain that part of the park not yet covered with gold. Sudaṭṭa let him have it; and on this ground the prince afterwards built a vestibule, which he gave to the order (f. 130).

The members of other orders (the tirthikas) in Râjagriha became jealous of the sudden popularity of the new order, so they complained to the king. Çariputra offered to demonstrate his greater worthiness by a trial of their relative magical powers (f. 131), out of which contest he came off victorious (f. 132). He also converted the chief of the tirthikas, "Red eye," or Raktâksha (*Mig-dmar*), and many of the spectators.

Then the tirthikas sought to kill Çariputra while the vihara was being built; but they were unable to execute their plan, and were finally converted, and became arhats (f. 135).

The vihara was built on the plan of one sent by the devas of the Tushita heaven, and contained sixty large halls and sixty small ones (f. 136).[2]

[1] Jeta was most likely the son of Varshikâ, a princess of kshatriya caste. See Dulva x. f. 126; he is there represented as a little older than Virudhaka, who succeeded Prasenadjit. Fah Hian, chap. xx., says that when he visited Çravasti (early part of the fifth century A.D.) there were very few inhabitants in it, perhaps about two hundred families.

[2] In Dulva xi. fol. 34[b], Anâthapindada asks the Buddha how the vihara must be ornamented with

When all was ready, Sudaṭṭa sent word to the Blessed One, and on his arrival at Çravasti he was received with great honours, such as were only shown to a king of kings (f. 138). After an entertainment, Anathapiṇḍada presented to the sangha the park and the vihara by pouring water on the Buddha's hands, as we have seen Bimbisara do in presenting the Bamboo grove. Then the Buddha, in honour of the two donors, called the place Jeta's park (*Jetavana*), the pleasure grove of Anathapiṇḍada (*Anathapiṇḍadârama*). Great was Jeta's joy when he heard his name placed first; so he had the vestibule he had built ornamented with all kinds of precious substances (f. 139b).

King Prasenadjit of Kosala having heard that the Blessed One was at Râjagriha in the Jetavana, visited him, and asked him how he could possibly pretend to be a Buddha when such old and respected sages as Pûrṇa-Kâçyapa, the Parivradjaka (Maskharin) Goçala, Sanjaya son of Vairaṭî, Ajîta-Keçakambala, &c., did not even lay claim to this title (f. 141b). Then the Buddha preached to him the sermon of the comparisons of young men, or *Kumara dristanta Sûtra*[1] (f. 140–141), by which the king was converted.

paintings (or bas-reliefs). The Buddha answers, "On the outside door you must have figured a yaksha holding a club in his hand; in the vestibule you must have represented a great miracle, the five divisions (of beings) of the circle of transmigration; in the courtyard, the series of births (jâtakas); on the door of the Buddha's special apartment (lit. hall of perfumes, *Gandhakûṭi*; see Burnouf, Intr., p. 262, and Childers, Pali Dict., s.v. *Gandhakûṭi*), a yaksha holding a wreath in his hand; in the house of the attendants (or of honour, *rim-gro*), bhikshus and sthaviras arranging the dharma; on the kitchen must be represented a yaksha holding food in his hand; on the door of the storehouse, a yaksha with an iron hook in his hand; on the water-house (well-house ?), nâgas with variously ornamented vases in their hands; on the wash-house (or the steaming-house *bsro-khang*), foul sprites or the different hells; on the medicine-house, the Tathâgata tending the sick; on the privy, all that is dreadful in a cemetery; on the door of the lodging-house (? text effaced), a skeleton, bones, and a skull."

[1] The Southern version of this sermon, *Dahara Sutta*, is in the Sanyutta-nikaya, and is very nearly identical with the Northern one. See Feer, Etudes Bouddh., ii. p. 63 *et seq.* The Tibetan version there translated (Mdo xxv. f. 458–460) differs slightly from that of the Dulva; not enough, however, to justify a new translation of it.

In this vihara of Jetavana the Buddha passed the season of *was* of the third year of his ministry.

We are not told where he passed the summer of the fourth year, but he was certainly at Jetavana in the fifth year, for it was from that place that he went to Kapilavastu in the sixth year of his ministry.

The Dulva does not chronicle any important conversion between that of Prasenadjit, king of Kosala, and that of the Çakyas of Kapilavastu in the sixth year.[1]

Part of the intervening time was most likely occupied in framing the regulations for the order of bhikshus, although the Dulva informs us that the most important rules of the code, which was afterwards called the *Pratimoksha,* were only formulated when Devadatta commenced sowing strife among the brethren, some ten or twelve years before the Buddha's death. At all events, our texts lead us to suppose that until after the conversion of Prasenadjit the mendicants of the order did not live together, and that the only rules laid down for their guidance were that they were obliged to beg their food, that they must observe the ordinary rules of morality (the çîla precepts), that they must own no property, and that they must preach to all classes of people. They may have adopted such rules as were in general usage at the time among ascetics, but it appears improbable that they had any regulating their dress,[2] for we are told that King Prasenadjit several times mistook doctors, &c., for Buddhist mendicants on account of their similar costumes, and that it was only then that the Buddha prescribed that the bhikshus should make their cloaks out of pieces of stuff dyed of different colours and sewn together (Dulva iii. f. 112[b]). Of course, the rule about shaving the head and

[1] See for this date Edkins, Chinese Buddh., p. 32; Schiefner, Tib. Lebens, p. 315.

[2] Thus in Dulva x. fol. 9, the bhikshus are prohibited from wearing the sacred cord (*Ts'angs pai skud*) of the Dvijas. Also, in the same vol. fol. 4[b], they were prohibited from drawing lines in white clay (on their persons), as do at the present day many Hindu sects, such as the Nimbârkas, the Râmânujas, &c.

beard was in force from the first days of the order, for this rule was common to all ascetics of those times.

Prasenadjit, shortly after his conversion, sent a message to Çuddhodana, king of the Çakyas of Kapilavastu, in which he told him, "Rejoice, O Râja, for thy son has found the drink of the cessation of death (*amrita*), and he is quenching the thirst of mankind with this nectar!" (D. iv. f. 142).[1]

Then Çuddhodana sent several messengers to his son at Râjagriha begging him to visit him at Kapilavastu; but they all entered the order, and came back no more to the king.

Finally he dispatched Kâludâyi[2] with a letter to the Buddha. Udâyi promised that he would come back, even if he entered the order in the meantime.[3] Hardly had he arrived at Râjagriha but the Buddha converted him, and Çariputra received him into the order (f. 143), after which the Buddha allowed him to return to Kapilavastu; but he instructed him to stop at the gate of the town, not to dwell in a house in the town, and to inform the king that when he himself came he would not stop in the town, but in a vihara, and that Jetavana was the model vihara (f. 144ᵇ).

Kâludâyi delivered the message[4] as it had been given him (f. 145), and King Çuddhodana had the vihara of the Banyan grove, or *Nyagrodhârama*, built on the plan of the Jetavana vihara for his son's reception (f. 146).

[1] Cf. Dulva vi. f. 93–102; and Feer, *op. cit.*, p. 43.

[2] The Nidânakatha, Rhys Davids, Buddh. Birth Stories, p. 120, says that Kâla Udâyin was born on the same day as the future Buddha, and had been his playfellow and companion. See also Feer, *op. cit.*, p. 38.

[3] The Nidânakatha, p. 120, says, "The Master spent the first Lent after he had become Buddha at Isipatana; and when it was over, went to Uruvila, and stayed there three months, and overcame the three brothers, ascetics. And on the full-moon day of the month of January he went to Râjagriha with a retinue of a thousand mendicants, and there he dwelt two months. Thus five months had elapsed since he left Benâres, the cold season was past, and seven or eight days since the arrival of Udâyin the elder" (*thera*). See also Bigandet, p. 169.

[4] The Nidânakatha, *loc. cit.*, says that Udâyin started for Kapilavastu on the full-moon day of March (*Phaggunipuṇṇamâ*). Also Bigandet, p. 170.

When all was ready, the Buddha started for Kapilavastu with his disciples, and first stopped on the banks of the Rohita near the city, where he and his followers performed all kinds of magical transformations in the presence of the king and the Çakyas who had come to meet them,[1] so that great was the astonishment of Çuddhodana and his people (f. 148). The king bowed at the Buddha's feet, much to the astonishment of his people; but he recalled to them how he had done so on former occasions when the Buddha was but an infant. He conversed with his son, recalling to him (in verse) the splendours and joys of his former life, to which, however, the Buddha opposed those of his present one (f. 150–152).[2]

After this first meeting the Buddha took up his abode in the Banyan grove, and by his first predication he converted his uncle Çuklodana and 70,000 Çakyas (f. 152[b]), "but Çuddhodana was not among them." At short intervals after this he converted Dronodana with 66,000 Çakyas, and Amritodana with 75,000 (f. 153).[3]

The Buddha was very anxious to convert his father, but he had not been able to make any impression on his mind, although he had sent Maudgalyayana to him, who had performed wondrous magical feats in his presence. One day a great number of gods came to the Banyan grove and built a marvellous hall, in which the Blessed One took his seat and explained the truth; and there his father saw him, surrounded by the four Lokapâlitas, by Çakra, Brahmâ, &c. (f. 155–156), and when the Lord had finished teaching the gods, he came and taught his father, who believed and entered the paths (f. 157).[4]

[1] The Nidânakatha, p. 122, says that the Buddha went to Kapilavastu attended by 20,000 mendicants, and that he took two months to travel the sixty leagues which separated it from Râjagriha. Bigandet, p. 170, says the same thing, but all this portion of his text is a translation of the Nidânakatha,—at least so it appears to me.

[2] Cf. Huen Thsang, B. vi. p. 318 *et seq.*

[3] These numbers appear fanciful. Beal, Rom. Leg., p. 351, speaks of "all the Çakyas of Kapilavastu, 99,000 in all."

[4] The Nidânakatha, p. 126, does not agree with this version. See Feer, *op. cit.*, p. 57.

The two following episodes seem out of place here, but it appears proper to preserve the arrangement of the text.

Çuddhodana offered the succession to the throne of Kapilavastu to Çuklodana, but he refused (f. 157), having become a Buddhist (bhikshu?); the king's other brothers refused for the same reason,[1] so they chose as Çuddhodana's successor Çakyarâja Bhadrika (f. 158[a]).

The following day Çuddhodana gave an entertainment to the Buddha and his disciples, and presented the Banyan grove to him by pouring water on his hands (f. 158[b]).

Shortly after this the Çakyas made a proclamation by which one man out of every family must enter the Buddhist order (f. 159[a]), and it is probable that to this decision, to which the Buddha was obliged to consent, was due a great deal of the trouble he afterwards had with some of the Çakya bhikshus whose names are mentioned farther on. I reproduce the following anecdote, not so much for its historic value, as to show the curious alterations some of these old legends have undergone during the ages in which they were preserved orally.

Dronodana had two sons, Aniruddha and Mahânâman; the former was his mother's favourite, but never took any part in the sports and amusements of his age, whereas his brother had learnt all kinds of field-work.[2] When the king's decree was proclaimed, their mother wanted Mahânâman to enter the order, but he told her that her favourite Aniruddha was better entitled to such an honour; and, to find out who was the more worthy, they made the following experiment. They took an empty basket in which they put a vase, which they covered over (at the mouth?) with sugar painted (or sealed) with

1 Çuddhodana could not have made this offer to his brothers until after the conversion of Nanda and Râhula, which, according to our text, only took place later on. So, likewise, it appears curious that the presentation of the Nyagrodha vihara only took place some time after the Buddha had taken up his residence there.

2 This is a reminiscence of the passage in the Southern version, in which Mahânâma describes to his brother the labour of the husbandman. See Spence Hardy, Manual, p. 235.

lac, and this they gave to a servant-girl with orders that if (f. 160) any one asked what was in the vase, to say that there was nothing. On the way to where Aniruddha was, Çakra filled the vase with pease, vegetables, and other kinds of food. Aniruddha asked the girl what she had in her basket. "Nothing," she answered him. "My mother loves me dearly, she cannot have sent this empty; surely it is a dish called 'nothing.'" So he opened the vase, and the fragrance of the contents pervaded the whole park and filled him with wonder and gratefulness toward his mother, so he sent her word begging that she would send him every day some of that "nothing" dish.

His mother, on hearing what had happened, wondered greatly and said to Mahânâman, "Seest thou that, my son?" "Yes, truly, mother." And by this means did they discover that Aniruddha was in truth entitled to the honour of entering the Buddhist order.

The mother told Aniruddha that he could enter the order, and she explained to him what this term implied.

Aniruddha sought his friend Çakyarâja Bhadrika (f. 161), and having embraced him, he told him of the king's proclamation and asked him to enter the order with him. Bhadrika objected that if he did so the throne would belong to Devadatta (f. 162), to the great prejudice of the people. Aniruddha then suggested that they should induce Devadatta to enter the order at the same time; so they obtained his promise, and as soon as they had it they caused to be announced in the streets of the city that Bhadrika, Raivata, Aniruddha, Devadatta, five hundred in all, were about to enter the order of the Blessed One.

Devadatta was greatly worried at this; he had hoped to be able to perjure himself and escape becoming a bhikshu, for that would put an end to all his hopes of reigning; but it was too late, and he had to submit. There appears to have been many more of the five hundred who entered the order under compulsion, and who afterwards aided Devadatta in bringing about a schism; the best known were Kokalika, Khandadvaja, Katamorakatisya, Sagaradatta, &c. (f. 163). Nanda,[1] the Buddha's half-brother, was also one of those who entered against his will. Nanda, says the Dulva x. (f. 102), was very much in love with his wife Bhadrâ,[2] but was led by the Buddha to the Banyan grove and there made a bhikshu. His fondness for his wife was so great that he tried several times to get back to her, and the Buddha was obliged to take him to the Trayastrimcat heaven, and also to hell, to convince him of the unworthiness of any worldly love.[3]

Çuddhodana, on hearing of the young Çakyas' determination, sent the royal barber Upâli (*Nye-bar-bkhor*) to shave their heads and beards. When he had finished doing so, they took off all their jewels and ornaments and gave them to him (f. 165[b]) and then went to bathe. Upâli thought, "If these young noblemen have given up wealth, the pleasures of youth, wives, and treasures, to become mendicants, it cannot then be seeming in me to care for these baubles; they would bring me but grief. If I had not had an evil birth,[4] I would have entered the order of the well-spoken dharma, and have devoted myself to crossing the stream and to freeing myself of all my bonds." Now Çariputra knew that Upâli would become famous as a bhikshu, so he went to where he was standing, and said, "Upâli, what troubles you?" and then he told him the thoughts of his mind. Çariputra led him to where the

[1] The Nidanâkatha (p. 128) says that Nanda was received into the order on the day of his marriage, the third day after the Buddha had reached Kapilavastu.

[2] In the Nidanâkatha (p. 128) she is called Janapada Kalyâṇî. Kalyanî = Bhadrâ, "good, beautiful."

[3] It was then that the Buddha spoke the famous gathâ, "When a citadel has been made of bones, plastered over with flesh and blood," &c. See Dhammapada, 150; Udânavarga, xvi. 22; and Dulva x. fol. 246–247, where there are many more verses of an equally instructive character.

[4] Can the Buddhist order have been in the first place only open to men of the higher castes? Upâli is the first bhikshu mentioned in the legends who did not belong to the brahman or kshatriya caste.

Blessed One[1] was, and told him that Upâli wanted to enter the order. "Come hither, bhikshu," the Blessed One said, "and lead a life of purity;" and forthwith Upâli's hair fell off and he stood arrayed in bhikshu's apparel, an alms-bowl in his hand, with the look of a bhikshu of eight years' standing.

When the young Çakyas arrived, the Blessed One consented to their admission into the order with misgivings, for he saw that some of them would soon become dissatisfied (f. 163). Upâli had been received while they were yet on their way, so they were obliged, on being received into the order, to do him homage, and to bow down before him. Devadatta, however, would not consent to this. "Son," the Buddha said to him, "bow down. Hast thou not entered the order to cast off pride?" But he still refused, and this was the first time that Devadatta disobeyed the Blessed One's orders (f. 167[a]).

One day while the Blessed One was out begging, Yaçôdhâra saw him from the palace, so she sought to win him back (f. 208[a]). She gave five hundred pieces to a charm-maker of Râjagriha, who gave her a philter which would bring the Buddha back to her. Yaçôdhâra gave this to Râhula, and told him to present it to his father. When the child came to where the Blessed One was, there appeared five hundred Buddhas, but Râhula recognised his father among them all,[2] and gave him the charm. The Buddha gave the food back to Râhula, and he ate it; after which he could not be prevented from following after the Buddha. Now the Lord saw that he was in his last birth, so he told Çariputra to admit the child into the order (f. 209), although he was only six years old.

Yaçôdhâra, foiled in this attempt, arrayed herself, and also Gôpâ, Mrigadjâ, and the 60,000 women of the palace,

[1] Bigandet (i. p. 183) says that he was in the village of Anupya, in the country of the Malla princes.

[2] It was on this occasion that the Buddha told the story of the clever thief who was recognised by his son. The Buddha had been the thief. See Schiefner, Tibetan Tales, p. 37; and Dulva iv. f. 209–214.

in all their finery (f. 214), and they placed themselves where they would be seen by the Buddha when he came to the palace to beg. The Blessed One performed all kinds of miracles in their presence, by which he filled them with awe and established them in the faith (f. 215). Gôpâ, Mrigadjâ, and the 60,000 other women entered the paths, but Yaçôdhâra, blinded by her love for her lost husband, would not see the truth, but continued to hope that she would be able to bring him back to her arms.[1] A little while later on, however, he converted her, and she also entered the paths. She entered the order (the following year?), became an arhati, and the Buddha said of her, "Yaçôdhâra, the mother of Râhula, is the most modest of all my female disciples" (f. 220[a]).

Amritodana had a son, Ananda by name, a boy of the same age as Râhula. Soothsayers had predicted that he would become the personal attendant of the Buddha, so his father sought to prevent them meeting. He took him to Vaisali when the Buddha came to Kapilavastu, and back to Kapilavastu when the Blessed One went to Vaisali.[2] The Blessed One perceived that it would be good for Ananda if he were converted (f. 233[b]), for "after my death he will find the amrita." So he went to Amritodana's house at Kapilavastu, and sat down in a room next to the one in which was Ananda. Suddenly the door opened, Ananda came in, and bowed to the Blessed One; then taking a fan, he stood on one side fanning him. Amritodana on seeing this bowed down at the Buddha's feet, and listened to the words of truth which he spoke. When the Buddha arose and went away, Ananda followed after him, and no one could keep him back. His father seeing this, consented that Ananda should enter the order,

[1] On this occasion the Buddha told the Rishyasringa jataka. See Schiefner, *op. cit.*, p. 253; and Dulva iv. f. 216, 219.

[2] We learn from a passage in Dulva xi. f. 328[a], that the Buddha on leaving Kapilavastu went into the Vridji country. The passage under consideration leads us to suppose that he made several visits to Kapilavastu at short intervals.

and on the morrow he led him in great pomp to the Nyagrodha vihara, where he was received into the brotherhood by Dâçabâla Kâçyapa (f. 334[b]).

While the Buddha was yet at Kapilavastu,[1] the Çakya women attempted to gain admission into the order. The story is told as follows in Dulva iii. f. 365–368:—

The Buddha had expounded the truth to the Çakyas three times, he had also taught Çuddhodana three times, and had made many converts (f. 366[a]). The Çakya Mahânâman had also heard the truth, and was so delighted with it that his wife was struck with his enthusiasm and asked him the reason. He told her about the Buddha and his doctrine, and said that he was their saviour. "He is the saviour of men, but not of women," she exclaimed. "Say not so," her husband replied; "his mercy extends to all creation. Go, seek him, and you will hear the truth from his mouth" (f. 366[b]). Mahânâman was unable, however, to get King Çuddhodana's permission for the women to go to the Banyan grove (doubtless the king suspected their purpose), but he interested Mahâprajapati Gautâmi (*Skye-dguhi-bdag tchen-mo*), the king's wife, in their undertaking, and she obtained the necessary authorisation (f. 367).

Mahânâman also persuaded five hundred [2] other Çakya women to go with them to the Banyan grove. Now Mahânâman's wife was young and beautiful, and she wore much jewellery on this occason. As she was approaching the Buddha with the other women, the Buddha's attendant[3] saw her, and reproved her for wearing such gorgeous apparel. She

[1] Already in the fifth century A.D. it was deserted and in ruins. See Fah Hian, chap. xxii.

[2] This number makes the story look suspicious. It reminds us too much of the episode of Bhadrika, Raivata, Aniruddha, &c. In fact, every episode relating to the female members of the order seems a copy of one concerning the bhikshus, and is evidently much more recent than the former.

[3] The text says Ananda, but this can hardly be if we follow the indications of D. iv. f. 51 and 232, for Ananda was the same age as Râhula, six years old, when this event happened. That this is the commonly received version is apparent from Spence Hardy, Man., p. 241, where we are told that Ananda was ordained "in the twentieth year after the teacher of the three worlds became Buddha,"

gave her jewellery to a maid-servant who had accompanied her, and who was very desirous of hearing the dharma, and told her to take her jewels home (f. 368[b]); but the girl was so distressed at being deprived of hearing the Buddha preach, that she died on the way to the city. She was, however, reborn as the Princess Ratnâvali (*Mu-tig-chan*), daughter of the king of Ceylon. Although the latter part of this legend occurred some years later, it is as well to reproduce it here, as does the Dulva.

It happened that some merchants of Çravasti (f. 370), pushed by contrary winds, came to the island of Ceylon, and through them Princess Ratnâvali heard of the Buddha, of his life and his doctrines. She wrote a letter to the Blessed One (f. 371[b]), asking him for the amrita, and the merchants carried it to the Buddha, who was then at Çravasti. He, knowing that the princess could be converted, told the merchants to speak his praise when they should return thither, and moreover he decided upon sending the princess his likeness. The artists who were called to paint his portrait were unable to do so. The Buddha told them to take a piece of cotton stuff, and to hold it up between him and the light, and by this means they traced the outlines of his person, and filled them in with different coloured paints (f. 372[b]). Below the portrait he had written the three refuges, the five prohibitions, the twelve nidanas, what was the truth (*lugs dang mthun*) and what was not the truth, and the holy eightfold way. Above it

which would make Ananda twenty at that time, the regulation age for ordination. See Dulva i. f. 108. If, on the other hand, we follow the legend which makes him of the same age as the Buddha, he was a hundred and twenty when he died, for he was head of the church for forty years after Mahâkâçyapa's death. Schiefner, Tib. Lebens, p. 309, says that Ananda was chief of the doctrine for forty years, and passed away when he was eighty-five. This cannot be considered as accurate, for it does not take into consideration the time during which Kâçyapa was patriarch, possibly ten or eleven years. Klaproth, Foe Koue Ki, p. 251, says that Ananda lived a hundred and thirty years, which would allow five years for Kâçyapa's patriarchate, forty-five for his own, and would make him the same age as the Buddha. Edkins, *op. cit.*, p. 42, says that Ananda was sixteen when he was chosen as the attendant of the Buddha.

were written the two verses, "Arise, commence new life," &c., and "He who leads a life of purity," &c.[1]

The merchants explained to the princess that whosoever observed all the rules written on the piece of cloth on which was the Buddha's likeness had found amrita (f. 374[a]).

When the merchants started for their home again, Ratnâvali gave them three dronas (bushels) of pearls (f. 375), one for the Buddha, one for the dharma, and one for the sangha.

With this legend the account given in the third volume of the Dulva of the first attempt of the Çakya women to found a female order of mendicants comes abruptly to an end. We must turn to the eleventh volume, f. 326[b]–338, to find the sequel.

When the Blessed One had finished preaching to the five hundred Çakya women in the Banyan grove, Mahâprajapati Gautami said to the Buddha, "If women could have the four fruits of the çramana, they would enter the order and strive for perfection. I beseech the Blessed One to let women become bhikshunis, and to live in purity near the Blessed One." But he answered her, "Gautami, wear the pure white dress of lay-women; seek to attain perfection; be pure, chaste, and live virtuously, and you will find a lasting reward, blessings, and happiness" (D. xi. f. 327). A second and yet a third time she renewed her request in the same terms, but she only elicited the same answer; so bowing down, she left his presence.[2]

When the Blessed One had remained at Kapilavastu as long as suited him, he took up his alms-bowl and

[1] See Çsoma, Tib. Gram., p. 164, where part of this episode is translated. Udânavarga, p. 23.

[2] It would be possible to make the Southern and Northern versions agree, to a certain extent, as to the time of the Buddha's life when Gautami entered the order, &c., if we take into consideration the facts mentioned in the Southern version of the first visit to Kapilavastu in the first year, and another at the time of his father's death in the sixth. In our text these two journeys are confounded. This, however, is of secondary importance.

cloak and went to the Natika[1] country in Vriji, and stopped at a place called Nakaikundjika (*sic*) (f. 328[a]). Gautami having heard this, she and the five hundred Çakya women shaved their heads, put on bhikshuni's clothing, and followed after him and came to where he was, wearied, ragged, wayworn, and covered with dust. When the Buddha had finished preaching to her and her companions, she renewed her request to be admitted into the order, but she received the same answer as previously (f. 328[b]). So she went and sat down outside the entrance of the house and wept, and there Ananda saw her and asked her what was the matter. She told him, and Ananda went to where the Buddha was and renewed Gautami's request (f. 329[b]). "Ananda," replied the Buddha, "ask not that women be admitted into the order, that they be ordained and become bhikshunis, for if women enter the order the rules of the order will not last long. Ananda, if in a house there are many women and but few men, thieves and robbers may break in and steal; so will it be, Ananda, if women enter the order, the rules of the order will not long be safe.[2] Or yet again, Ananda, if a field of sugar-cane is blighted (*btsah-nad*), it is worthless, good for nothing; so will it be, Ananda, if women enter the order, the rules of the order will not last long (f. 330[a]). However, Ananda, if Gautami accepts the eight following rules, she may enter the order:—1st, To thoroughly understand the nature of a bhikshuni; 2d, a bhikshuni being near bhikshus, shall be taught every half-month; 3d, a bhikshuni shall not pass the season of *was* in a place where there are no bhikshus; 4th, a bhikshuni during *was*

[1] Fah Hian, ch. xxi., speaks of a town called Na-pi-ka, twelve yojanas south-east of Çravasti. The Natika of our text must have been east of Kapilavastu, whereas that of Fa Hian was less than a yojana to the west of it.

[2] Elsewhere (Dulva x. f. 127[b]) the Buddha says, "There are five kinds of dangerous serpents—the angry, the spiteful, the hating, the ungrateful, and the venomous one; so likewise there are five kinds of dangerous women—the angry, the spiteful, the hating, the ungrateful, and the venomous women." See also p. 152, where Ananda's conduct on this occasion is severely reproached by him.

shall be sufficiently separated from the bhikshus so as not to see and hear them or fear the proximity; 5th, a bhikshuni by words or by reviving recollections shall not damage the morals of a bhikshu; 6th, a bhikshuni shall not be wrathful, abusive, or do anything sinful; 7th, a bhikshuni shall confess her sins to the bhikshus (?) every fortnight; 8th, a bhikshuni, though she has been ordained since an hundred years, shall always speak kindly to a bhikshu, even if he be recently ordained; she shall honour him, rise before him, reverence him, and bow down to him" (f. 331). Gautami accepted all these rules, and so she and the other women were received into the order, and among them was Yaçôdhâra, the Buddha's wife.

From here the Blessed One went on to Vaisâli.[1] I take the following description of this celebrated city from Dulva iii. f. 80:—"There were three districts in Vaisâli. In the first district were 7000 houses with golden towers, in the middle district were 14,000 houses with silver towers, and in the last district were 21,000 houses with copper towers; in these lived the upper, the middle, and the lower classes, according to their positions." The people of Vaisâli (who were the rulers, f. 79) had made a law that a daughter born in the first district could marry only in the first district, not in the second or third; that one born in the middle district could marry only in the first and second; but that one born in the last district could marry in any one of the three; moreover, that no marriage was to be contracted outside Vaisâli.[2]

Their chief magistrate was called Nâyaka (*Sde-dpon*) (f. 82), and he was elected by the people, or rather by the ruling clans of Licchavis, for the people of the country were called Vrijians, or inhabitants of the land of

[1] See Schiefner, Tib. Lebens, p. 268. Dulva iv. f. 334[b] says that the Buddha on leaving Kapilavastu went to Râjagriha, where Jivaka cured an abscess on Ananda's head; and from there he went to Çravasti and abode in the Jetavana vihara (f. 336).

[2] I have followed Schiefner's translation in W. Ralston's English rendering of it. Tibetan Tales, page 77.

Vriji (*Spong-byed*).[1] Vaisâli is invariably described in the Dulva as a kind of earthly paradise, with its handsome buildings, its parks and gardens, the singing-birds, and continual festivities among the Licchavis. "Nanda Upananda!" exclaimed the Chabbaggiyâ bhikshus when they visited Vaisâli; "the Blessed One never saw the like of this, even when he was among the Trayastrimcat devas" (Dulva x. f. 2).

Sakala (*Dum-bu*), a minister of King Virudhaka of Videha, had been obliged to flee from his country on account of the jealousy of the other ministers of the king; so he went to Vaisâli together with his two sons, Gopâla (*Sa-skyong*) and Sinha (*Seng-ge*). Sakala soon became a prominent citizen in Vaisâli, and after a while he was elected Nâyaka (f. 82). His two sons married at Vaisâli, and Sinha had a daughter whom they called Vâsavî (*Gos-chan*); it was foretold that she would bear a son who would take his father's life, set the diadem on his own head, and seize the sovereignty for himself. Sinha's wife bore him, moreover, another daughter, whom they called Upavâsavî (*Nye-gos-chan*), and the seers declared that she would bear a son provided with excellent qualities.

Gopâla was fierce and of great strength, so he ravaged the parks of the Licchavis. To restrain him, the popular assembly (*Don-du ts'ogs*) gave him and his brother a park; and thus it is said by the sthaviras in the sûtras, "The Blessed One went out from Vaisâli to the sala forest of Gopâla and Sinha" (f. 82).

When Sakala died, the people appointed Sinha, his son Nâyaka; and Gopâla, slighted at this, departed from Vaisali and took up his residence at Râjagriha in Magadha, where he became the first minister of Bimbisara (f. 83).

A little later on King Bimbisara married Vâsavî, Gopâla's niece, and as she was of a family from Videha,

[1] Dulva v. f. 284–288, Ajatasatru ravages the territory of Vriji, and it is the Licchavis who defend it.

she became known as Vaidehi (f. 85). After a while she bore a son, who, on account of the prediction made to his mother, received the name of Adjatasatru, or "the enemy (while) not (yet) born" (*Ma-skyes dgra*)[1] (f. 8).

We will farther on have frequent occasion to speak of this prince, who is one of the prominent personages in the history of the last years of the Buddha's life.

The history of two other persons from Vaisâli who played an important rôle in this story is told as follows in Dulva iii. f. 87–107:—There lived at Vaisâli a Licchavi named Mahânâman. From a kadali tree in an amra grove in his park was born a girl, lovely to look upon, perfect in all parts of her body, and he called her name Amrapâlî (*Amra skyong-ma*). When she was grown up, as there was a law of Vaisâli by which a perfect woman was not allowed to marry, but was reserved for the pleasures of the people (f. 88), she became a courtesan.

Bimbisara, king of Magadha, heard of her through Gopâla; he visited her at Vaisâli, though he was at war with the Licchavis, and remained with her seven days.

Amrapâlî became with child by him, and bore him a son whom she sent to his father. The boy approached the king fearlessly and climbed up to his breast, which caused the king to remark, "This boy seems not to know fear;" so he was called Abhaya or "fearless" (f. 92).

King Bimbisara, "who was always longing after strange women," had a child by the wife of a merchant of Râjagriha, and the mother had the child left in a chest before the palace gate (f. 92[b]). The king had the chest opened, and asked his son Abhaya if the child was living (*jiva*), so it was called Jivaka; and having been provided for by Abhaya, it was moreover called *Kumarabhanda* or Jivaka Kumarabhanda (*Hts'o-byed gdzon-nus-gsos*).

When Abhaya and Jivaka were grown up, they deemed

[1] Burnouf, Lotus (p. 340 and 482), says that the name of Adjatasatru's mother was Çrîthadrâ.

it proper to learn some trade, so Abhaya learnt coach-making and Jivaka studied medicine at Takchaçilâ with Atraya (*Rgyun-shes-kyi-bu*), and soon became a master in the healing art.

The Blessed One was once stopping at Râjagriha in the Veluvana Kalantaka nivasa. There then lived in Râjagriha a householder called Subhadra, whose wife was with child. One day the Blessed Buddha, having put on his mantle and taken his alms-bowl, went into the town to beg. Wandering on through the town begging alms, he came to the house of Subhadra. Then he and his wife came to the Blessed One, and Subhadra asked him, "Blessed One, if this my wife be with child, what kind of offspring will she bring forth?"

The Buddha replied, "She will bring forth a male child; he will make his family renowned; he will enjoy the pleasure of gods and men; he will enter the priesthood of my order, and, casting off all the miseries of sin, he will become an arhat."

Then they filled the Blessed One's alms-bowl with the choicest food, both hard and soft, and handed it back to him. . . .

A short time after this one of the Nirgranthas thought, "The Çramana Gautama has been prophesying something to them in this house, the only one where we can get anything. I must go and see what he has told them." So he went and asked them. Now this Nirgrantha was a soothsayer; so he took a lot of white pebbles, and having made his reckoning, he saw how exact was all that the Buddha had said. Then he thought, "If I praise this prophecy I will cause this householder to go over to the Çramana Gautama's doctrine, so I will say a little good and a little evil of it." Then he clasped his hands and changed the expression of his face, so that Subhadra asked him, "Sir, why clasp you your hands and change your expression?" "Householder," he replied, "part of that prediction is true and part is a lie." "What, sir, is true and what a lie?" "Householder, when he said, 'She will bring forth a male child,' that is true; that 'he will be renowned in his family' is true, for 'renowned' or '*prakasa*' is a man's name; but it is this child's lot to be burnt up in his house a short time after his birth. That 'he will enjoy the pleasures of gods and men' is a lie, for there are but few (*i.e.*, there are none) men who enjoy the pleasures of gods and men, or who ever see the gods. That 'he will enter the priesthood of my order' is true, for when he is without food or raiment he will certainly be a member of the Çramana Gautama's order. That 'he will cast off all the miseries of sin and become an arhat' is a lie, for the Çramana Gautama himself has not cast off all the miseries of sin and become an arhat; how much less then can one of his disciples?"

Subhadra was greatly distressed at this, and asked what he must do. "Householder," the Nirgrantha replied, "enter only our order, and by learning our precepts you will find wisdom," and with that he departed.

(After this Subhadra tried to bring on an abortion, but being unable to do so, he took his wife into the woods, where she died, and his servants and friends came and put the corpse on a bier and carried it to the Çitavana cemetery.)

The Nirgranthas, on hearing all this, were greatly delighted; so they erected canopies, flags, and streamers, and went about saying to every one in the streets, the lanes, and in the cross-roads of Râjagriha, "Listen, sir; the Çramana Gautama prophesied that Subhadra's wife would bring forth a male child, &c. (as above); and now she is dead, and they are carrying her to the Çitavana!"

Two young men, one a believing kshatriya, the other an unbelieving brahman, were out walking, and the brahman told the news to his companion; but the kshatriya youth, who did not think the words of the Blessed One could be untrue, answered him in this verse:—

"The moon with all the stars may fall to earth;
This earth, its hills and forests, may reach the sky;
The waters of the mighty deep may all dry up,
But by no chance can the mighty Rishi tell a lie."

. . . Subhadra having had firewood made ready, put his wife's remains on it and set fire to the pyre. When all her body had been consumed there still remained as it were a ball of flesh, which burst open, a lotus appeared, and lo! in the centre of the lotus was a child, beautiful and of pleasing appearance.

All the vast multitude saw this, and exceeding great was their astonishment; but the Nirgranthas suffered in their might, in their pride, in their haughtiness.

The Blessed One said to Subhadra, "Householder, take your child;" but he looked at the Nirgranthas, who said, "No one has ever entered a roaring fire without being burnt to death;" so he would not take the child.

Then the Blessed One said to Jivaka, "Doctor, take the child." He, thinking the Blessed One would not bid one do what was impossible, entered the fire without hesitation and took the child. Then it went from mouth to mouth, "At the Conqueror's bidding he entered the flames; he took the child in the fire; by the Conqueror's might the fire harmed him not!" . . .

The Buddha said to Subhadra, "Householder, take this child." But he, putting his trust in false doctrines, would not take it, and turned to the Nirgranthas, who said, "Householder, it is undeniable that this thing will be burnt by fire; if you take it to your house, your dwelling will burn, and you will lose your life." So he, thinking that his own preservation was of paramount importance, left the child.

Then the Blessed One said to Çrenika Bimbisara, king of Magadha, "Mahârâja, take the child;" and he, filled with the deepest respect for the Buddha, held out his hands and took it.

He asked the Buddha what name it ought to receive. "Mahârâja," answered the Buddha, "as this child has been born from out the fire, let it be called Jyotishka (*Me skyes*) or 'Born of the fire'" (*jyotis*).

(Bimbisara had the boy reared with every care, but finally the father was persuaded by his brother-in-law to take his child.)

According to universal custom, as long as the father lived the son's name was not mentioned, but after a while the householder Subhadra died, and young Jyotishka became the head of the house. Filled with faith in the Buddha, he sought his refuge in the dharma, the sangha, and the Buddha. He had a vihara built on the spot where he had been (preserved from) the death that (awaited him at the hands of) Subhadra. He fitted it up with everything of the most perfect description, and gave alms to the clergy of the whole world. Therefore is it said in the sûtranta of the sthaviras, "The Blessed One was stopping at Râjagriha, in the ârama of the 'rubbed side'" (*dku mnyed-pai ts'al*).

Now the agents of Subhadra in foreign parts heard of his death, and that Jyotishka had become head of the house, also that he was a firm believer in the Buddha, the dharma, and the sangha. On hearing this they took an alms-bowl of sandal-wood, which they decorated with jewels and sent it to Jyotishka. He had it put on the end of a long pole, with this notice appendent, "No one may have this by using a ladder, steps, or a hook (to reach it), but whatever çramana or brahmana can get it by using only magical or superhuman means shall have whatever he wishes."[1]

Some tirthikas came along, after washing on the river-bank, and saw this, so they asked the householder what it was there for. When he had explained it, they said, "Householder, you are a believer in the Çakyaputra

[1] Comp. Bigandet, *op. cit.*, vol. i. p. 212 *et seq.*

çramanas; they will get (the bowl);" and with that they went their way.

After a while the bhikshus and sthaviras came into Râjagriha to beg, and they also saw it. They asked Jyotishka what it was; so he explained it to them. Then they said, "Householder, the Blessed One has said the bhikshu's virtues must be concealed and his sins made public; this is applicable in the case of this alms-bowl," and with that they departed.

After a while the venerable Dâçabâla Kâçyapa came that way, and he asked the householder the same question. When its purpose had been explained to him, he thought, "It is long since I have put away all sin (*kleça*), and have been made clean, and the householder would be very glad to know which of the tirthikas or myself is the greater adept in magical performances," so he extended his hand as an elephant would his trunk and took the pâtra and carried it off to the vihara.

(When the Buddha heard of what Kâçyapa had done he forbade bhikshus showing magical feats, and moreover he prohibited them from having alms-bowls made of any other substance than iron or earthenware.)

. . . (f. 34[b].) One day King Bimbisara said to Jyotishka, "Young man, you who are enjoying the pleasures of gods and men, how comes it that you have never invited me to your house?" "I invite your majesty." "Go then and get ready your servants." "I myself will wait on your majesty, though he who knows the joys of gods and men has many servants."

So the king went to Jyotishka's house, . . . and passing through a jewelled door, he saw before him like a lake of water, in which fish were made to move by machinery. The king, desiring to enter (the room), commenced undoing his shoes, when Jyotishka said, "Sire, why are you getting ready to bathe?" "Because I must wade in the water," he replied. "Sire," Jyotishka answered, "it is not water, it is a floor of jewels which looks like water."

"But those fish which seem to move about?" "Sire, they are made to move by machinery."[1]

The king could not believe it, so he threw down a ring; and when he heard the noise it made on striking the floor, great was his amazement.

Then he entered the room and sat down on a throne. When the women came and bowed down at his feet, they had tears in their eyes. The king asked, "Why are the women crying?" "Sire," answered Jyotishka, "they are not weeping (in grief); 'tis the smoke from the wood in the artificial sun which brings tears to their eyes" (*lhai-na-bzah-la shing-gi dud-pai dri dgah-bas*).[2]

Here we will leave Jyotishka for the time being. The end of his history will find place in the latter part of our narrative, after Adjatasutra had begun to reign.

Çampa, which was a part of the kingdom of Magadha, and where the Buddha made frequent excursions, was the birthplace of the two following heroes, whose stories have been preserved to us in the third and fourth volumes of the Dulva.

Mrigadhara (*Ri-dags hdzin*), first minister of Prasenadjit of Kosala, had seven sons, the youngest of which was called Visâkha (*Sa-ga*), whom he married to Visâkhâ (*Saga-ma*), the daughter of Balamitra (*Stobs-kyi bshes-gnyen*), an illegitimate son of King Aranemi Brahmadatta, who was living at Çampa, where he had been exiled (f. 126[a]). She soon became celebrated for her intelligence, cleverness, and wisdom (f. 115–124), which was so great that her

[1] There are several other stories in the Dulva about mechanical devices; one is given p. 108. See also Dulva xi. f. 166, the story of the elephant which a mechanic made for Bharata, minister of King Tchaṇḍa Pradyota. The same story occurs in Rodger's Buddhaghosha's Parables, p. 39, and Schiefner, Mem. de l'Acad. de St. Petersb., xxii. No. 7, p. 36. In the Mongol history entitled Bodhimur (Schmidt, Sanang Setsen, p. 342), we read of the Nepalese princess, wife of the Tibetan king Srong-btsan-sgam-po, building a temple on Mount Potala, at Lhasa, in which was also a crystal floor. The king was also deluded when he first saw it. The whole passage of the Bodhimur seems to be a copy of our text.

[2] Taken from the Jyotishka Avadana, Dulva x. f. 17–38. The Sanskrit text is in the Divya Avadana. See Burnouf, Introd. à l'Hist. du Buddh., p. 199.

father-in-law asked permission of the Buddha to call her his mother (f. 126), and so she is called in Buddhist legends "Visâkhâ, the mother of Mrigadhara." Likewise, King Prasenadjit was so faithfully nursed by her in a severe illness that he called her his sister. She built a vihara near Çravasti, in what had formerly been a park, and made it over to the clergy. Therefore it is said in the sûtranta of the sthaviras, "The Blessed One was residing at Çravasti, in the vihara of Mrigadhara's mother, Visâkhâ, in what had been a park (*pûrvârama*)."

At another time Visâkhâ brought forth thirty-two eggs, which she placed in cotton, each in a separate box, on the Buddha's advice, and on the seventh day thirty-two sons came forth, who all grew up to be sturdy, very strong, overcomers of strength (f. 127[a]). They once had a quarrel with the purohita's son, so he sought means to get rid of them. The hillmen had defeated the king's troops seven times (f. 127[b]); Visâkhâ's sons were sent against them, but they defeated the hillmen, took from them hostages and tribute, and came back. Then the purohita tried to make the king destroy them, for they were dangerous to his power, so strong were they. The king therefore invited them to a feast, and there he drugged them, and while stupefied he had their heads cut off (f. 128[b]), which he sent in a basket to their mother, who was then entertaining the Buddha and his disciples. The Buddha consoled her by telling her of the evil deeds which her sons had committed in a former existence.[1]

At about the same time as the previous events were taking place, there lived also at Çampa a rich householder named Potala[2] (*? Grur-hdzin*), to whom a son was born while he was on a trip to Râjagriha. A person ran to the householder and told him that he had a son. So great was

[1] See also Schiefner, Tibetan Tales, p. 110 *et seq.* Fah Hian (Beal's), p. 78, where she is called Visâkhâ-matawi.

[2] It is probable that this is a mistake for *gro-dzin* = Çrona. The following story is taken from Dulva iv. f. 314–325. Cf. the Pali version in Mahavagga, v. 1, and Sûtra in Forty-two Sections, sect. 33.

his delight that he made the messenger repeat the news three times, and would have had him repeat it again, but the man thought he was laughing at him, and would not speak. The householder told him that he was mistaken, and that for every time he had told him he would fill his mouth once with gold. Moreover he sent word to his treasurer to distribute twenty koṭis of gold to celebrate the event. As the child had been born under the constellation Çrona (*Gro-dzin*), he was called "Crona-twenty-koṭis," or *Çronavimçatikoṭi*. On the soles of his feet were tufts of golden-coloured hair four fingers long (f. 315[b]). The Buddha desiring to convert him, sent Maudgalyayana to him, who appeared to him in the orb of the sun, and talked to him of the Buddha. Çronavimçatikoṭi filled his bowl with food of extraordinary fragrance, and this he carried back to the Buddha in the Kalantaka bamboo grove. Just then King Bimbisara came to visit the Buddha, and smelling the sweet odour, he asked from whence the food came. The Buddha told him that it was from his own land of Çampa, and related the young man's history. The king decided to go and see this wonder, but the people of Çampa, fearing that the king's visit would be dangerous for them, sent him word that the young man would come to Râjagriha. As he was not accustomed to walk, they prepared for him a boat in which he could journey to the capital of Magadha (f. 321[a]). . . .

The king came down to the Ganges, and had dug a canal from there to the capital, by which means the boat was brought to Râjagriha amid great rejoicing. . . . The king having asked the young man if he had ever seen the Buddha, learnt that he had not, so they went together to the Bamboo grove, and there Çronavimçatikoṭi was converted and became a bhikshu (f. 323[a]).

After that he retired to the Çitavana cemetery of Râjagriha, and gave himself up to the rudest penances, but it did not bring him the passionlessness he sought. The Buddha called him to him and asked why he had been so severe in his penances. "When you were at home did you know how to play on the lute?"

"I did, Venerable One."

"When the strings were excessively stretched, was the sound of the lute agreeable, pleasing, harmonious, correct?"

"It was not, Venerable One."

"But when the strings of the lute were too loose, was the sound of the lute agreeable, pleasing, harmonious, correct?"

"It was not, Venerable One."

"When the strings were neither too much stretched, nor too loose, was the sound agreeable, pleasing, harmonious, true?"

"It was, Venerable One."

"Çrona, in like manner, too much application brings distraction, and too much relaxation brings indolence. Be moderate, unselfish, and pious, and you will reach excellence."

Following this advice, he gave himself up to no more excesses, and in a short time he became an arhat.[1]

'Twas not very long after his departure from Kapilavastu that the Buddha thought of introducing his doctrine into Kauçambî. The history of the conversion of the king of that country is told as follows in the sixteenth volume of the Mdo f. 337-339. I reproduce the intro-

[1] Huen Thsang, iii. p. 66, relates this story. In a passage of the Punyabala Avadana (Mdo xxx. f. 1, 33) occurs the following passage, which happily illustrates the character of some of the principal disciples of the Buddha:—"A great many of the bhikshus were gathered together, and were talking about the best thing conceivable. Then the ayuchmat Nanda, the cousin of the Blessed One, and the son of his aunt, the ayuchmat Çronavimçatikoti, the ayuchmat Aniruddha, the ayuchmat Çariputra, came and sat down in the midst of the assembly. Then spoke the ayuchmat Nanda, 'Venerable sirs, the best thing conceivable is a fine appearance.' 'Venerable sirs,' quoth Çronavimçatikoti, 'diligence is the best conceivable thing.' 'Venerable sirs, skilfulness is the best thing,' said Aniruddha. The venerable Çariputra said, 'Venerable sirs, of a truth wisdom is the best thing that man can conceive.' But the Buddha declared that moral merit was the best thing for man." See also Mdo xvi., Anguli-maliya Sûtra, f. 243-260.

ductory passage of this story, though I have found no mention of this event in the Vinaya:—"The Blessed One was teaching his doctrine to the multitude in the city of Varanasi, when perceiving that the time for the conversion of Udayana (*Tchar-byed*), king of Vadsala (Kauçambi?), had arrived, he, together with his disciples, departed for the Vadsala country.

"Udayana, king of Vadsala, had assembled his army with the intention of conquering the city of Kanakavati (*Gser-chan*), when, seeing the Blessed One approaching, he exclaimed in anger, 'All such messengers of bad luck must be put to death!' and with that he took a sharp arrow and shot it at the Blessed One. As it flew through the air these words were heard:—

> "From malice is misery brought forth.
> He who here gives up to strife and quarrels,
> Hereafter will experience the misery of hell.
> Put then away malice and quarrelling."

"When the king heard these words, he became submissive to the Blessed One, and with clasped hands he sat down near the Buddha, who preached to him on giving up strife and quarrelling, on conquering, not human enemies, but egotism, that great and mighty foe. 'Let discernment (*rnam-rtog*) be your sword; faith, charity, and morality your fort; virtue your army, and patience your armour. Let diligence be your spear, meditation the bow you bend, and detachment the arrow.'"[1]

While the Blessed One was once stopping at Kapilavastu in the Banyan grove,[2] the steward of the Çakya Mahânâman died, and he appointed a young brahman in his stead steward of the hill-people. Desirous to possess this world's good and not to see his race die out, this

[1] This is the substance of his sermon, not a literal translation.

[2] This must have been in the early part of his ministry, for, as we will see, Mallikâ's son Virudhaka had reached man's estate long before the end of the Buddha's life. I only give the general outlines of the story, which is too long to be given here *in extenso*. It is taken from Dulva x. f. 121–134.

brahman married a woman of the same caste as his own, who after a while bore him a daughter, whom they named Tchandra (*? Zla-ba*).

She grew up to be shrewd and well-bred, and her pretty face gained the hearts of all the hill-people. After a while her father died, and the hill-people went and told Mahânâman of his death. "Sirs," he inquired, "had he collected the taxes and dues?"

"Lord, he had certainly collected the greater part of them, but he used it to procure remedies for his cough. He did not recover, however, and he even made other loans besides, so that to-day the little he has left belongs to his creditors. But he had a house, a son and daughter, and the latter is shrewd and good-looking, a favourite among the hill-people."

So Mahânâman took the daughter into his house. His wife was old, and it was her duty to cook the food and to gather flowers. Then she said, "My lord, I am very old, and my hands are unable to accomplish both my tasks, so I pray thee let Tchandra help me." To this he consented, and the old woman said, "Tchandra, go to the garden and gather the flowers while I cook the food." Mahânâman was so well pleased with the way in which she made the wreaths that he changed her name to Mallikâ (*Phreng-chan*), or "the wreath girl."

Now it happened that one day Mallikâ had gone into the garden with her food, and just then the Blessed One passed that way collecting alms. Mallikâ was greatly struck with his beautiful appearance, and wished to give him her food, but she felt so poor that she held back, hesitating. He, knowing her heart, held out his bowl, and she put her offering in it, wishing the while, "May this make me some day to be no longer a slave or poor."

One day Prasenadjit, king of Kosala, carried away by his horse in the heat of the chase, came to Kapilavastu alone, and wandering here and there, he came to Mahânâman's garden. There he saw Mallikâ. "Maiden," he said, "whose garden is this?"

"It is the Çakya Mahânâman's."

He got off his horse and said, "Bring me some water to wash my feet."

A little while after he said, "Maiden, bring me water to wash my face." Then she, pushing away with her hand the surface water, took water which was neither too warm nor too cold, and with that he washed his face.

Again he said, "Maiden, bring me some drinking water." Then mixing[1] the water thoroughly, she took cool water in a leaf cup and gave it to the king. When he had drunk it he asked Mallikâ, "Young girl, are there three different pools in this garden that thou hast brought me three kinds of water?"

Then she explained what she had done, and Prasenadjit praised her shrewdness. After that he requested her to rub his feet with a towel, and she willingly complied, but scarcely had she touched his feet when he fell asleep. Mallikâ thought, "These kings have many enemies. If any one should harm him while thus asleep, it would be a slur on my master's reputation, so I will close the gate." Hardly had she done so when she heard cries of "Open" from a crowd of men who wanted to get in, but she opened not the gate; and the king awakening, asked what was the matter. When he heard why Mallikâ had closed the gate, he admired still more her shrewdness and wisdom.

Having found out who she was, he went to Mahânâman, and asked him for the girl to make her his wife. Mahânâman consented, so the king took her with him in great state to Çravasti.[2]

Now Prasenadjit's mother was displeased that her son had married a servant-girl of humble birth. But when Mallikâ went to salute her and took hold of her feet,

[1] My translation is conjectural. The text is *tchu rnam-par glongs-nas*. I think that *glongs* may be derived from *klong*, "a wave."

[2] Cf. Huen Thsang, B. vi. p. 317.

she at once fell asleep. When she awoke, she thought, "Surely a maiden with such a touch is of noble birth, worthy of the family of Kosala!" At that time the king of Kosala had two wives, Varshikâ (*Dbyar-ts'ul-ma*), celebrated for her beauty, and Mallikâ, renowned for her wonderful touch[1] (f. 127).

After a while Mallikâ had a son, whose name was given him by his grandmother. She had said of Mallikâ that surely she was of noble birth, so she called the child Virudhaka (*Hphags-skyes-po*), or "the high-born."[2]

At the same time the wife of the purohita of King Prasenadjit brought forth a son amidst great suffering, so they called his name Ambârisha (*Ma-la gnod*), or "Harmful to his mother."[3]

Virudhaka was brought up as became the heir to a great kingdom, and Ambârisha as became a young brahman. He learnt the theories and practices of the brahmans, to say Om, to say Bhu, the truth-speaking Veda (*Rik*), the sacrificing Veda (*Yajur*), the hymns (*Sama*), the Veda for taking care of the sacred things (*Atharva*). He learnt about rishis of old, about the firmament, the cause of earthquakes, and about atmospherical space, also the six occupations of a brahman (f. 131).

One day Virudhaka and Ambârisha while deer-hunting came to Kapilavastu and entered the Çakyas' park. The keepers went and told the Çakyas, saying, "Sirs, Virudhaka is in your park!"

Then the Çakyas, who were not forbearing, exclaimed, "If that be the case, let us go and kill him!" So they put on their armour and started.

[1] Cf. Feer, Annales Musée Guimet, v. p. 65, note 4. *Dbyar-byed* is the Varshakara minister of Adjatasatru who figures in the Parinirvana Sûtra. See p. 123. Varshikâ was probably Bimbisara's sister. See Spence Hardy, Manual, p. 227; and for the Southern version of Mallikâ's story, p. 293 *et seq.*

[2] There are two other personages by this name mentioned in Buddhist legends, one of the four great kings of space, and a king of Videha.

[3] M. Feer, Annales Musée Guimet, v. p. 69, thinks that his name may *possibly* be Mâtraparadhaka. I have followed Schiefner, Tib. Lebens, p. 326. For another version of these events, see Edkins, *op. cit.*, p. 45.

The elders seeing them, asked them where they were going.

"Virudhaka is in our park, and we are going to kill him!" they cried.

"Young men," the old Çakyas replied, "you are overhasty; resent not his wickedness and turn back." And the young men obeyed them.

Virudhaka, who had heard them, went after his troops (who had accompanied him in the chase); and returning, he introduced them into the park.

Then the keeper of the park went and told the Çakyas, "Sirs, Virudhaka has entered the park with all his troops. It is not right to let the park be spoiled by dirty elephants and horses."

The Çakyas, greatly exasperated, and disregarding the words of their elders, started out to kill Virudhaka. But he, hearing that the Çakyas of Kapilavastu were coming to kill him, said to one of his men, "I am going to hide (with all the troops); if the Çakyas ask you anything about me, tell them that I have gone away."

So the Çakyas came to the park, and not seeing Virudhaka, they asked the man, "Where is that son of a slave?"

"He has run away," he answered them.

Then some of them cried, "If we had found him we would have cut off his hands;" others said, "We would have cut off his feet;" others would have killed him. "But since he has run away, what can we do?"

So they decided to have the park purified. "Clean up the park," they said to the workmen; "and wherever this son of a slave has been, clean it and sprinkle fresh earth (over his footprints). Whatever part of the walls he has had hold of, plaster it over and make it new. Take milk and water and sprinkle it about, and also scented water; strew about perfumes and flowers of the sweetest kind."

Now Virudhaka's man, who had heard all this, went and told him what the Çakyas had said. Virudhaka was greatly incensed, and exclaimed, "Gentlemen, when my father is dead and I am king, my first act will be to put these Çakyas to death. Promise me that you will give me your support in this undertaking."

All those present promised, and Ambârisha said, "Prince, you must certainly do as you have resolved, (and remember) the virtuous man is steadfast in what is right."

And from that time he sought means to take possession of the throne of Kosala.

Shortly before the Buddha's death Virudhaka ascended the throne and executed his plan against the Çakyas, as will be seen in the next chapter (p. 116 *et seq.*)

Not wishing to reproduce in this narrative those legends which have already been translated from Tibetan into any European language, I will devote but a few lines to one of the most celebrated victories of the Buddha, viz., the one he gained over the six brahmanical teachers assembled at Vaisali. This important event took place in the early part of the Buddha's public life, most likely in the sixteenth year of his ministry.

Buddhist works mention six principal philosophical masters who were the chief opponents of the Buddha. Their names are frequently met with in Tibetan works (Dulva iv. f. 141, 409, *et seq.*) They were Pûrṇa-Kâçyapa, (Maskari)-Goçala, Sanjaya son of Vairatî, Ajita-Keçakambala, Kakuda-Katyâyana, and Nirgrantha son of Jnâta. We will have occasion, in speaking of the conversion of King Adjatasatru, to mention their principal theories; for the moment we will content ourselves with mentioning that they all claimed to be great magicians, and as they felt that the Buddha was depriving them of their popularity, they decided to have a public trial, which would establish their supernatural powers and their superiority over the Çramana Gautama. Prasenadjit, king of Kosala, had everything made ready (Dulva xi. f. 239) in a place between Çravasti and Jetavana; the Buddha performed such wonderful feats (f. 241–249) that the tirthikas dared not show their inferiority, so they fled in dismay[1] (f. 250). The most prominent of these six was Pûrṇa-Kâçyapa, "a man who went naked in the villages before all the world" (f. 252). When his disciples asked him, "Master, tell us what is the truth" (*tattva*), he told some of them, "The truth is that this world is eternal." To others he said, "It is not eternal." To others, "It is eternal and perishable." To others, "It is neither eternal nor perishable." To others, "The finite and the infinite exist." "There is no finite, no infinite." "Vitality (*srog*) and the body are one. Vitality and the body are separate. On departing this life there is a hereafter. There is not. There is and there is not. The truth is that on departing this life there is a hereafter and there is no hereafter. The other (teachers) are fools;" and with these and similar reasons he upset their minds[2] (f. 251[a]). He could no longer reason, so with wandering mind he also ran away. As he went along he met a eunuch, who recognised him and said, "Whence comest thou, thus crestfallen, like a ram with broken horns? Ignorant though thou art of the truth (taught by) the Çakya, thou wanderest about without shame like an ass." Then Pûrṇa-Kâçyapa told him that he was seeking a lovely pool full of cool water, in which he wished to clean himself of the dirt and dust of the road. When the eunuch had pointed it out to him, he went there, and fastening around his neck a jar full of sand, he threw himself into the water and was drowned.[3]

After defeating the tirthikas the Buddha vanished from amidst his disciples and went to the Trayastrimcat heaven, where, seated on a slab of white stone in a beautiful grove

[1] Cf. Bigandet, vol. i. p. 215 *et seq.* He places the contest of Buddha with the heretics immediately after the story of Daçabala Kâçyapa and Jyotishka's jewelled bowl, see p. 69. Huen Thsang, B. vi. p. 304, says that the Buddha converted the heretics.

[2] I do not think that this is intended to illustrate the habitual teaching of Kâçyapa, but only what he said when his mind was troubled by his defeat. For Pûrṇa-Kâçyapa's doctrines, see p. 100.

[3] For a full account of the Buddha's miracles and the subsequent events, see Dulva xi. f. 230–252, also Der Weise und der Thor,,chap. xiii., and Burnouf, Intr. à l'Hist., p. 162 *et seq.*

of parijâtaka and kobidaraka (*sic*) trees, he instructed his mother and a host of devas. He was prompted to leave Varanâsi lest the people should suppose that the great wonders he had shown were intended as a means of acquiring gifts and honours.[1]

The disciples were greatly worried at the Buddha's disappearance, and questioned Maudgalyayana, who told them where the Blessed One was. When three months had passed away the disciples sought Maudgalyayana again, and told him that they wanted to see the Buddha, that they thirsted after him. Maudgalyayana, by the power of samadhi, went to the Trayastrimcat devas' heaven, and told the Buddha how all the people of Jambudvipa longed to see him. The Blessed One bid him return and tell the disciples that after seven days he would return to them, and would be at the foot of the udumbara tree of the Avadjaravana (*sic*) of the town of Sâmkaçya in Jambudvipa. Then the Buddha visited many other abodes of the devas, teaching them all the truth; after which he descended to the earth by a vaîdurya (lapis lazuli) staircase, while Brahmâ, bearing a jewelled yak tail, descended a golden one on his right together with all the gods of the Rûpaloka, and Çataketu (Indra), bearing a hundred-ribbed parasol over him, descended by a crystal staircase on his left accompanied by all the devas of the Kamaloka.

Now the bhikshuni Utpalavarṇâ[2] saw the Blessed One descending to earth, so she took the appearance of an emperor (*Chakravartin*), and came to honour him. Udayin, who was also there, recognised her by the sweet odour that her body emitted; but the Blessed One rebuked her, saying, "It is not seeming in a bhikshuni to perform magical feats in the presence of the Master." Then he

[1] Conf. Bigandet, i. p. 224, and Spence Hardy, *op. cit.*, p. 308.

[2] See on Utpalavarṇâ, Schiefner's Tib. Tales, p. 206 *et seq.;* and Hdjangs-blun (Der Weise und der Thor), chap. xxv. According to Tibetan authorities (Schiefner, Tib. Lebens, p. 315), the Buddha passed the seventeenth summer of his ministry in the Tushita (here Trayastrimcat) heaven.

sent her away, and the Buddha told his disciples the story of Susroni.[1]

There lived at about that time in Koçala a celebrated brahman called Pushkarasarin (*Padma snying-po*, in Pâli *Pokkharasâdi*), who had a very learned disciple called Appriya (? *Ma-sdug*). Hearing that the Blessed One was at Çravasti, he sent Appriya to him to see if the reports concerning the Buddha's learning were really true.

So Appriya came and entered into conversation with the Buddha, who compared the different occupations of çramanas and brahmanas with what their occupations ought to be (see Brahmajala Sûtra), and asked him many of the questions contained in the sermon known in the Pâli version as the Tevidja Sûtra, or "On the Knowledge of the Vedas." Appriya returned to Pushkarasarin, and told him that the çramana Gautama was worthy of all the praise bestowed on him, and he repeated the conversation he had had with him. So greatly was the master enraged with the way in which his messenger had behaved that he hit Appriya on the head with his shoe (f. 520), and then and there he decided to go see the Buddha himself. He drove to where the Buddha was, taking with him a supply of pure food, and he found him attended by Ananda, who was fanning him.

The Buddha soon remarked how devoured he was by pride, for he wanted to fix the ceremonial that should be used when he and the Buddha met, so he sought to dispel it. He talked to him of charity, of morality, &c. When he saw that he had gladdened, incited, rejoiced him, that his mind was free from obstacles, intent, that it was prepared to receive the highest truths, then he explained the highest truths, namely, suffering, the cause of suffering, the cessation of suffering, the path. Just as a clean cloth,

[1] See for the descent from heaven, Dulva xi. f. 308–315; and for the story of Susroni (in Tib. *Sho-shum-pa*), Dulva xi. f. 316–325; and Schiefner's Tibetan Tales, p. 227 *et seq.* This translation of Schiefner's is not, however, literal. Conf. also Fah-Hian, p. 62; and Hiuen Thsang, B. iv. p. 237.

free from black spots and ready for dyeing, takes the colour when put in the dye, thus the brahman Pushkarasarin while sitting there discerned the four blessed truths of suffering, the cause of suffering, the cessation of suffering, the path (f. 523[b]). Then the brahman Pushkarasarin having seen the truth, having found the truth, having discerned the truth, having fully mastered the truth, having penetrated the whole depth of the truth, having crossed over beyond uncertainty, having dispelled all doubts, dependent on the favour of no one else (f. 524[a]), not having found it by another, having found the incontrovertible doctrines in the teaching of the Master, rose from his seat, and throwing his cloak over one shoulder, turned with clasped hands to the Blessed One, and said to the Blessed One, "Lord, glorious, truly glorious! Lord, I take my refuge in the Buddha, in the dharma; I take my refuge in the fraternity of bhikshus; may I be received among the lay followers. From this day forth, while life lasts, I take my refuge and I put my trust (in them)."[1]

We have seen (p. 54) that Devadatta and quite a number of Çakyas had been made to enter the order much against their will when the Buddha visited Kapilavastu in the sixth year of his ministry. Devadatta was the leader of this dissatisfied portion of the fraternity, and his name became in later times synonymous with everything that is bad, the object of the hatred of all believers. We read in Dulva iv. f. 453, that while the Blessed One was at Çravasti, Devadatta started for Kapilavastu with the intention of stealing Gôpâ, the Buddha's wife. He came up to her and took her hand, but she gave it such a squeeze that the blood spurted out, and then she threw him from the terrace where they were standing into the Bodhisattva's pleasure pond. The Çakyas heard the noise

[1] This passage, which is continually repeated in the Dulva, is reproduced to show how exactly the Tibetan text and the Pâli agree. I have used Rhys Davids' expressions wherever it was possible, so that the comparison might be made by those who cannot avail themselves of the original texts.

of his falling. When they found out that Devadatta had penetrated into the inner apartments of the Bodhisattva,[1] and had tried to seduce his wife, they wanted to put him to death; but they remembered that the Buddha had once predicted that Devadatta would inevitably fall into hell, so they let him go.

Another time, while the Blessed One was stopping at Râjagriha at the Kalantaka nivâsa Bamboo grove, there was a dire famine, and it became difficult to get alms. So the bhikshus who had magical powers, and who knew the country called Jambudvipa (or the island of Jambu), used to go there and fill their alms-bowls with delicious jambu, myrobolan, or vilva fruits, and bring them back and divide them with the other bhikshus. Others would go to Purvavideha, or to Aparagaudani, or to Uttarakuru, where they would fill their alms-bowls with the wild rice which grew there, and with this they lived, dividing what was left over with the fraternity of bhikshus; or they would go to the four Lokapâlitas heaven, to the Trayastrimcat devas' heaven, and fill their alms-bowls with nectar (*amrita*); or yet again they would go to distant countries where there was prosperity and plenty and fill their alms-bowls with all kinds of savoury viands, with which they lived in plenty, dividing what was left over among the bhikshus.

Then Devadatta thought that it would be a great thing for him to be able to do like these bhikshus with magical powers. So he went to where the Blessed One was, and asked him to teach him magic. But the Buddha,

[1] The use of the term *Bodhisattva* in this legend, and in another (Dulva iv. f. 454) which we will have occasion to relate farther on, seems to imply that the Buddha had not reached enlightenment at the time when it took place, or, at all events, that his wives were not aware of it. In the legend of f. 454, Yaçôdhâra is the heroine, and the story is said to have occurred shortly before Devadatta's death, which took place when Adjatasatru was king (*i.e.*, during the last five years of the Buddha's life). On the other hand, we have learnt (p. 57) that Yaçôdhâra became a bhikshuni. It is impossible to make these different accounts agree, but the legend is interesting as illustrative of the Buddhist ideas of the characters of the Buddha's wives.

who well knew the evil intentions lurking in his mind, answered, "Gotama, devote yourself to virtue, and by that means you will acquire magical and other powers. Gotama, devote yourself to acquiring spiritual insight and superior knowledge, and you will acquire magical and other powers."

So, seeing that the Buddha would not teach him magic, he went to Adjnata Kaundinya, Açvadjit, Bhadrika, &c., and asked them to teach him, but they knew the Blessed One's opinion, so they each one successively answered him, "Devadatta, learn to rightly understand rûpa, and you will acquire magical and other powers. Devadatta, learn to rightly understand vedana, sandjna, sanskâra, vidjnâna, and you will acquire magical and other powers."

Then Devadatta went to Daçabala Kâçyapa, saying to himself, "The sthavira Daçabala Kâçyapa has no superior far or near; he is without guile, an honest man, the master of my elder brother, Ananda (*bdag-gi phu-nu-bo-rgan pa kun dgah-bo*); he can teach me the way to acquire magical powers."

Kâçyapa taught him the way; then Devadatta kept from sleeping during the night, and having reached the first stage of dhyana, he acquired the irrdhi of the way of the world. So he became able, from being one, to multiply himself; and, having multiplied himself, he could become one again. With the eye of wisdom he could make himself visible or invisible. He could go from one side of a wall or of a mountain to the other side without any more trouble than if it had been air. He could do what creatures on the earth or above it do, or what birds[1] or fishes do. He could walk on water, without sinking, as if he were on dry land, or sit cross-legged in the air like a winged animal. He could become smoke or fire, appearing like a great heap of fire. He could bring a stream of water out of his body as if he was a whale

[1] The text has *byeu zul byed de*, but I read *bjeu ts'ul.*

(*makara*). Through the might of the great magical powers he had acquired he could give to himself the splendour of the sun and moon.

Then he thought, "If I could get the greatest person in the land of Magadha to become my disciple, the common of mortals would follow his example without any difficulty." Then he thought of Prince Adjatasatru, who would be the ruler of the kingdom at his father's death; so transforming himself into an elephant, he entered the front door of Prince Adjatasatru's house and went out by the wicket, and having entered by the wicket, he came out by the front door. After that he transformed himself into a horse, into a bhikshu, and passed before him in the same manner, Prince Adjatasatru thinking the while, "Why, this is the venerable Devadatta!" Then he transformed himself into a golden necklace; encircling the prince's neck, he fell into his bosom, entwined himself around his person, &c., and he knew that Adjatasatru thought, "Why, this is the venerable Devadatta! Why, there is no greater teacher than the venerable (*ayuchmat*) Devadatta; great are his magical powers!" So the prince believed in him; and after that each morning he would go with five hundred chariots, and would give him and his friends five hundred bowls full of different kinds of food, on which Devadatta and his five hundred adherents did feast.[1]

Devadatta became so infatuated with the gifts and honours which Adjatasatru was lavishing on him that he said to himself, "The Blessed One is getting old and decrepit, and it wearies him to exhort the bhikshus and lay followers, both male and female. What if the Blessed One turned over the direction of the congregation to me? I will guide them, and in the meanwhile the Blessed One will be able to live in comfort, without any pre-occupation." Hardly had he conceived this idea but his magical

[1] Dulva v. f. 430–439. See also Dulva iv. f. 249–255; conf. Spence Hardy, Manual, p. 327 *et seq.*

powers commenced decreasing, and finally left him entirely, although he knew it not. But Maudgalyayana was informed of the fact by a deva from the Brahmâloka[1] (who had been the son of Kaundinya), so he went and informed the Buddha just as Devadatta was coming to make him the above-mentioned proposition. When the Blessed One heard him he replied, "Thou fool! thinkest thou that I will commit the care of the congregation to an eater of filth and spittle like thou (*ro dang hdra-ba mtchil-ma za-ba*), when I do not intrust it to virtuous men like Çariputra or Maudgalyayana?"

Devadatta was indignant with the Blessed One; he was provoked and dissatisfied, so he shook his head three times, and with the words, "Let us abide our time," he went out of the presence of the Blessed One.[2] It was probably after the preceding events that Devadatta brought about the first schism in the Buddhist order of which we have any record. The five rules which seem to have been the distinguishing features of his reformation are given as follows in Dulva iv. f. 453:—"Sirs," said Devadatta to his hearers, "(1.) The çramana Gautama makes use of curds and milk; henceforth we will not make use of them, because by so doing one harms calves. (2.) The çramana Gautama makes use of meat; but we will not use it, because, if one does, living creatures are killed.[3] (3.) The çramana Gautama makes use of salt; but we will not use it, because it is produced from a mass of sweat (*rngul khrod-nas byung*). (4.) The çramana Gautama wears gowns with cut fringes; but we will wear gowns with long fringes, because by his practice the skilful work of the weavers is destroyed. (5.) The çramana Gautama lives in the wilds; but we will live in

[1] Spence Hardy (*op. cit.*, p. 328) calls him Kakudha.

[2] Dulva v. f. 436–439, and Dulva iv. f. 256–258.

[3] The Buddha allowed the use of meat, but it was not lawful to make use of it if it had evidently been prepared for the bhikshu, if it had apparently been prepared for him, or if it was presumable from circumstances that it had been prepared in his intention. See Dulva iii. f. 38. On the third rule see Wassilief, Buddh., p. 56.

villages, because by his practice men cannot perform works of charity (*dana*)."[1]

When the Buddha was about fifty years old,[2] he said to the bhikshus, "Bhikshus, I am bent down with age and infirmities, and worn out through giving counsel to my followers; you must appoint a bhikshu who will attend to my wants."

Kaundinya asked to become his attendant, but the Buddha told him that he was too old and would require an attendant himself. Açvadjit, Subahu, and all the other great sthaviras asked for this place, but he told them that they were all too old. Then Maudgalyayana bethought him that Ananda would be a fit person and acceptable to the Lord; so he took Çariputra with him and went and asked Ananda if he would accept this most honourable place. Ananda at first refused, "for," he said, "it is a difficult matter to wait on a Buddha. As it is difficult to approach a mighty sixty-year-old elephant of the Mâtanga (forest), strong, with great curved tusks and deep-set chest, revelling in the fight, when he is ready for the fray, so is it difficult to serve the Blessed Buddha and to attend on him; therefore, venerable Çariputra, choose me not as the Blessed One's attendant."

Finally he consented, but on three conditions: (1.) That he should never have to partake of the Blessed One's food, use his underclothes (*smad gyogs*), or his cloak; (2.) That he should not have to accompany the Blessed One when he went to a layman's house; (3.) That he might at any time see and revere the Blessed One. The Buddha agreed to these conditions, and from that day on Ananda became his inseparable attendant, and was the foremost among those who heard much, who understood what they heard, who remembered what they had heard.[3]

[1] See also Udânavarga, p. 204, where the third rule is still less intelligible, but might be rendered "because it is produced from the semen of Mahesvara," whatever that means. Cf. Spence Hardy, Manual, p. 338.

[2] See Spence Hardy, Manual, p. 241.

[3] See Dulva iv. f. 240–243.

While Devadatta was enjoying his short-lived popularity in Râjagriha the Buddha went to Gâya, and while there he learnt of Adjatasatru refusing to send him gifts, reserving them all for Devadatta. Then he told his disciples the following story:—"Bhikshus, in days of yore there lived in the desert wild, in a hermitage surrounded by every variety of fruit and flower trees, a number of rishis (hermits) who fed on roots or fallen fruits, and who clothed themselves with bark. Now there was a mango-tree near by, and when on its fruit-laden branches the fruit was ripe and ready to eat and the hermits tried to take any, the selfish deity who lived in the tree would not let them have any.

"It happened one day while the hermits were away looking for roots and fruit that a band of five hundred robbers came to the hermitage and espied the mango-tree. They wanted to get the fruit, so their chief said, 'Let us cut down the tree with an axe and eat the fruit.'

"(On hearing this) the deity let all the fruit fall to the ground; the robbers ate their fill and went away.

"When the rishis came back, they asked (one of their number whom they had left behind) who had eaten the mangoes. Then he spoke this verse—

'To the peaceful and righteous-doing
The tree's fruits are not given;
To the thief, to the wicked-doer,
The fruits of the tree are given.'

"They asked him how it had come about, and he told them. So it was that the avaricious deity would not give the fruit to the peaceful hermits, but gave it to the lawless thieves."

Then the Blessed One added, "What think ye, bhikshus! He who was then the deity is now Adjatasatru, and the robber chief is now Devadatta."[1]

Adjatasatru, impelled by Devadatta and also by his own ambition, sought to take his father King Bimbisara's

[1] Dulva iv. f. 272–273.

life by shooting an arrow at him, but he failed in the attempt. When the Buddha heard of this he laid all the blame on Devadatta, and he told the Bhikshus the story of the guilty dogs (D. iv. f. 332), of the grateful animals (f. 333–335), and of the ichneumon, the snake, and the mouse (f. 335–336).[1]

Bimbisara having found out that Adjatasatru's object was to become king, made him viceroy of Çampa, and there he and Devadatta gave themselves up to plundering the people, so that they complained to the king.

Bimbisara imagining that if his son's domains were vaster he would be less rapacious, gave him the whole of Magadha, with the exception of his capital, Râjagriha; but even this did not arrest his exactions. Then the king relinquished also Râjagriha, only reserving his treasures; but as Devadatta suggested to Adjatasatru that the real sovereign was the one who had the treasures, he prevailed on the king to relinquish these also. Bimbisara complied, but at the same time he implored his son to give up his wicked associate Devadatta. Exasperated at this, Adjatasatru had his father cast in prison, there to die of hunger; but Queen Vaidehî, the only person admitted to see him, brought him food in a bowl. Adjutasatru heard of this through the jailers, and forbade the Queen doing so on pain of death. Then Vaidehî had her body anointed with a quantity of nutritious powders, and filled her ankle rings with water; by this means she kept the king alive. This device was also found out, and she was no longer allowed to visit the king. Then the Blessed One walked on the Vulture's Peak, in a place where Bimbisara could see him from his window, and the joy that this gave him kept him alive. Adjatasatru found this out, and had the window walled up and the soles of his father's feet scarified.

The Blessed One then sent Maudgalyayana, who entered

[1] All of these stories have been translated in Schiefner's Tibetan Tales.

the prison through his magical power, and comforted the king with the assurance that he would come to life again in the region of the four great kings.

It happened that at that time Udayibhadra, son of Adjatasatru, had a gathering on his finger, which made him cry, though his father took him in his arms and kissed him. Then Adjatasatru put the finger in his mouth and sucked it, which broke the sore and relieved him. Just then Vaidehî came in, and seeing what Adjatasatru was doing, she told him that his father had once done the same thing for him. Great was the king's distress at the way he had treated his father, and he wished that he were still living. "Ah!" he cried, "if any one could tell me that the old king was alive I would give him my kingdom!" A great crowd rushed to the prison with shouts of joy, but when Bimbisara heard them, he thought that they were going to inflict some new torture on him, so, filled with terror, he heaved a deep sigh and passed away.[1]

According to the Li-yul-gyi lo-rgyus pa, f. 429[a] (see p. 233), Adjatasatru became king of Magadha five years before the Buddha's death, but this is a very little time for the accomplishment of all the events enumerated in the next chapter. The Southern recension[2] says that it was eight years after Adjatasatru's coronation that the Buddha died. This is a little better, though still a very short period.

[1] Dulva iv. f. 336–341. Conf. Spence Hardy, *op. cit.*, p. 328 *et seq.*

[2] See Dipawansa, iii. 60.

CHAPTER IV.

FROM THE COMMENCEMENT OF ADJATASATRU'S REIGN TO THE DEATH OF THE BUDDHA.

SHORTLY after Adjatasatru had become king of Magadha, and while the Buddha was on the Vulture's Peak near Râjagriha, in the abode of the yaksha Kumbhira, Devadatta asked the king to assist him in becoming Buddha, "For you owe your crown to me," he said.

Devadatta had a skilled mechanic called from Southern India, and made him construct a catapult in front of the Buddha's residence. He stationed 500 men to work it, 250 more were stationed so as to kill the Buddha in case the machine missed him, and Devadatta took up a position so as to be able to do the deed himself if the others failed.

Just as the men were about to let off the catapult, they saw that it would kill the Buddha; so they would not do so, but went away; and descending a magical staircase which the Buddha had caused to appear, they came and sat down at his feet, and he converted them.

Devadatta thinking that the deed was done, climbed to the top of the Vulture's Peak, and from there he saw the men seated at the feet of the Buddha, and then the mechanic, to whom he had given as a reward a pearl necklace worth a hundred thousand pieces (of gold), ran away down the magic steps. Devadatta managed, however, to hurl a stone from the catapult at the Buddha, and though a yaksha called Vadjrapani shattered it, and the yaksha

Kumbhira sacrificed his life in trying to arrest it, a fragment struck the Buddha on the foot and made a dangerous wound.

Jivaka visited him three times, and prescribed a kind of sandal-wood called *Tsan-dan sa mtchog*, a very rare substance, which was only procured with great difficulty. But the Blessed One had lost a great deal of blood, and though Jivaka made him drink the milk of a young woman, the hemorrhage could not be stopped. Then Daçabala Kâçyapa exclaimed, "Blessed One, if it be true that thou carriest alike in thy heart thy sons and thy enemies, let the hemorrhage stop!" and forthwith the blood stopped trickling forth.[1]

King Adjatasatru had a very ferocious elephant called Ratnapala (or Vâsupala, *Nor-skyong*), which wounded so many persons each time it was brought out, that the people had been obliged to request the king to have a bell rung to warn the people whenever he was about to be led out. Now it happened one day that a rich citizen of Râjagriha had invited the Buddha and his disciples to come eat at his house. Devadatta hearing of this, went and told the elephant-tamer that he would give him a necklace worth a hundred thousand (pieces of gold) if he would let out the elephant. He consented to do so, but only with the king's consent, which Devadatta feigned to obtain. Then the bell of warning was rung, and the man who had invited the Buddha ran to the Bamboo grove and begged him not to come into the town. The Blessed One told him to fear nothing, and, together with five hundred disciples, he started out for the city. Devadatta went on to the palace terrace to see the Buddha killed, but when the elephant came rushing at the Buddha, who had been abandoned by all his disciples save Ananda, he tamed it with a few words, and the ferocious beast followed him submissively to the house where he was going to eat. So that the elephant

[1] Dulva iv. f. 349, 361.

might continue to look at him, the Buddha changed the walls of the house into crystal, but the king caused a wall to be put up between the elephant and the house, when, deprived of the sight of the Blessed One, it died of grief and was reborn in the heaven of the four great kings.[1]

Devadatta sought by every means to make the bhikshus doubt the truth of the Buddha's word, and to make them disobey the disciplinary rules which he had established. Çariputra and Maudgalyayana went to where Devadatta was teaching his five hundred followers, with Kokalika on his right side and Kandadvaja on his left. Çariputra exhorted the misguided bhikshus to return to the true doctrine, and Maudgalyayana performed all kinds of magical feats before them; so that finally their eyes were opened, and they asked to be led back to the Blessed One. The "perfect pair" took them back, and caused a ditch to appear across the road, which arrested Devadatta, who, with Kokalika, Kandadvraja, Katamorakatisya, and Sagaradatta, had started in pursuit, hoping to turn them back. The misled bhikshus were presented to the Buddha; they confessed their sin, and were readmitted into the order without a word of reproach, the Blessed One only repeating to them the theory of causes and effects, and vindicating the truth of his doctrine.[2]

We left in the preceding chapter (p. 70) Jyotishka, the wealthy householder of Râjagriha, in peaceful enjoyment of all human pleasures, but when Adjatasatru, beguiled by Devàdatta, had killed his righteous father, placed the crown on his own head, and become king, he called Jyotishka, and said to him, "Householder, you and I are brothers,[3] let us divide our household property."

Then Jyotishka thought, "He who has killed his

[1] Dulva iv. f. 374–376.

[2] Dulva iv. f. 396–399. Conf. Spence Hardy, *op. cit.*, p. 339.

[3] It must be remembered that Bimbisara had brought up Jyotishka.

righteous father, who has put the crown on his own head, and made himself king, will perhaps kill me. He wants to deprive me of my house, but he will be foiled." So he said, "Sire, how do you want to divide?"

"I will take your house, and you will take mine."

Jyotishka answered, "So let it be."

Then Adjatasatru moved into Jyotishka's house, and he into Adjatasatru's; but all the splendour of the first residence passed into Jyotishka's new one, and he had to change with the king seven times.

Adjatasatru thought, "Since I cannot get Jyotishka's jewels by this means, I will try another." So he commissioned robbers and thieves to go and steal the jewels in Jyotishka's house. They were discovered by the women of the house, and Jyotishka learnt from them that they had been sent by the king. Adjatasatru, on hearing that they had been caught, sent a messenger to Jyotishka saying, "I am the culprit; let them go."

The householder dreading lest the king should kill him, made up his mind to enter the Buddhist order; so he gave his wealth to the needy, to the forlorn, to the poor, and to the sick, and the paupers he made rich. Then, with the consent of his friends, kindred, neighbours, and sons, he went to the Blessed One and became a bhikshu.[1]

The Blessed One was at Râjagriha, in the mango grove of Jivaka Kumarabhaṇḍa,[2] where he was passing the summer.

Then it happened that the son of Vaidehî, the king of Magadha, Adjatasatru, knowing that it was the night of the full moon of the mid-summer month, went on the terrace of his palace, into the brightness of the full moon, surrounded by all his courtiers.

Then he said to his courtiers, "Sirs, 'tis midsummer; of

[1] See Dulva v. f. 36–38.

[2] According to Schiefner, Tib. Lebens, p. 315, the Buddha passed the thirty-sixth summer in this place; but this does not agree with our text. It cannot be placed earlier than the forty-first summer, or in his seventy-fifth year.

a truth 'tis the night of the full moon of the midsummer month, for the moon has risen full as the sun. What can (we) do?"

Then said one of the women of the palace to the son of Vaidehî, to the king of Magadha, Adjatasatru, "Sire, as it is midsummer, the night of the full moon, &c., having all that heart can wish, let then your majesty rejoice, be glad, make merry. That, methinks, would be well."

Another of the women suggested decorating all around Râjagriha, and "let then your majesty rejoice, be glad, and make merry," &c.

Prince Udayibhadra suggested a campaign against some other kingdom in commemoration of the day. One of the king's old ministers said, "There is Purṇa Kâçyapa,[1] who has a retinue, who is a teacher of many, who is honoured by many, revered by many. He is exceedingly old, the master of five hundred, and he is passing the summer at Râjagriha. Let your majesty go and pay his respects to him."

Another old councillor made the same remark about the parivradjaka (Maskarin), son of Gôçâli, Sanjayin, son of Vairattî, Ajita Keçakambala, Kakuda Katyayana, and Nirgrantha Djnatiputra, who had retinues, who were teachers of many (rest as above), who were passing the summer at Râjagriha.

Now Jivaka Kumarabhanda was present among the courtiers while this was going on, so the king said to him, "Say you nothing, Jivaka? Why do you remain silent?"

"Sire, there is the Blessed One, who has a retinue, who is a teacher of many, who is honoured by many, who is revered by many, and who is passing the summer here at Râjagriha in my mango grove; let your majesty go and pay your respects to him, and that, methinks, would be well."

[1] How can this be, for we have seen, p. 80, that Purṇa Kâçyapa drowned himself near Çravasti in the sixteenth year of the Buddha ministry? It is useless to seek to explain all the discrepancies we meet with in these legends. All that can be done is to try and arrange them so that the contradictions are not too evident.

Then the heart of the king of Magadha, Adjatasatru, the son of Vaidehî, turned toward the Blessed One, flowed toward the Blessed One, went toward the Blessed One; so he said to Jivaka Kumarabhaṇḍa, "Go, Jivaka, and have got ready my best elephant; I will mount it and go visit the Blessed One." "Sire," replied Jivaka, "be it as thou dost command." So he had the king's great elephant got ready, and five hundred female ones on which rode five hundred women of the palace bearing torches, and then he went to the king of Magadha, Vaidehiputra Adjatasatru, and said to him, "Sire, the time has come, and your elephant is ready." So the king mounted his great elephant, and, preceded by the five hundred women with torches on female elephants, he went forth from Râjagriha to visit the Blessed One.

Now at that time Vaidehiputra Adjatasatru, king of Magadha, was not on friendly terms with the Vrijians;[1] so hardly had the king left Râjagriha but he was filled with fear, thinking, "May not this Jivaka Kumarabhaṇḍa

[1] In Dulva v. f. 284 *et seq.*, we read, "It happened that Vaidehiputra Adjatasatru, king of Magadha, was not on friendly terms with the Licchavis of Vaiçali; so the king of Magadha assembled his *chaturanga* army and commenced ravaging the territory of Vriji (*Spong-byed*). The forces of the people of the territory of Vriji informed the Licchavis of Vaiçali that Adjatasatru had assembled his army and was ravaging the territory of Vriji, and they called on them for help. When the Licchavis of Vaiçali heard this, they also got together their army and started out from Vaiçali. As they were starting out, they met Maudgalyayana entering Vaiçali to get alms. So they asked him—for, they argued, there is nothing that he does not know—if they would be victorious. He answered them, 'Men of Vasistha's race, you will conquer.' Then they were pleased, greatly delighted, their hearts were rejoiced, and without one moment's hesitation they attacked King Adjatasatru, who, taken by surprise, was defeated, panic-stricken, and driven to the shores of the Ganges. Then the king of Magadha thought, 'These Licchavis of Vaiçali are cruel and hard-hearted. If I jump into the Ganges, they will draw me out with a net or a noosed rope (? *htchil-pas dbyung-pas*), or some such contrivance, and I will be brought to great misery. 'Tis better to die.' So having made up his mind to die, he rallied his army, beat the Licchavis, terrified them, conquered them, and put them to flight. They entered Vaiçali in great disorder, and shutting the gates, they remained behind their walls. King Adjatasatru having conquered them and subdued the territory of Vaiçali, went back to Râjagriha." See also Ananda's remark shortly before his death, p. 165.

want to kill me, ensnare me, or may he not wish to deceive me, or deliver me over to the executioner, to my adversaries, or to my enemies?" And he was so sorely disturbed in mind that he broke out in a profuse sweat. Then he said to Jivaka Kumarabhaṇḍa, "Jivaka, do you not want to kill me, ensnare me, or do you not wish to deceive me, or deliver me over to the executioner, to my adversaries, or to my enemies?"

"Sire," he answered, "I do not intend [to do any of these things]."

Then Vaidehiputra Adjatasatru said to Jivaka Kumarabhaṇḍa, "Jivaka, what is the number of the Blessed One's followers?"

"There are twelve hundred and fifty bhikshus (with him)."

"Ah! Jivaka, how can it be that thou dost not wish to kill me, to ensnare me, to deceive me, or to deliver me over to the executioner, or to my foes, or to those who are not my friends, for here is the Blessed One with such a great number of followers, and I hear not even the sound of a cough or a whisper!"

"Sire, the Blessed One likes a low voice, he delights in a low voice, he speaks in a low voice; and as he extols a low voice, his disciples speak softly. Sire, push on your elephant, for there is the light of the lamp in the courtyard (*hkhor-gyi khyam-na*)."

So the king of Magadha, Vaidehiputra Adjatasatru, pushed on his elephant, and having ridden as far as was right, he alighted and entered the vihara on foot.

Now at that time the Blessed One was seated in the midst of his disciples as in the middle of a calm and placid lake; so when the king of Magadha, Vaidehiputra Adjatasatru, had come to the middle of the court, he asked Jivaka Kumarabhaṇḍa, "Jivaka, which is the Blessed One?"

"Sire, the Blessed One is he who is sitting in the midst of the congregation of bhikshus as in the middle of a calm and placid lake."

Then Vaidehiputra Adjatasatru, king of Magadha, went up to the Blessed One, and throwing his cloak over one shoulder, he touched the ground with his bended knee, and with clasped hands he spoke to the Blessed One as follows: "My lord (*btsun-pa*, *Bhante* in Pâli), would that Prince (*Kumara*) Udayibhadra had a spirit as controlled and dispassionate as are the minds of the bhikshus of the order of the Blessed One."

"Good, good, Mahârâja; great is the love thou hast shown him. Be seated, Mahârâja."

Then Vaidehiputra Adjatasatru, king of Magadha, bowed down his head at the Blessed One's feet, and sat down to one side. While thus seated he said to the Blessed One, "If the Lord, the Blessed One, will permit it, I will ask him a question."

"Mahârâja, ask whatever question you like."

"My lord, there are many kinds of trades and professions, such as wreath-makers, basket-makers (? *smyug-mkhan*), weavers (*gdan-pa mkhan*), grass-gatherers, trainers, elephant-riders, horsemen, chariot-drivers, swordsmen (*ral-grii thàbs*), archers (*gdjui hdsin stangs-pa*), body-servants (*djam hbring bgyid-pa*), scribes, dancers (*bro-gar len-pa*), rajâputras warlike and valorous, jesters (*mnyen-par byed-pa*), barbers, and bathers. Any one of these exercising his trade or profession gives in charity, does good, tends the sick (*gso-ba rnams gso-djing*); he acquires the five kinds of desirable things (*i.e.*, all that he can wish for), he enjoys himself, is happy, and partakes of the pleasures of this world; is there any such visible reward for one who devotes himself to virtue?"[1]

"Mahârâja, have you ever propounded this question before to any çramâṇa or brahmâṇa?"

[1] In Tibetan *yang-dag-par mthong-bai dge-sbyong-gi ts'ul*. The last two words, *dge-sbyong-gi ts'ul*, or, in Pâli, *samanna-phala*, have become the name of this sermon, which has been translated by Burnouf, Lotus de la Bonne Loi, p. 448 *et seq.*, and by Gogerly. See Grimblot, Sept Suttas Pâlis, p. 113 *et seq.* Conf. Spence Hardy, *op. cit.*, p. 333 *et seq.*

"My Lord, I have. Once, my Lord, I went to Purṇa Kâçyapa, and I asked him [the same question as above].

"'Râja,' he answered, 'here is my theory.' Then he said, 'Offerings, sacrifices, and burnt-offerings exist not, righteousness is not, neither is unrighteousness. Rewards for righteousness or for unrighteousness are not. This world is not, the other world is not. Father and mother are not; there is no such thing as opapâtika birth;[1] there is no birth. They who here in this world have reached the truth, who have entered into the truth, who understand this their present life, have perfectly understood that this life and another life (lit. world) are severed (the one from the other), that their being born is at an end. They live a life of purity and do what ought to be done. They do not know that there are other existences but this one, so there are none who go (to another existence). In this very life they will come to an end, decay, die, and come not forth again after death. The body of man is composed of the four great elements, and when he dies the earthy part of his body returns to earth, the watery part to water, the fiery part to fire, and the airy part to air. The perceptive powers are scattered in space. The corpse is carried by men to the cemetery and burnt, and is at an end. The burnt remains are ashes, and the bones become the colour of wood-pigeons. Thus both the fool and the wise man who pretend that they will receive anything for their charity speak empty, foolish, lying words.'

"Then did he talk of both the fool and the wise man being destroyed, decaying, and having no hereafter when once dead. My Lord, if a man had asked about mangoes and one had talked to him about bread-fruit (*labuja*, but in the text *la-ku-tsai hbras-bu*), or if he had asked him about bread-fruit and he had talked to him about mangoes, so it was that Purṇa Kâçyapa, when I asked him con-

[1] *Sems - chan brdzus - te skye - ba emdo.* Conf. the Pâli *n'atthi sâtta opapâtikâ.* The Pâli attributes these theories to Ajita Keçakambala.

cerning the visible reward of the çramaṇa, talked to me about not being.

"Then, my Lord, I thought 'twould not be seeming in me to openly deprecate such a person, such a learned and highly respected man, such a çramâṇa and brahmâṇa residing in my land. So, my Lord, without praising or blaming Purṇa Kâçyapa's words, I arose from my seat and went away.

"Then I went to the son of Gôçali (Maskarin), and I asked him [the same question].

(f. 411.) "'Mahârâja,' he answered, 'here is my theory.' Then he said, 'There is no cause or reason for human defilement; beings are defiled without cause or reason. There is no cause or reason for human puṛity; beings are pure without cause or reason. There is no cause or reason for beings ignoring or for their not perceiving; beings ignore and do not perceive without cause or reason; and so there is no cause or reason for beings knowing and perceiving; beings know and perceive without cause or reason. There is no power, no ability; there is no power and ability. There is no personal action, no external action; there is no personal and external action.[1] There is no personal ability, no ability of another; there is no personal and impersonal ability of another. All sentient beings, all living creatures, all creation are without power, force, might, will, control; they are subject to the existences which are inherent to their natures; and this is how creatures in the six forms of existence experience the different kinds of pleasure and pain.'

"This was what he said, my Lord. If a man had asked about mangoes, &c. So I arose from my seat and went away.

"Then I went to Sanjayin, the son of Vaîratti, and I asked him [the same question].

(f. 412.) "'Mahârâja,' he replied, 'here is my theory.'[2]

[1] *Skyes-bui rtsal medo, pha rol gnon pa medo. Skyes-bui rtsal dang pha-rol gnon pa medo. Bdag-gi rtsal medo gdzan-gyi rtsal medo. . . .* Comp. the Pâli *purisa-kâre . . . purisa-parakkame.*

[2] The Pâli attributes these theories to Pûrṇa Kâçyapa.

Then he said, '(There is such a thing as) to do, to cause to be done, to mutilate, to cause mutilation, to burn, or to cause burning, to strike, or to cause to be struck, to inflict pain on living creatures, to steal, to commit adultery, to prevaricate, to drink intoxicating liquors, to break into houses, to untie knots (*? mdud pa hgrol-ba*), to rob in arms, to make ambuscades on the high road (*? lam hgog-ching hdug-pa*), to plunder villages, to plunder cities, to plunder the country. In this world all sentient creatures are whirled around on the circle of a wheel; so if one mutilates, torments, strikes, tears to pieces, he only does something to a little flesh, to an accumulation of flesh; and having only done something to a little flesh, to an accumulation of flesh, there is no sin in any of these actions, no sin will accrue from such deeds. If a man on the south bank of the Ganges hurts everything, tears to pieces everything, mutilates everything, or if a man on the north bank of the Ganges makes offerings, gives alms, from these actions there is neither sin nor merit; by so doing there will be no future punishment nor acquisition of merit.' Thus did he speak of the non-existence of merit in charity, good conduct, self-restraint, in seeking what is right, in liking what is right. My Lord, if a man had asked about mangoes, &c., &c. So when I asked him about the reward of virtue, he talked to me of irresponsibility (*byed-pa nyid-ma min*).

Then, my Lord, I thought 'twould not be seeming, &c., so I arose from my seat and went to Ajita Keçakambala, and I asked him [the same question].

(f. 413^b.) "'Mahârâja,' he replied, 'here is my theory.' Then he said, 'The seven following kinds of corps are not made or caused to be made, they are not emanations or caused to emanate,[1] they do not conflict (*gnod-par bya-ba ma-yin-pa*); they are eternal, they stand like a pillar. These seven are earth, water, fire, wind, pleasure, pain, and

[1] *Ma sprul-pa sprul-pas ma byas-pa.*

vitality is the seventh.[1] These seven corps are not made or caused to be made, &c.; they stand like a pillar. They are not moved for the production of merit or demerit, for that of merit and demerit, nor for the production of pleasure or pain, nor for that of pleasure and pain, in either bringing them about or arresting them. The man who cuts off another man's head does nothing to a being moving or existing in the world, but the sword in penetrating between the seven elements injures a living being, and that is all. To kill, to bring about death, to think or to cause to think, to exhort or to cause to exhort, to know or to cause to be known, none of these exist. The foolish and the wise have 14,000 principal kinds of births, 60,000 (or) 600 great kalpas;[2] there are five(fold) actions, or three(fold), or two(fold), or simple actions or half actions; there are 62 paths, 62 medium kalpas, seven senses (*sandjna*), 120 hells (*nayakas*), 130 organs (*dbang-po*), 36 elements of dust, 49,000 nâgas, 49,000 of the garuda species, 49,000 of the parivradjaka species, 49,000 of the akelaka species, 49,000 of the nirgrantha species, seven modes of conscious existence, seven of unconscious existence, seven as asuras, seven as pisatchas, seven as devas, seven human; there are seven (or) 700 lakes, seven (or) 700 (kinds of) writing (? *hbri-ba*), seven (or) 700 dreams, seven (or) 700 proofs (? *sad-pa*), seven (or) 700 kinds of

[1] *Grog-gson-ba nyid ni bdun-pa ste.* This resulted from reading in the original; *sattame* instead of *satta me.*

[2] The text is *rtog-patchen-po*, which can only mean literally "great consideration, alternative;" but this is so very unsatisfactory that I venture to suggest that *rtog-pa* may here be used to translate the Sanskrit *kalpa*, which admits of the double signification of "thought" and "age, cycle." At all events, this would be very uncommon, for the Tibetan word *bskal-pa* = *kalpa* is of continual occurrence, and it can only have been because this phrase was rather obscure for the Tibetan translators that they substituted *rtog-pa* for *bskal-pa*. The same difficulty recurs a little farther on, where we find *rtog-pa bar ma*, which I have translated by "medium kalpas." All this is very uncertain. It may be that *rtog-pa* is intended to translate *vikalpa*, "doubt, uncertainty;" but this is not much more satisfactory than the sense I have adopted in the text. See the Chinese version of the text, p. 258, where the expression "great remembrances" also occurs, without, however, the phrase being more intelligible.

precipices; there are six social degrees, ten kinds of ranks, eight kinds of mahâpurushas; and all must inevitably go on transmigrating through 84,000 great kalpas before they reach the end of misery.

"'It is as if a ball of thread was dropped in space; it unwraps itself to its full length; so likewise both fools and sages must go on in the inevitable round for 84,000 great kalpas ere they reach the end of misery.

"'Therefore çramâṇas and brahmâṇas who say, "By morality, religious observances, penance, a life of purity, I will mature this action and the action which has matured will be wiped out," talk senselessly. Pleasure and pain exist, and there are no ascending or descending births.'

"Thus did he speak, saying that transmigration was given out equally to all. My Lord, if a man had asked about mangoes, &c.; so I arose from my seat and went to Nirgrantha, son of Djnati, and I asked him [the same question].

(f. 416.) "'Mahârâja,' he replied, 'here is my theory.' Then he said, 'All impressions experienced by beings are the result of a previously produced cause. From the fact that former deeds are wiped out by penance, recent deeds cannot be arrested by any dam. Whereas, there being no future misery (*asrava*), there will be no actions as there is no misery; actions being ended, affliction will be at an end; affliction being at an end, the end of affliction is reached.'[1]

"Thus did he speak, saying that by the extinction of asrava one reaches the end of affliction.

"My Lord, if a man had asked about mangoes, &c.; so when I questioned Nirgrantha Djnatiputra concerning the reward of virtue, he talked to me about first causes. My Lord, then I thought, &c.; so I arose and went to Kakuda Katyayana, and I asked him [the same question].

(f. 417.) "'Mahârâja,' he replied, 'here is my theory.'[2] Then he said, 'If any one asks me if there is another life,

[1] Dr. Leumann informs me that these theories agree with Jain doctrines, as shown by their canon.

[2] The Pâli attributes these theories to Saṃjaya.

I answer his question by "There is another life." If they inquire of me, saying there is no other life, or the other world (life) is or is not, or it is and is not, or it is not not existing, or the other world is so and so, or it is not thus, or it is another way, or it is not another way, or it is not not another way, I reply to their questions by "The other world (*i.e.*, future life) is not another way, (or) it is not not another way."'

"Then I thought the greatest fool of all the men of religion in Râjagriha, the stupidest, the most hypocritical, is this Kakuda Katyayana. But still it occurred to me 'twould not be seeming in me, &c.; so, without extolling or yet blaming the words of Kakuda Katyayana, I arose from my seat, and (now) I have come to the Blessed One, of whom I ask [the same question]."

"Mahârâja, I will question you concerning this inquiry of yours. Answer me as you see fit.

"Mahârâja, let us suppose that you have a slave, an attendant, without a will of his own, who knows no pleasure of his own. This man, seeing you in your palace, in possession of everything which can gratify the senses, living in the midst of more than human bliss, amusing and diverting yourself, thinks, 'Vaidehiputra Adjatasatru, king of Magadha, is a man, and I also am a man; but Adjatasatru, because he has formerly accumulated good deeds, now lives in a palace, in the midst of more than human joys, amuses and diverts himself, and I also may become like him if I perform meritorious acts. I will shave my head and beard, put on an orange gown, and, filled with faith, I will give up a home life and retire from the world.' Then, cutting the rope (which holds him to the world), he shaves his head and beard, and, filled with faith, gives up a home and retires from the world. He abstains from taking life, from stealing, from fornication, from joking (*pra-ma*), from mocking, reviling, coveting, slandering, and from malice. Now if your emissaries should meet him, and, thinking, 'This was a slave, an attendant, without a will of his own, of Vaidehiputra, king of Magadha, &c., &c.; he abstains from slandering and from malice; let us go and tell the king.' If then coming to where you are, they should say, 'Does your majesty know that his slave, his attendant, &c., &c., is living abstaining from slandering and from malice?' would your majesty on hearing this say, 'Bring the man here; he shall again be my slave, my attendant, without a will of his own'?"

"Not so, my Lord; but in whatever place I met him I would speak respectfully to him, bow before him, rise in his presence, join my hands to him (make an anjali), and show him every possible kind of respect; and as long as he led such a life I would provide him with clothes, food, lodgings, and medicines."

"What think you, Mahârâja? In such a case as this have I not demonstrated that there is a visible reward for a life of virtue?"

"Of a truth you have, my Lord. In such a case the Blessed One has shown that there is a visible reward for a life of virtue."[1]

The Buddha continued to converse with him until the king was finally gained over to the Buddhist creed.

After Adjatasatru's conversion by means of the Çramana-phala Sûtra, he would no longer admit Devadatta's followers into the palace, but had them all turned away. One day Devadatta came to the palace and was refused admission. Just then he espied the bhikshuni Utpalavarṇa entering the palace for alms, and he thought, "It is for such bald-pates as this that they have quarrelled with me." Then he said to Utpalavarṇa, "What have I done thee that thou hast deprived me of alms?" and with that he struck her. "Persecute not the righteous," she meekly said. "How can you, a relative of the Blessed One, treat so badly one who is a Çakya who has renounced the world? Be not so harsh with me." But he struck

[1] See Dulva iv. fol. 405 *et seq.*; and for the end of the sûtra, Burnouf, Lotus, p. 461–482.

her with his fist on the head. She reached the abode of the bhikshunis, though suffering great pain, and shortly after she died.[1]

Devadatta having failed to reach eminence as a religious teacher, still retained some hope of being able to become king of the Çakyas. Now the Çakyas had thought of putting Yaçôdhâra on the throne, so Devadatta went to Kapilavastu and ascended the terrace of the palace where Yaçôdhâra was. He took her hand and besought her to become his wife, that they would reign over Kapilavastu. On hearing such a proposition she sprang up from her seat and threw him to the ground. "Thou shameless fool," she cried, "I cannot bear thy touch. My husband must be one who will become an universal monarch or a bodhisattva." The Çakyas, on hearing of this new insult of Devadatta to the Buddha, told him to go and beg the Blessed One's pardon, and that if he granted it they would make him their king.

Devadatta filled underneath his nails with a deadly poison, intending to scratch the Buddha's feet. When he drew nigh the Buddha and cast himself at his feet he tried to scratch him, but the Blessed One's legs had become of adamantine hardness, so that Devadatta's nails broke off.[2] The Buddha granted him forgiveness, but on condition that he professed his faith in the Buddha. If, however, he should do so with a lie in his heart, he would at once fall into hell. Devadatta, who was in great pain, exclaimed, "To the very marrow of my bones I seek my refuge in the Buddha." Hardly had he uttered the words but he fell into hell.

But even there the Buddha's mercy followed him, for he sent Çariputra and Maudgalyayana to visit him in hell, and to tell him that, though he was then suffering for having tried to divide the brotherhood and for having killed Utpalavarna, he would on the expiration of a kalpa become a pratyeka buddha.[3]

[1] See Dulva iv. f. 448–449.

[2] Conf. Huen Thsang, B. vi. p. 302, and Fa-Hian, p. 80. The Hdzangs-blun gives another version of Devadatta's death.

[3] See Dulva iv. f. 455–457.

The bhikshus came to the Buddha and said, "Lord, see to what grief Devadatta has come because he hearkened not to the words of the Blessed One."

The Blessed One answered them, "Bhikshus, 'tis not only now that grief has come to him because he hearkened not to my words. Listen how the same thing happened to him in days of yore.

"Bhikshus, in times gone by there lived in a mountain village a master-mechanic (*hkhrul-hkhor-gyi slob-dpon*) who married a woman of the same caste as his own, . . . who after a while gave birth to a son. Twenty-one days after his birth they had a naming-feast, and, tenderly nurtured, the child grew apace.

"After a while his father died, and (the lad) went to another mountain village where lived another master-mechanic, and with him he commenced learning his trade.

"In yet another mountain village there lived a householder whose daughter's hand (the young man) asked of her father. The father replied, 'If you can get here on such-and-such a day, I will give her to you, but on no other day.'

"Then (the young man) said to his master, 'Master, in such a village there lives a householder whose daughter's hand I have asked of her father. He told me that if I could get there on such-and-such a day he would give her to me, but on no other.'

"The master-mechanic said, 'Since that is the case, my lad, I will go (with you) myself and get her.'

"So on the appointed day they mounted together a wooden peacock, and the same day they reached the mountain village, to the great astonishment of all the people. They took the girl, and mounting the same machine, they went to (the young man's) own home. Then (the master-mechanic) took the machine and said to the youth's mother, "Your son does not know how to manage this machine, so do not let him have it."

"After a while (the young man) said, 'Mother, please

let me have the machine, so that I may astonish the people' (*skye-boi ts'ogs dbang-du bgyio*).

"'My son,' she answered, 'your master said that you did not know how to manage it, and that I must not let you have it. You do not understand it; it will bring trouble on you. I will not let you have it.'

"'Mother,' he said, 'I can make it go forward and backward; the master only refused it through jealousy.'

"Women's hearts are tender, so seeing how much he longed for it, she let him have it.

"Then he got on the machine and started off, to the great delight of the people; but the master-mechanic saw (him on) the machine and cried out, 'Go away, and do not try this again!' But he went on flying about farther and farther until he flew to the ocean. Then the deity caused a deluge of rain to fall on the ocean, and the parts (*sbyor-kha-rnams*) (of the machine) were soaked. No longer able to manage it, he was wrecked (lit. came to trouble).

"A deity then spoke this verse—

> 'When one's words of loving-kindness,
> One's cautious instructions, are not heeded;
> When one stops not and remembers nought,
> He is carried off by the wooden bird.'

"Bhikshus, what think ye? At that time I was the master-mechanic and Devadatta the apprentice. At that time he would not listen to my words of caution, and through his ignorance he got into trouble; so likewise now, hearkening not to my words, he has gone to suffer the torments of hell."[1]

Çariputra and Maudgalyayana shortly after their visit to Devadatta in hell had told the Cûlekasataka[2] tirthikas in Râjagriha that they had seen their master in hell, and that he had admitted to them the falsity of the doctrines

[1] See Dulva iv. f. 462–464.

[2] The text reads *dbyug thogs spyi phud-chan*, which I have taken as synonymous with *gtsug-phud ras-gchig*. This, however, may be a mistake, but I have not met elsewhere with the former expression.

he had taught. His disciples were so enraged at this that they resolved to avenge themselves on the calumniators. They at first tried to quarrel with Çariputra, but he passed on; so they attacked Maudgalyayana, whom they met in Râjagriha a little later. They pounded him like sugar-cane and beat him through the whole town, and would have killed him then and there if Çariputra had not come to his rescue, and having changed him into a little child, carried him off in his cloak to the Veluvana vihara.[1] The news of this attempted assassination spread like wild-fire, and a great crowd with King Adjatasatru came to the vihara. The king had the heretics seized. He asked Maudgalyayana why he, who was such a great magician, had not been able to escape. He told him that such was his destiny on account of bygone deeds (he had in a former existence treated his father and mother in like manner). Adjatasatru sent all his physicians to Maudgalyayana, and told them that if he was not cured within seven days they would all be degraded (*? dbang-thang bchad*). They were greatly worried at this, for Maudgalyayana's condition was hopeless, and nothing less than a miracle could cure him. This they told to the wounded man, who promised that in seven days he would be in Râjagriha begging his food; and he did as he had promised; but after having shown himself in Râjagriha, he went to "the town with the wooden paling" (*? Grong-khyer shing-thags-chan*), and died on the afternoon of that same day. Çariputra, who was at Nalanda, was taken ill the same day, and died at the same time as his friend, and 77,000 ordinary bhikshus also died at this time.[2]

[1] Conf. Bigandet, *op. cit.*, ii. p. 25, and Spence Hardy, Manual, p. 349.

[2] Dulva xi. f. 652, we are told that when Çariputra died 80,000 bhikshus died; and that at Maudgalyayana's death 70,000 died, and at the Buddha's death 18,000 passed away. By this may also be understood that from the first founding of the order until the time of Çariputra's death 80,000 bhikshus had died, &c. Bigandet, *op. cit.*, vol. ii. p. 9, places Çariputra's death in the forty-fifth or last year of the Buddha's ministry. He recounts it after the Blessed One's illness at Beluva. See p. 130. His version of this event is much fuller than that of our text.

When Çariputra's disciples had finished cremating his body, they carried his ashes (*ring-bsrel*), his alms-bowl, and his cloak to the Blessed One at Râjagriha.

The Blessed One after their arrival left Râjagriha and went to Çravasti and stopped at Jetavana. Now, when Anathapiṇḍada heard that Çariputra was dead, and that his ashes were in the hands of Ananda, he went and asked permission of the Buddha to build a cairn (*tchaitya*) over his ashes, in consideration of their long-standing friendship. The Buddha having given his consent, Anathapiṇḍada carried the remains to his house, put them in a high place, and honoured them in the presence of his friends and relatives with lamps, incense, flowers, perfumes, wreaths, and sweet-scented oils (*byug-pa-rnams*); and all the people of Kosala, King Prasenadjit and queen Mallikâ, the royal family and Varshikâ, the rishi Datta, the elders, Visakhâ Mrigadhara's mother, and many other believers came and honoured them.

Then Anathapiṇḍada inquired of the Buddha how the cairn or tchaitya ought to be built. "It must have four storeys, gradually decreasing in size, and it must contain a vase, and there must be one, two, three, four, thirteen baldachins, and it must have roofs to protect it against the rain (*tchar-khab-dag bdjag-par-byao*).[1]

Moreover, Anathapiṇḍada asked permission of the Buddha to found a feast which should be celebrated at a certain time at the tchaitya of Çariputra. The Buddha gave his consent, and King Prasenadjit had proclaimed

[1] The text adds, "For a pratyeka Buddha there shall be no rain-court (*tchar-khab*); for an arhat there shall be four festoons (? *dgugs*); for a sakridagamin three; for an anagamin two; for a crotapanna one; as to ordinary people, their tchaityas must be plain" (*byi-bor* = *byi-dor* ?). We see from this that the tchaitya of Çariputra was similar to that made for a Buddha. See Dulva xi. f. 53–68 for the preceding episode. We will not insist on the death of Mahâprajapati Gotami, and of the other Çakya women who had founded with her the female order of mendicants. They are said to have died shortly before the Buddha, while he was at the banyan grove of Kapilavastu. Prajapati Gotami was aged 120 at the time of her death, but she had retained her youthful appearance, and her hair had not become white. See Dulva x. f. 180–185, also Spence Hardy, Manual, p. 317 *et seq.*

with sound of bell, "Give ear, ye people of Çravasti, and all ye foreigners! At the time of the feast of the tchaitya of the venerable Çariputra, all merchants who may come thither with goods will have to pay no duties or tolls or ferry fees; they may come freely."

We may as well note here that Dulva xi. f. 53 gives the following directions for disposing of the corpse of a bhikshu. His body must be burnt, but in case wood cannot be found, it may be thrown into a river. If there be no river in the neighbourhood, it must be interred in a shady spot, the head to the north, lying on the left side, on a bed of grass. Then it must be covered with green grass and leaves. Previously to being interred the body must be washed. A cairn or tchaitya (*mtchod-rten*) must be raised over the remains.

We have seen in the preceding chapter (p. 79) that Virudhaka, son of King Prasenadjit of Kosala, and heir-apparent, was very desirous of becoming king, so as to avenge himself on the Çakyas of Kapilavastu. He then commenced conspiring against his father, and trying to gain over to his interests all the five hundred councillors of Prasenadjit; and they all promised him their support, with the exception of Dirghâchârâyana[1] (*Spyod-pai-bu ring-po*), the chief minister, who was devoted to his lord. On a certain occasion, while Dirghâchârâyana was at Virudhaka's dwelling on business, the prince spoke to him about his desire to avenge himself on the Çakyas as soon as he became king, and he proposed assassinating his father, so that he might the sooner reign. The minister persuaded him to desist from such a crime, "for," he said, "the king is old, and in a little while you will ascend the throne, for there is no other heir but you." Virudhaka

[1] Conf. Feer, Annales Musée Guimet, v. p. 65. He there translated this name Dîrgha, son of Cârî. Since then he has written to me that in the Avadanâ-Cataka he is called Dîrgha Cârâyana, translated in Tibetan *Rgyu-bai-bu ring-po*, "Dîrgha, son of the walker." I have no doubt that in our text *Spyod-pai-bu* is intended as a translation of Cârâyana. I have, therefore, availed myself of M. Feer's remark, and have adopted this restitution of the name instead of Schiefner's Dirghachâriya.

gave in to his reasons, but bound the minister over to secrecy as to what had just passed between them.

Now the Blessed One was stopping in a little town of the Çakyas called Metsurudi, when one day Prasenadjit having got on his chariot with Dirghâchârâyana driving, started out. On the road he saw a hermit living in solitude, shunning sin and the company of man, and the king bethought him that that was the way in which the Blessed One lived; so turning round to the minister, he asked him if he knew where the Blessed One then was, for it had been some time since he had been to pay him his respects. Dirghâchârâyana told him that he had heard that the Blessed One was in a Çakya town called Metsurudi. "Is it far off?" asked the king. "It is about three yojanas from where we are," answered Dirghâchârâyana. "Drive me, then, to the village of Metsurudi."

When they had come to Metsurudi, the king alighted from his chariot and went to the ârama on foot. The Blessed One was passing the day inside of the dwelling with closed doors, and the bhikshus outside were walking about with their cloaks off. The king went up to them and asked where was the Blessed One. "He is passing the day in the house with big doors. If you want anything, Mahârâja, go and knock gently on the door, and the Blessed One will have it opened." So the king handed over to Dirghâchârâyana the five insignia of royalty which he wore, his crown, his parasol, his sword, his jewelled yak-tail, his richly embroidered shoes, and having knocked gently, the Blessed One opened the door and he went in.

Dirghâchârâyana thought, "The king has given me the five insignia of royalty; I will accomplish the prince's secret intention!" So mounting the chariot, he drove off to Çravasti and made Virudhaka king.

Prasenadjit, having bowed down at the feet of the Buddha, wiped his face and mouth and then said, "Blessed One, it has been a long time since I have seen you. Sugata, it has been a long time since I have seen you."

Then the Buddha said, "Mahârâja, why are you so very humble, so excessively humble towards the Tathâgata?"

"Venerable One, it is because I believe that the Blessed One is the Tathâgata, the Arhat, the Perfectly Enlightened One. Well spoken your doctrine, excellent your disciples and the order."

"But, Mahârâja, why do you believe in me?"

"Venerable One, I have seen those çramanas, those learned brahmans, filled with pride in their learning, acting and speaking accordingly. I have seen their self-sufficiency and their intolerance for all other opinions. . . . Venerable One, I have yet other reasons for believing in your doctrine. Venerable One, I am of Kosala, and the Blessed One also is of Kosala; I am of kshatriya caste, and so is the Blessed One; I am aged and decrepit, fourscore years old, and the Blessed One is aged and decrepit, and (nearly) fourscore years old. Venerable One, I am the anointed king of the country, and you are the king of the exalted Dharma."

When they had finished conversing, the king came out of the house. Mallikâ and Varshikâ (his wives) had seen Dirghâchârâyana, and learning from him that the king was at the village of Metsurudi, they started out on foot to find him. When the king heard from the bhikshus that Dirghâchârâyana had abandoned him, he continued his road on foot, going in the direction of Râjagriha.[1] After a while he met Mallikâ and Varshikâ. "How came you here on foot?" he exclaimed. "Sire," they answered, "Dirghâchârâyana has put Virudhaka on the throne, so we who are of your majesty's family went away."

"Mallikâ," the king replied, "'tis thy son who is in possession of the throne; go and enjoy his sovereignty with him; I and Varshikâ will go to Râjagriha." So, with sorrow and tears Mallikâ went away as she had been told.

[1] I think this must be a mistake for Çravasti, for it was only after meeting his wives that he heard of Dirghâchârâyana's treason; then he turned his steps toward Râjagriha.

The king and Varshikâ set out for Râjagriha; after a while they reached it, and wandering about, they came to one of King Adjatasatru's parks, which they entered. Then the king said to Varshikâ, "Go and tell King Adjatasatru that Prasenadjit, king of Kosala, is in his park." So she went and told the king, who cried out in anger, "What, sirs! this king has a mighty host, and he has quietly come here without any of you knowing it!"

Then Varshikâ[1] said, "Sire, where is his army? His son has usurped his throne, and he has come here alone with his handmaid."

The king, well pleased with Prasenadjit's confidence in him, ordered everything to be made ready to show him respect, and he had announced to the people that whereas Prasenadjit the king of Kosala was in the park, every one must accompany the king with flags and banners to receive him.

After waiting a long time for Adjatasatru, King Prasenadjit became irritated and sick from inanition, so he went to a turnip-field near the park, and the gardener gave him a handful of turnips, and he ate them, tops and all (*la-pug-gi-rdog-ma dang lo-ma-dag zos-pa dang*). This made him very thirsty, so he went to a pool of water and quenched his thirst. Suddenly his hands stiffened, and, seized with cramp in the stomach, he fell in the road and died, suffocated by the dust caused by the wheels of (passing) vehicles.

When King Adjatasatru and all the people reached the park, they searched everywhere, but could not find Prasenadjit. The king sent messengers all about, one of whom came to the turnip-field and learnt from the gardener that a man had been there, had taken a handful of turnips and gone toward the pond. The messenger went that way, and found Prasenadjit lying dead in the road. So he went and told Adjatasatru, and he came there followed by a great concourse of people. On seeing the disfigured corpse,

[1] She is here called *Dbyar-byed*, instead of *Dbyar-ts'ul-ma*.

he said, "Sirs, Prasenadjit was a sovereign king, and it is very unfortunate that he has died in my realm. You must show him every honour in accompanying his remains to the cemetery; and, so that I may show him the highest marks of respect, I will go and consult the Blessed One." So they carried the corpse to the cemetery while the king went to the Blessed One. The Buddha told him to render to the deceased monarch whatever honours he was able to, and this Adjatasatru accordingly did.[1]

Hardly had Virudhaka become king of Kosala but his minister, Ambharisha, reminded him of his oath to destroy the Çakyas, and the king got ready his army hoping to be able to surprise them. The Buddha, who knew Virudhaka's intentions, went out from Çravasti on the road to Kapilavastu, and sat down under an old *shakotaka* tree on which was no bark; a crooked, leafless tree that could offer no shade, and there he passed the day. Virudhaka found him there, and asked him why he had chosen this tree which afforded him no shade. "Mahârâja," the Blessed One replied, "my relatives and kindred make it shady." Then Virudhaka thought, "The Blessed One is filled with compassion for his kinsfolk," so forthwith he turned back and returned to Çravasti.[2]

Now it occurred to the Buddha that if the Çakyas of Kapilavastu knew the truth, they would not be subject to rebirth in case they were destroyed by Virudhaka. So he started up and went to the Çakya country, and coming to Kapila, he entered the Banyan grove. The Çakyas hearing that he had come to their country, flocked to see him, and he taught them the four truths, so that great numbers were converted, and many entered the order.

(F. 146.) Ambharisha persuaded the king to march again against the Çakyas. So Virudhaka reassembled his troops, marched to Kapila, and pitched his camp near the city.[3]

[1] See Dulva x. f. 133–143.

[2] Cf. Huen Thsang, B. vi. p. 305.

[3] Schiefner, Tib. Lebens, p. 288, adds here, "Darauf kommt ein Sohn Agâtaçatru's mit seinen Truppen zu Hülfe und schliesst die Stadt ein." I have found no mention of this in the Dulva.

Mahâmaudgalyayana having heard of Virudhaka's intended attack, went and asked the Blessed One to allow him to carry the whole of Virudhaka's army to another part of the world, or to perform some other magical feat which would save the Çakyas; but the Blessed One replied that nothing would avail; that the Çakyas must bear the consequences of their former deeds.

As soon as the Çakyas of Kapila heard that Virudhaka had come with all his troops to destroy them, they got together their army, sallied forth and repulsed him. Those among them who had been converted by the Blessed One, and who refrained from killing anything, carried cudgels and goads; they cut the bow-strings and the strappings, and shot arrows into the ear ornaments (*rna-rgyan-la mdah hphel-par byed*).

After repelling Virudhaka's army, the Çakyas re-entered the city, shut their gates, and remained watching on their walls, sounding their trumpets the while.

Ambharisha rallied the troops of Kosala and inspired them with fresh courage. "We run no danger," he said. "The Çakyas are Buddhists (lit. righteous); they would not kill anything that has life; no, not even a black beetle. See, they have not killed any one among us." So they remained (encamped around the city).

The Çakyas issued a proclamation prohibiting any one from attacking Virudhaka or his army. If any one did so, he would be no kinsman of theirs, no Çakya. There happened to be a Çakya called Shampaka who was off working for himself on the hills,[1] and who had not heard the proclamation of the Çakyas. Filled with rage on hearing of Virudhaka's attack, he sallied forth towards Virudhaka's army, overthrew a great number of persons, the

[1] Cf. Huen Thsang, B. vi. p. 318, who says that there were four men working in the fields. M. Feer, however, Annales Musée Guimet, vol. v. p. 72, does not translate the Tibetan text as I have done. Huen Thsang, *loc. cit.*, says that one of these men became king of Udyâna, the second king of Bamyan, the third king of Himatala, and the fourth king of Çâmbî.

greater part of whom he killed outright. Virudhaka, greatly discouraged, said to Ambharisha, "Are these your righteous people who will not kill even a beetle? If they all kill as many of us as this one man, there will not be left a soul living among us!"

When Shampaka tried to enter Kapilavastu, the people would not let him, for he had violated their law, and though he pleaded that he had had no knowledge of it, he was obliged to go away with his attendants. Before leaving the country he went to the Blessed One, and besought him to give him some memorial of his person (f. 149). The Buddha gave him by magic some of his hair, some nail-parings, and a tooth,[1] and bearing them with them, he set out for the country of Vaku.[2] Shampaka was made king of the country by acclamation, and was called King Shampaka. He built a stupa for the relics of the Blessed One, and it was called Shampaka's stupa. He married a woman who was a pagan, converted her to Buddhism, and established a regular government. He, moreover, organised means for protecting the forests, and taught the people not to kill the deer (f. 150).

Meanwhile Virudhaka said to Ambharisha, "Now that the Çakyas have closed their gates and remain cringing behind their walls bewailing, what is to be done?"

The minister suggested that they should try to foment dissensions among the inhabitants, and that by that means the city would soon fall into their hands. So the king sent a messenger to the Çakyas, saying, "Sirs, although I have no fondness for you, yet I have no hatred against

[1] Dulva x., f. 169[b], it is prescribed that a bhikshu shall circumambulate the chortens (cairns) which contain hair and nail-parings of the Tathâgata. See also same vol. f. 198.

[2] Huen Thsang, B. iii. p. 141 *et seq.*, gives the history of four Çakyas who were obliged to leave their country for having fought with Virudhaka. One of them (the Shampaka of our text) founded the kingdom of Udyâna. Huen Thsang, p. 131 *et seq.*, gives a description of Udyâna, a country of Northern India, watered by the river Swat, a tributary of the Kabul. There is also a region south-east of Kachmere which was called Tchampâka, a name which forcibly reminds us of the hero of our story. It is on the north-western frontier of Lahul.

you. It is all over; so open your gates quickly." Then the Çakyas said, "Let us all assemble and deliberate whether we shall open the gates." When they had assembled, some said, "Open them;" others advised not doing so. Some said, "As there are various opinions, we will find out the opinion of the mậjority." So they set about voting on the subject.

Then Mâra, the Evil one, thought that it was a good occasion to revenge himself on Gautama's kinsmen for his former defeats by the Buddha; he took the form of the headman (*rgan-po*) of the Çakyas, and advocated opening the gates, and they all voted in the same way. So they sent Virudhaka word that he could enter the city, and he made his entry with all his army. Hardly were they in but the king cried out, "I will shut up the Çakyas' mouths; I will exterminate the Çakyas!" And with that he commenced having the Çakyas slaughtered with wild vociferations (*ku-cho tchen-po hdon-to ?*).

Mahânâman hearing the noise, and filled with anguish for his people, ran to Virudhaka, and said, "Sire, you came here on a promise; make me a promise, I beseech you!"

"What do you ask?"

"Spare the people, O king!"

"I will not spare your people," replied the king, "but you and your family may leave the place."

"Sire," said Mahânâman, "let as many of my people escape as may while I can remain in the water without sinking."

Then the king's courtiers said to him, "Sire, this Mahânâman is a compatriot (*yul-mes*) of yours, and he was a friend of your father's, so grant him his request."

The king told him to do as he wished; so, filled with anguish for his people, he went down into the water of a pool. On the edge of the pool there grew a sala tree, the branches of which fell into the water; they got entwined in Mahânâman's hair-knot, so that he was pulled under and drowned.

In the meanwhile some of the Çakyas of Kapilavastu got out of the city without any of their goods, and hastened away. Some of them went to Bal-po (Nepal), some to different towns and villages, some to the Râja-(griha?) country (*rgyal-poi yul-hkhor*), and to different castles (*pho-brang de dang de dag-tu*) (f. 151). Some of the Çakyas, thinking of their property, went out of one gate and came in by another, and Virudhaka's courtiers called his attention to this. "Go," said the king, "and see if that countryman of mine has sunk yet." So they went, and looking, they found him dead. When they told this to the king, he became enraged, and said to his courtiers, "Prepare me a seat. I will not leave it until the blood of the slain runs down this road in streams." But the blood that flowed from the men and women he had killed was not in sufficient quantity (to make a stream), so his courtiers poured on the road one hundred thousand jars of red lac. Seeing this, Virudhaka thought, "Now I may depart, for I have fulfilled my promise." He had massacred in this way 77,000 Çakyas, the greater part believers. Moreover, he took five hundred youths, and a like number of maidens, whom he carried off to the ârama of the Parivradjaka tirthikas called the "Place of the Sow;[1] but Ambharisha advised the king to have them also put to death. Then Virudhaka tried to have the young men trampled to death by elephants, but they overcame the elephants and kept off their tusks; so he had them thrown into a pit and covered over with iron plates.

Virudhaka sent a man to the Blessed One with instructions to listen to what he might say (about the massacre), and to come and repeat it to him. The Buddha went to where the young Çakyas had been cast in a pit covered over with iron plates, and as there still remained a little life in them, they cried out when they saw him; and

[1] In Tibetan, *phag-moi gnas*. This may possibly be an abbreviation for *rdo-rje phag-moi gnas*, "the place of Vadjravarahi."

shortly after they died and were reborn in the Trayastrimcat heaven. Then the Buddha sat down to one side, and told the bhikshus that in seven days the house of Kosala would be destroyed, that Virudhaka and Ambarisha would be burnt up, and be born in the bottomless hell (*Avitchi*).

In the meanwhile Virudhaka returned to Çravasti. It happened that Prince Jeta had gone on to the terrace of his palace, and was amusing himself there when Virudhaka noticed him and asked who it was. When his courtiers told him that it was Jeta, he ordered them to call him to him. When he had come he said, "Jeta, I come from putting to death my enemies, and you have remained here amusing yourself!"

"Sire," answered the prince, "who are your enemies?" "The Çakyas," he answered. "If the Çakyas are your enemies," replied Jeta, "who are your friends?"

Then the king said, "Have him sent to where the Çakyas are!" So Jeta was put to death, and he also was reborn in the Trayastrimcat heaven.

Virudhaka tried to put the five hundred Çakya maidens in his harem, but they mocked at him and would not go. Then he was angered and exclaimed, "When the vipers are killed, still their young are poisonous; so cut off their hands and feet, and then let them go back to their people."

Then they took the five hundred Çakya maidens to the bank of a pâtali (*dmar-bu-chan*) pond, and there they cut off their hands and feet, for which reason the pond became known as "the pool of the severed hand" (*lag-pai dong-gi rjing*).[1] The Blessed One came to them, had their wounds dressed, and, while they felt some relief from their sufferings, he unfolded to them the law, so that they died in the faith and were reborn in the region of the four great kings (f. 159). From thence they came back to visit the Blessed One at Jetavana during the night, and there they obtained the reward of çrotapanna.

[1] See Fah-Hian, p. 87, and Huen Thsang, B. vi. p. 307.

When Virudhaka's messenger came and told him what the Buddha had said, he was filled with trouble. Ambharisha comforted him with the assurance that Gautama had only said this because the king had killed so many of his people. Moreover, he advised him to have a kiosque built in the water, and there to pass the seven days. The king followed his advice, and retired to the kiosque with all his harem. On the seventh day, as they were preparing to return to Çravasti, and the women were arraying themselves in all their jewels, the sky, which until then had been overcast, cleared up, and the sun's rays falling on a burning-glass which was on a cushion, set fire to the cushion, and from that the flames spread to the whole house. The women ran away and made their escape, but when the king and Ambharisha tried to do likewise, they found the doors shut, and with loud cries they went down into the bottomless hell.[1]

In the following pages will be found an abstract of the Tibetan version of the Mahâparinirvâna Sûtra, or as Professor Rhys Davids has happily translated it "The Book of the Great Decease," in which are related the events which took place during the last year of the Buddha's life—that is to say, his seventy-ninth year. This work has been considered as perhaps the oldest one extant in the Pâli canon, and as having been composed before the time of the first synod held after the Buddha's death.[2] There appears to me no reason to believe that this narrative has been handed down with any more or any less care than the history of the first years of the Buddha's ministry, for example; but as this sûtra is confessedly very important, I have thought it advisable to give an analysis of the Tibetan version. Wherever the text of this and the Pâli version agree, I have used Professor Rhys

[1] See Dulva x. f. 133, 161; also for parts of it, Feer, Annales du Musée Guimet, vol. v. p. 65, 76; Schiefner, Tib. Lebens, p. 287–289; and Huen Thsang, B. vi. p. 307–308.

[2] See Oldenberg's Vinaya Pitakam, vol. i., p. 26.

Davids' translation,[1] so that the similarity of the two texts may at once be detected.

The Blessed Buddha was stopping at Râjagriha on the Vulture's Peak mountain. Now at that time Vaidehiputra Adjatasatru, king of Magadha, was not on friendly terms with the Vrijians; so he said to his courtiers, "I will conquer these Vrijians, I will crush them, I will put them to rout for their turbulence; rich, mighty, happy, prosperous, numerous though they be."

So Vaidehiputra Adjatasatru said to the brahman Varshakâra (*Dbyar-byed*), one of the great nobles (*sna-tchen-po la-gtogs* = *Mahâmatra*)[2] of Magadha, "Varshakâra, go to where is the Blessed One; bow down on my behalf at his feet, and ask him for me if he is free from illness, if he is suffering or not, if he is comfortable (*bskyod*), at ease, in vigorous health, happy, free from trouble (f. 536[a]); then tell him, 'Lord, Adjatasatru Vaidehiputra, the king of Magadha, and the Vrijians are not on friendly terms, and (the king has said to his courtiers), &c.,' [as above], and bring me word what the Blessed One says when he hears this. Because, Varshakâra, the tathâgatas, arhats, perfectly enlightened ones never say anything which does not come true."

Then the great noble of Magadha, the brahman Varshakâra, having hearkened to the words of Vaidehiputra Adjatasatru, king of Magadha, said, "Sire, be it as you command." So he mounted a pure white chariot with splendid horses, a golden seat (*khang*), as if he was going to carry the globular anointing vase (for a coronation), and went out of Râjagriha to see the Blessed One and to offer him his respects. He went to where was the Blessed One, riding as far as was practicable,

[1] Sacred Books of the East, vol. xi. p. 1–136. Conf. also Bigandet, *op. cit.* (3d edit.), vol. ii. p. 1–95; and Spence Hardy, *op. cit.*, p. 355 *et seq.* My text is from Dulva xi. f. 535[b]–652[b]. There exist several other works in the Bkah-hgyur on the nirvana of the Buddha. They are—(1.) In Mdo, viii. f. 1–231, entitled *Mahâ parinirvâna sûtra*; (2.) Do., f. 231–234, same title; and the section called *Myang-hdas* or Nirvâna, in two volumes.

[2] See Buddh. Trigl., p. 27[a].

then alighting and climbing the Vulture's Peak on foot (f. 536b). When he approached the Blessed One, they exchanged different greetings and congratulations, then he sat down to one side. While thus seated, the brahman Varshakâra, the great noble of Magadha, [delivered the king's message, and when he had finished, he said], "What does the Blessed Gautama say to this?"

"Varshakâra (the Buddha replied), they were once disunited. Varshakâra, I was once staying near the Rtseb-pa[1] tchaitya of the Vriji country (f. 537a), and there I taught the Vrijians the seven conditions of welfare; and as long as they continue to keep these seven rules of welfare, so long as they keep present to their minds these seven conditions, so long will the Vrijians' prosperity increase and not diminish."

"Gautama, I do not know the particulars of these summarily mentioned facts. I beg Gautama to repeat to me what he then said, so that I may be able to appreciate his words."

Now at that time the venerable Ananda was standing behind the Blessed One holding a fan, with which he was fanning him. Then the Blessed One said to the venerable Ananda, "Have you heard, Ananda, whether the Vrijians assemble frequently and from afar?"

"Lord, I have heard [that they do]" (f. 537b).

"Well, Varshakâra, so long as the Vrijians [do this], so long will the Vrijians' prosperity increase and not diminish."

(The six other conditions of welfare which he inquires about in the same terms as above are)—(1.) Whether the Vrijians sit in harmony, rise in harmony; whether the Vrijians' plans and undertakings are carried out in harmony? (2.) Whether the Vrijians do not edict anything not desirable, or abrogate anything desirable, whether they follow the institutions made by the Vri-

[1] This word does not appear to be Tibetan. It is most likely a misprint, but I am unable to correct it. The Pâli version calls the place the Sârandada cetiya (p. 3).

jians? (3.) (F. 538[a].) Whether, among the Vrijians, Vrijian women, Vrijian maidens are protected by their fathers, mothers, husbands, brothers, mothers-in-law, fathers-in-law, by their relatives and kinsfolk; whether they do not by promises or stealth take other men's wives; whether they do not put them away as of little value, as they might throw away a wreath of flowers; whether Vrijians are murdered in abductions?[1] (4.) Whether the elders of the Vrijians, the upper classes and parents are honoured by the Vrijians, revered, venerated, respected; whether they hearken to their words and act as they direct? (5.) Whether the tchaityas, in whatever part of the territory of Vriji they be, are revered, venerated, respected by the Vrijians, and whether they have not done away with the time-established honours due them? (6.) Whether among the Vrijians arhats receive the strong protection and support (*dran-ba nye-bar-gnas*) that is due them, and whether arhats who are not travelling are invited, and whether those who are travelling (through their country) are made happy (f. 538[b]), and receive the necessary robes, alms, bedding, medicine?"

"Varshakâra, so long as the Vrijians shall continue to keep these seven rules of welfare, so long as the Vrijians keep before them these seven conditions of welfare, so long will their prosperity increase and not decline" (f. 540[a]).

"Gautama, if the Vrijians have any one part (of these conditions of welfare), Vaidehiputra Adjatasatru, king of Magadha, would not be able to subdue them; how much more so if they are possessed of them all! Gautama, I have much to do, so I must depart."

"Go, Varshakâra; you know what is best for you." So the great noble of Magadha, the brahman Varshakâra, well pleased with the words of the Blessed One, went away.

[1] The latter part of this phrase is obscure, and I feel some uncertainty as to the way in which I have translated it.

Shortly after his departure the Blessed One said to the venerable Ananda, "Go, Ananda, and cause all the bhikshus who are stopping on the Vulture's Peak to assemble in the service hall." When Ananda had hearkened to the words of the Blessed One, he replied, "So be it;" and he went, and having assembled in the service hall all the bhikshus then stopping on the Vulture's Peak (f. 540[b]), he went back to the Blessed One, and having bowed down reverentially at his feet, he stood to one side, and while thus standing he said to the Blessed One, "Lord, all the bhikshus stopping on the Vulture's Peak are assembled in the service hall; may the Blessed One do as he deems proper."

Then the Blessed One went to the service hall and took his seat in the midst of the congregation of bhikshus, and then he said to them, "Bhikshus, I will explain to you seven consecutive conditions of welfare; listen well and be attentive and I will explain them." (Then follows (f. 540[b]–544[b]) different series of conditions of welfare. The text does not materially differ from that of the Pâli version, except that of the 5th and 7th condition in the first series; but as we only have to do with the historical portion of the narrative, I must refer those whom the question interests to the text.)

(F. 545[a].) From the Vulture's Peak (*Gridhrakuta parvata*) the Buddha went toward Pâtaligâma (*Dmar-bu-chan-gyi-grong*) and stopped at Ambalatthika (*Od-mai dbyug-pa-chan*), in the king's house, and there he explained the four truths to his disciples; "For," he said, "both you and I, from not having perceived them, have been wandering about for a long time in the orb of regeneration."

From thence he went to Pâtaligâma, and stopped near the tchaitya of Pâtaligâma,[1] and the people having heard of the Buddha's arrival, went to him, and he told them

[1] Or, Pâtalitchaitya, as it is frequently written. Beal, Sacred Books of the East, xix. p. 249; Bstan-hgyur, Mdo, 94, f. 90.

of the fivefold loss of the evil-doer (f. 546) and of the fivefold gain of the well-doer[1] (f. 547).

At that time the great noble of Magadha, the brahman Varshakâra,[2] was having built the fortress of Pâtaligâma for the purpose of subduing the Vrijians; and at that time in the village of the Patali there were many powerful dêvas (*lha*), who haunted the whole place. Now the Blessed One, while passing the day at his abode, saw with his divine sight, which surpassed that of men, the many powerful fairies who were haunting all the ground of Pâtali(gâma); and when he had seen them he bore it in mind, and, entering into his house, he sat down in the midst of his disciples. While thus seated, the Blessed One said to the venerable Ananda, "Ananda, have you heard who was building the fortress of Pâtaligâma?"

"Lord, it is the great noble of Magadha, the brahman Varshakâra, who to subdue the Vrijians (f. 549[a]) is building the fortress of Pâtaligâma."

"Ananda, just so, just so! Ananda, the great noble of Magadha, the brahman Varshakâra, is as wise as if he had held council with the Trayastrimcat dêvas. Ananda, while I was passing the day (near this place), I saw with my divine sight, which surpasses that of men, [a quantity of powerful fairies]. Ananda, whatever spot is haunted by powerful fairies, they influence the minds of powerful men to build there. Whatever spot is haunted by fairies of medium or inferior power, they influence the minds of medium or inferior men to build there. Ananda, this place of Pâtaligâma is haunted by powerful fairies, therefore they will influence the minds of powerful men to build here. Ananda, among the abodes of high-class people, among famous places, among famous marts and mercantile em-

[1] See Rhys Davids, *op. cit.*, p. 16, *et seq.*

[2] The Pâli version, p. 18 (Rhys Davids, *op. cit.*), speaks of two personages, Sinîdha and Varshakâra. The Chinese Buddhacharita (Beal, Sacred Books of the East, vol. xix.), p. 250, also alludes to two persons, although it does not give their names. Not so, however, the Tibetan version of the Buddhacharita (f. 90[b]), which only mentions *Tchardbyings* or Varshakâra.

poriums (*zong-bgram sar*), Pâtaliputra (*Dmar-bu-chan-gyi grong-khyer*[1]) (f. 549[b]) will be the greatest. Three perils will menace it—fire, water, and internal dissensions."

When Varshakâra heard that the Blessed One was at Pâtaligâma, he went to the Blessed One, and having exchanged compliments and greetings with him (f. 549[b]), he invited him with his disciples to a meal on the morrow (f. 550[a]). When the meal was over, the Blessed One left the village by the western gate; then turning northward, he passed the Ganges at a ferry (or ford), and these were called Gotama's Gate and Gotama's Ferry (f. 551[b]).

(F. 552[a].) After this the Buddha went to Kotigâma (*Grong-khyer spyil-po-chan*), and stopped in a çinçapa grove north of the village,[2] where he taught the brethren the meaning of morality, meditation, and wisdom. On leaving this place he went to Nâdika (*Grong-khyer sgra-chan*), and resided in the gunjaka[3] (or brick hall) of Nâdika (f. 552[b]).

Now the lay disciple Karkata (*sic*) had died, as had also the lay followers Nikata (*Nye-ba*), Katissabha (*Kat-ii-khyu-mtchog*), Tushti (*Mdjes-pa*), Santushti (*Nye-mdjes-pa*), Bhadra (*Bzang-pa*), Subhadra (*Shin-tu bzang-pa*), Yaças (*Grags-pa*), Yaçodatta (*Grags-byin*), &c.; and when the bhikshus found this out, they went and asked the Blessed One what had become of them (f. 553[a]). After having told them (f. 553[b]–554[a]), he explained to them the Mirror of Truth[4] (*dharma*), which enables one to see what will be his future, and which would help them when he would be no more (f. 554[b]).

After this the Blessed One went to Vaisali and stopped at Amrapalî's grove (f. 555[b]). When Amrapalî heard of the Buddha's arrival, she went to see him, attended by a great number of waiting-women. The Buddha seeing her coming, cautioned the bhikshus. "Bhikshus," he said,

[1] Usually Pâtiliputra is rendered in Tibetan by *Skya-nar-gyi-bu*. In the Tibetan Buddhacharita (f. 90[b]) it is *Pa-ta-li-yi-grong*.

[2] Cf. Rhys Davids, *op. cit.*, p. 23.

[3] The text has *Kunjikai gnas-na bdjugs-so*. There can be no doubt that this is an error for Gunjaka.

[4] See Rhys Davids, p. 26–27.

"Amrapalî is coming! Be mindful, wise, and thoughtful," &c.[1] (f. 556). When Amrapalî had come near to him, she bowed down at his feet, and, sitting down to one side, the Blessed One instructed, aroused, and gladdened her by his words, after which she invited him and the bhikshus to take their meal with her on the morrow (f. 557ᵃ). The Blessed One accepted the invitation by remaining silent, and Amrapalî departed.

The Licchavis of Vaisali also heard of the arrival of the Blessed One, so they mounted their chariots . . . and went to see him [2] (f. 557ᵇ). Seeing them coming, the Buddha called the bhikshus' attention to them: "Bhikshus, you who have not been in the parks of the Trayastrimcat dêvas, these are like unto them for the glory of their appearance, their riches, and the beauty of their apparel" (f. 558ᵃ).

The Licchavis saluted the Blessed One, and then he instructed, incited, and gladdened them by his words. When he had finished speaking, a brahman youth called Kapila (*Ser-skya*) rose up (f. 558ᵃ) and said, "Blessed One, may I venture; Tathâgata, may I give vent (to my feelings)?" And when the Blessed One had authorised him, he spoke these verses:—

"A room of jewels the king of Anga keeps,
And great the wealth owned by the lord of Magadha;
But in that country the living Buddha
Obtains admiration great as Himavat.

See the Teacher like the radiant sun,
As a lovely full-blown lotus,
As the sweet scent of the open Karṇikâ (*donka*),
Like the sun shining brightly in the sky!

Wisdom is the Tathâgata's might;
See how as a beacon in the night
Now flashes his illumined eye,
Dispelling the darkness in those around him!" (F. 558ᵇ.)

[1] See Rhys Davids, p. 28, where his admonitions do not seem to allude to the coming of the famous courtesan.

[2] Our text does not mention their meeting with Amrapalî, or give any hint that it knows of it. See Rhys Davids, p. 31.

The Licchavis were so much pleased with his verses that each one of them gave him the cloak he was wearing. Again the Blessed One instructed, incited, and gladdened them by his words, and the Licchavis asked him to eat with them on the morrow, but he refused, having accepted the courtesan's invitation; then the Licchavis having saluted him, departed.

After their departure the brahman youth Kapila begged the Blessed One to accept the five hundred cloaks which he had received; and the Buddha, to please him, acceded to his request. Then having taught him concerning the five wonders which attend Buddhas in this world (f. 559–560), Kapila took his leave.

On the morrow, after eating at Amrapalî's (f. 561[a]), she sat down on a low stool and listened to the Buddha's discourse on liberality and its merits.[1]

On leaving Vaisali the Buddha went to Beluva (*Od-ma chan-gyi-grong*) in the Vriji country (f. 561[b]), and stayed in a çinçapa grove to the north of the village (f. 562[a]).

Now at that time there raged a famine, and it was a difficult matter for all the bhikshus to find food; so the Blessed One told them to go and dwell in the Vriji country round about Vaisali during the rainy season, wherever they had friends and acquaintances. He decided to pass the rainy season with Ananda at Beluva (f. 562[a]). While spending the rainy season there, a dire illness fell upon the Blessed One, and sharp pains came upon him even unto death. Then the Blessed One thought, "The sharp pains of a dire illness have come upon me even unto death, but the congregation of bhikshus is scattered, and it would not be right for me to pass away while the congregation of bhikshus is thus scattered. I will by a strenuous effort dispel the pain, so that I may retain a hold on this body until it has accomplished its task. I will keep this body until all my projects have been

[1] The text does not mention the gift of her residence to the order, for which see Rhys Davids, *op. cit.*, p. 33.

accomplished."[1] So he overcame the pains and kept his hold on life (f. 562[b]).

Ananda came to him (when he was convalescent) and gave vent to the sorrow he had felt. "My body was as stiff as if I had taken poison; the cardinal points (*phyogs*) became confused; I forgot the lessons I had heard; there was yet a hope in my heart (lit. throat), for I thought the Blessed One would not pass away before he had made a final exhortation to the congregation of bhikshus, however brief it might be" (f. 563[a]).

The Buddha reproached him for thinking that he had withheld any part of his doctrine. "Think not, Ananda, that the Tathâgata withholds what he does not deem suitable for certain persons. I am not (one of those) teachers unwilling to lend his books[2] (f. 563[b]). Moreover, Ananda, the Tathâgata has reached fourscore years; his body has become bent down and decrepit, and he lives holding the two parts together (with difficulty). Just as an old cart is only kept in order by binding (tight) together the two portions of it, so the Tathâgata, having reached fourscore years, his body bent down and decrepit, only lives holding the two parts together (with difficulty). Therefore sorrow not, Ananda, neither give yourself up to grief. . . . Ananda, let the truth be your island; let the truth be your refuge. There is no other island, no other refuge."

Then the Blessed One went with Ananda to Vaisali, and there they abode in the mansion built on the edge of the monkey pond. In the morning (after his arrival) he went into Vaisali accompanied by Ananda to collect alms, and when he had finished his meal and washed his bowl, he went to the Tsapala (*i.e.*, Kâpâla) tchaitya (f. 565[b]), and

[1] The text here is difficult; it is, *Mts'an-ma thams-chad yid-la mi mdzad-pas sems-kyi ting-nge-hdzin mts'an-ma med-pa skus mngon sum-du mdzad-pa bsgrubs-nas djugs-te.* I have translated *mts'an-ma* (=*lakshana*) by "project," because I did not see that any other sense could be made out of it, but I have no authority for so doing.

[2] In Tibetan *slob-dpon-gyi dpe mkhyud;* conf. the Pâli *âkariya mutthi*, which Rhys Davids, p. 36, very happily translates by "the closed fist of a teacher who keeps some things back."

sat down near a tree to pass the day. Then he said to Ananda, "Ananda, how delightful a spot is Vaisali, the Vriji country, the Kâpâla tchaitya, (the tchaitya of) the seven amra trees (*Sattambaka*), the Bahuputra (*Bu-mang-po*) (tchaitya), the banyan tree of Gautama, the twin sala trees, the Brtson-pa-gtong (?), and the crested tchaitya of the Mallas (*makuta bandhana tchaitya, chod-pan htching-pai mtchod-rten*), and many other spots in Jambudvipa," &c., &c. (see Rhys Davids, p. 40–48).

After having conversed with Ananda, he told him to call the brethren together at the Kâpâla tchaitya, and there he exhorted them to practise the four earnest meditations, the fourfold great struggle against sin, &c. (see Rhys Davids, p. 60–61) (f. 670).

Then the Buddha went to Kusinagara (*? Kus-tii-grong*) (f. 571[a]), and as he and Ananda were passing through Vaisali, he turned his whole body to the right as would an elephant (*Bal-glang*) and looked at (the city). Ananda asked him why he did so, and then the Buddha told him that it was the last time he would ever see Vaisali, for he was about to pass away in a grove of sala trees (f. 571[b]).

Then the Blessed One journeying in the Vriji country passed through different villages called Amragâma (*Amrai-grong*), Jambugâma (*Hdzam-bui-grong*), Bhaṇḍagâma (*Rjo* (*rje?*) *grong*), Shur-pai-grong (?), Hasthigâma (*Bal-glang ltar-gyi-grong*), villages of the Vrijians and Mallas, and he came to Bhoga-nagara (*Long-spyod-grong*), and there he stopped in a çinçapa grove to the north of the village (f. 572[b]). And while he was there the earth trembled, and he explained the reason to his disciples, attributing earthquakes to three natural causes.[1] On leaving this place the Blessed One went to "the village of the earth" (? *Sa-pai-grong*[2]) (f. 578[b]). Proceeding

[1] The text does not exactly agree with the Pâli version, for which see Rhys Davids, p. 44. Our text says that it was here that he spoke of "the three great references." See R. D., p. 67 *et seq.* In the Tibetan text they are to be found, f. 573[a]–577[a], but it is much more developed than the Pâli version, and gives many more rules.

[2] It may be that *Sa-pai* is an error for *Pa-vai*, as the letters which

then from Bhoga-nagara, and journeying in the Mallas country (Malya in the text), he came to "the village of the earth," and stopped in the Jalûkâ mahâvana (*Dza-lu-kai ts'al-mang-pa*) (f. 579[a]), and the people of the place having heard that he was there, came to him and he taught them. Now at that time there was a man called Kunda (*sic*), a worker in metals, among those assembled to listen to the Blessed One, and he sat there until all the people had left (f. 579[b]); then he arose and invited the Buddha and his disciples to eat with him on the morrow, and the Blessed One assented by remaining silent.

Before the night was over, Kunda, the worker in metals, had prepared for the Blessed One a quantity of delicious food, and when the Buddha came on the morrow, he filled an iron bowl with food which had been expressly prepared for the Buddha and placed it before him with his own hands; but a wicked bhikshu took the bowl and the food which had been offered to the Blessed One and hid it in his bosom, and though both the Buddha and Kunda saw him do so, they said nothing. Then Kunda went and had another iron bowl filled with other delicious kinds of food and presented it to the Buddha, and the brethren he treated to delicious food, both hard and soft, and he waited on them himself [1] (f. 580[a]). When the Buddha had finished eating, he spoke some verses to Kunda (f. 580[b]–581[a]), after which he said to Ananda, "Let us go to Kusinârâ" (*Grong-khyer rtsa-chan*). So passing through Pâvâ (*Sdig-pa-chan*) the Blessed One entered the wilderness on the other side of the Hiranyavati river (*Tchu-bo dbyig-chan*), and then he said to Ananda, "Ananda, my back (*nga rgyab*) pains me. I would like to rest. Fold

compose these two words are very much alike, but Pâvâ, which was the home of Kunda (acc. to the Pâli version), is elsewhere rendered in Tibetan *Sdig-pa-chan*. On f. 581[b] we hear that to go to Kusinârâ he passed through Pâvâ; the Jalûkâ mahâvana was probably on the farther side of Pâvâ (*Sa-pai-grong*).

[1] It is curious that the text contains no mention of the pork which is said to have caused the inflammation, the cause of Buddha's death. See Rhys Davids, p. 71. Our text omits § 18, 19 of the Pâli version.

in four the Tathâgata's robe." Then he laid down on his right side and drew his feet together; having done which, he asked Ananda to go to the Kakustana river[1] (*sic*) and fill his bowl with water to drink (f. 582[a]).

Ananda went with the bowl to the river, but five hundred waggons had just crossed it and had stirred it up; Ananda filled the bowl and brought it back to the Blessed One. He told him, however, that the water was muddy, and added, "My Lord, I beg you to only wash your feet and to rinse your mouth with this water. A little way hence is the Hiranyavati river, and if the Blessed One only drinks of its waters, his body will once more be whole" (*sku-la yang gdab-par bgyio*). So the Blessed One only washed his feet and rinsed his mouth, and sitting down patiently, his legs crossed and his body erect, he was soon lost in meditation (f. 582[b]). Now at that time one of the great nobles of the Mallas, a man called Pushkasa (*Gyung-pa*), was travelling on this road, and seeing the Buddha in all his splendour seated at the foot of a tree, he approached him, and having respectfully saluted him, he sat down to one side. The Buddha asked him what teacher he followed, and he said that Arata Kalama was his master. Then the Buddha having told him what had happened to him while in a room at Atuma during a violent storm[2] (f. 583–584), converted him, and Pushkasa told one of his attendants to bring him a piece of chintz the colour of burnished gold, and he offered it to the Buddha (f. 585[a]); then having listened to his teaching, he saluted him and went his way. Now as soon as Pushkasa had left, the Blessed One said to Ananda, "Take the chintz the colour of burnished gold,

[1] Spence Hardy, *op. cit.*, p. 356, calls the river in which the Buddha bathed the Kukutthâ. Bigandet, vol. ii. p. 39, calls it the Kakanda, an arm of the little Gundak. "It is at present dried up, but up to this day are to be seen several marks indicating the ancient bed of that stream." See also his note, p. 40, on the Hiranyavati. The Pâli version does not mention the name of the river. Kaçyapa reproached Ananda for his conduct on this occasion. See p. 153.

[2] See Rhys Davids, p. 76 *et seq.*

cut off the fringes and give it to me, for I will wear it." Then Ananda did as he had been told; and when the Buddha put on the robe, lo! his body became exceedingly brilliant, so brilliant that Ananda said, "Lord, I have been in attendance on the Blessed One twenty years and more, but never before has the Blessed One's body been bright as at present. What may be the reason of it?" Then the Buddha told him of the two occasions on which a Buddha's body becomes resplendent[1] (f. 586).

Thence they went to the Hiranyavati river, and when they had come to the bank of the river, the Blessed One put aside all his garments but one, and going down into the river he bathed; then crossing the stream, he dried himself and sat down. Then he told Ananda that Kunda, the worker in metals, must not feel remorse because he died after eating a meal at his house (f. 587[a]).

Then they departed, journeying to Kusinârâ through the wilderness between the Hiranyavati river and that town. Again he asked Ananda to arrange him a couch, for he was weary and would fain rest a while; so he laid down and went to sleep (f 587[b]). When he awakened he exhorted Ananda to steadfastness and the bhikshus to walk in the way of the truth, and to follow the Sûtranta, the Vinaya, and the Mâtṛika, &c., &c. (f. 588–589[a]); and then they resumed their journey to Kusinârâ, and stopped in the twin sala tree grove.[2] Now, knowing that his time had come, he told Ananda to place the Tathâgata's couch (*khri tchos*) between the twin sala trees, with his head to the north, "for in the middle watch of this night I will utterly pass away." Ananda did as he was bidden, and the Blessed One laid down on his right side, drew his feet together, and gave up his mind to thoughtfulness, to the thought of light (*snang*), to the thought of nirvâṇa (f. 590). Ananda stood by his side holding on to his couch, and the tears flowed from his eyes as he thought, "Soon the

[1] See Rhys Davids, p. 81.
[2] See on the position of this grove, Bigandet, vol. ii. p. 46.

Blessed One will utterly pass away; soon the Sugata will utterly pass away; the eye of the world will soon pass away," . . . and he went out and wept.

The Buddha noticed his absence, so he asked the bhikshus who pressed around him to call Ananda, and he said to him, "Ananda, thou hast ever been attentive to the Tathâgata by acts of love, kind and good" . . . (f. 590–591[a]); and then he explained to the brethren that as there were four wonderful qualities in a king of kings, so likewise there were four in Ananda[1] (f. 591[b]–592[a]). When the Blessed One had finished speaking, Ananda said, "Lord, there are the six great cities of Çravasti, Saketa, Çampa, Varâṇasi, Vaisali, Râjagriha, and others besides; why then has the Blessed One seen fit to reject these and to decide to die in this poor village, this sand-hole (*dgon-dung*), this straggling village (*mkhar-ngan*), this suburb, this semblance of a town?" The Buddha rebuked him for thus speaking of Kusinârâ, and then he narrated the history of King Mahâsudarçana (*Legs-mthong tchen-po*) and of his glorious capital Kusâvati, which had become Kusinârâ[2] (f. 592–607).

Now the venerable Upâvana (*Dpe-chan*) was standing in front of the Blessed One, and the Buddha told him, "Bhikshu, stand not in front of me."

Then Ananda said, "Lord, I have attended on the Blessed One twenty years and more, but I have never heretofore heard him speak harshly to the venerable Upâvana."

Then the Blessed One told the former history of Upâvana, which accounted for what he had said to him[3] (f. 608–609).

[1] See Rhys Davids, p. 95–99.

[2] This agrees very exactly with the Mahâsudassana Sutta; cf. Pâli Digha Nikâya. See Rhys Davids, *op. cit.*, p. 237–289.

[3] Cf. Rhys Davids, p. 87 *et seq.* The Tibetan version does not mention the facts related in § 10–15. Bigandet, vol. ii. p. 49, says that it was the Bhikshuni Utpalavarna who was standing in front of the Buddha. See, however, what has been said, p. 106.

After this incident Ananda asked the Blessed One how they must honour him after his death.

"Ananda," he replied, "take no trouble about that; the brahmans and householders who are believers will attend to that."

"How then, Lord, must the brahmans and householders who are believers honour the Blessed One's remains?" asked Ananda (f. 610[b]).

"Ananda, they must treat them as those of a king of kings" (*Chakravartin*).

"Lord, how do they treat the remains of a king of kings?"

"Ananda, the body of a king of kings is wrapped in bands of cotton, and when it has thus been wrapped it is covered with five hundred layers (*? zung*) of cotton. After that it is put in an iron case filled with oil, and it is covered with a double cover of iron; then a funeral pile of all kinds of odoriferous woods is built; (the remains) are burnt and the fire is put out with milk. Then they put his bones in a golden casket, and in the cross-roads they build a tchaitya over his remains, and with baldachins, flags and streamers, perfumes, garlands, incense and sweet powders, with the sounds of music, they honour, praise, venerate, and revere him, and celebrate a feast in his honour. So likewise, Ananda, must they treat the Tathâgata's remains.

"Go, Ananda, and tell the Mallas of Kusinârâ, 'O, Vâsishtas (*Gnas-hjug-dag*), your master will finally pass away at midnight to-day, leaving every particle of the skandas behind;'" and he invited them to visit him (see Rhys Davids, p. 101), (f. 611[a]).

The Mallas came to him, and he instructed them, after which Ananda presented all the Mallas to the Buddha in the first watch of the night (f. 611–612).

Then there occurs in the text (f. 613–616) what appears to be an interpolation; it is the history of the conversion of the king of the Gandharvas, called Abhinanda (*? Rab-dgah*).

(F. 616[b].) Now there then lived at Kusinârâ a parivradjaka called Subhadra[1] (*Rab-bzang*), old, well stricken in years, decrepit, one hundred and twenty years of age. He was a man greatly respected, revered, and honoured by the people of Kusinârâ, who deemed him an arhat. The parivradjaka Subhadra had seen many things during the Buddha's life which had led him to believe in his authority, so when he heard that he was about to pass away so near where he was, he decided to visit him; . . . and having been introduced to his presence, he asked him concerning the truth of the doctrines of Purṇa Kâçyapa, Maskharin, son of Gôçâli, &c. (see f. 618–619). The Buddha answered him, "Subhadra, he who does not know the holy eightfold way is no true çramana of the first, second, third, or fourth degree. Subhadra, he who professes a doctrine and discipline in which is the holy eightfold way, he is a man of true saintliness of the first, second, third, and fourth degree," &c. (f. 619[b]).

And Subhadra became yet another among the arhats, and as soon as he had attained arhatship he thought, "It would not be right in me to witness the utter passing away of the Blessed One, so I will pass away before him." So he went to the Blessed One and said, "Would that I might pass away before the Blessed One," and the Buddha granted him permission (f. 621[b]); so after performing divers wonders, by which five hundred Mallas who were standing by were converted, he utterly passed away.

Now the bhikshus were astonished that he should have obtained such a great privilege, so they questioned the Blessed One, and then he told them this birth-story:—

"Bhikshus, in days gone by there lived in a valley a deer, the leader of a herd of a thousand deer; he was prudent, wide-awake, and of quick perception. One day a hunter espied him, who went and told the king. So

[1] Cf. Bigandet, vol. ii. p. 61 *et seq.* Rhys Davids, p. 127 note, says that Subhadra was "a young man of high character." None of the authors I have been able to consult disagree with our text. See also Hiuen Thsang, B. vi. p. 337.

the king assembled all his army and came and surrounded all the deer and their leader. Then the leader thought, 'If I do not protect these deer they will all be destroyed;' so looking about the place in which they were penned, he espied a torrent flowing through the valley, but the current was so swift that the deer feared that it would carry them away. The leader at once jumped into the water, and, standing in the middle of the stream, he cried, 'Come, jump from the bank on to my back, and from there to the other bank; it is the only means of saving your lives; if you do not do so you will surely die!' The deer did as he told them, and although their hoofs striking his back cut the skin and tore the flesh off to the bone, he endured it all. When the deer had thus crossed the stream, the leader looked back and saw a fawn who could not get over. Then, with body torn, with every joint racked with pain, he took the fawn on his back, crossed the stream and put it on the bank, and thus he saved them to still enjoy the pleasures of life. Knowing that all the deer had crossed and that death was approaching, he cried, 'May what I have done to preserve the pleasures of life to these deer and this fawn make me cast off sin, obtain unsurpassable and perfect enlightenment; may I become a Buddha, cross over the ocean of regeneration to perfection and salvation, and pass beyond all sorrow!'

"What think ye, bhikshus! I am he who was then the leader of the herd; the deer are now the five hundred Mallas, and the fawn is Subhadra."

Then he told another story about Subhadra, in which he had also played a part, but I am forced to omit it as it is too long (f. 625–629).

When he had finished telling it he spoke to his disciples about keeping virtuous friends (*kalyanamitra sevaṇa*), (f. 629[b]–630[a]).

Then the Buddha said to the bhikshus (f. 630[b]), "If hereafter any of my kinsmen, the Çakyas, shall come bearing the insignia of the heretics, and desire to enter the order and be ordained, they shall receive the requisites of bhikshus, and be ordained (at once), and this because I have made this concession in favour of my kinsmen the Çakyas.

"If any other heretical parivradjakas (with the exception of the fire-worshipping Jatilas, who must be treated like the Çakyas) shall come wishing to be received into the order and ordained, the bhikshus shall give them probationers' robes, which they must wear for four months when they can be ordained, if, at the expiration of that time, the bhikshus are satisfied with them"[1] (f. 631).

Then the Buddha enumerated the different parts of the sacred writings (1.) Sûtranta, (2.) Geya, (3.) Vyakarana, (4.) Gâthâ, (5.) Udâna, (6.) Nidana, (7.) Avadana, (8.) Itivritaka, (9.) Jâtaka, (10.) Vaipulya, (11.) Adbhutadharma, (12.) Upadeça; and he exhorted the bhikshus to study them, and recommended them to hold half-monthly meetings, in which they should recite the Prâtimoksha Sûtra[2] (f. 631[b])

Moreover he said, "Let the assembled congregation make a selection of the minutiæ of the precepts (*bslab-pai gdzi*) and of the minor matters (*phran-ts'egs*), so that they may be able to dwell in harmony"[3] (f. 631[b]).

"The novices must not hereafter call the elders by their names, by their patronymic names (*rus-nas bod-par-mi bya*), but they must use no other expression than 'Venerable' (*Bhadanta, btsun-pa*), or Ayuchmat (*Ts'e-dang-ldan-pa*). The elder bhikshus must provide the novices with alms-bowls, robes, nets (*dra-ba*), cups, and girdles, and they must incite them to steadfastness, to reading, recit-

[1] Cf. Mahâvagga, I. xxxviii. 11. Rhys Davids, Sacred Books of the East, xiii. p. 190.

[2] All this passage is evidently an interpolation.

[3] The text is difficult; it reads, *Dge-hdun ts'ogs-nas skab dbye-djing bde-ba-la rig-par gnas-par-byao.* In Dulva xi. f. 73[a], the Buddha, while lying between the twin sala trees, explains to his disciples how they must understand the rules he had laid down. Unfortunately the Tibetan text is very obscure. See, however, my translation of it in "Revue de l'Hist. des Religions," 1884.

ing, and they must exhort them to delight in yoga" (devotion).

After having spoken to his disciples of the four places which believing men will visit and where they will build stûpas,[1] he said, "Brethren, if there be any doubt among you concerning the Buddha, or the doctrine, or the order, or concerning misery, its origin, its arresting, or concerning the way, inquire freely and I will explain it, so that you may not think, 'While we had our master before us we did not venture to make him explain.' Let bhikshu ask bhikshu and friend friend, and then question me and I will give you an explanation" (f. 633[b]).

But they were silent, so that Ananda exclaimed, "Of a truth there is no bhikshu in this assembly who has any doubt or misgiving," &c.[2]

Then the Blessed One uncovering his body, said to the bhikshus, "Brethren, look at the Tathâgata's body. Brethren, look well at the Tathâgata's body; for it is as hard to find a Tathâgata, Arhat, Samyaksambuddha as to see a flower on a fig tree. Bhikshus, never forget it; decay is inherent to all component things!" and these were the last words of the Tathâgata (f. 634[a]).[3]

As soon as the Blessed One expired the mighty earth was shaken, thunderbolts did fall, and the gods in the sky did shriek with (or like) sound of drum (f. 635[a]). At that time the venerable Mahâkâçyapa was stopping in the Kalantakanivasa Bamboo grove at Râjagriha; and when the earth quaked he sought what might be the reason, and he saw that the Blessed One had utterly passed away. . . .

[1] See Rhys Davids, Sacred Books of the East, xi. p. 90. These places are — 1. Where the Buddha was born; 2. Where he became Buddha; 3. Where he first preached; 4. Where he died.

[2] See Rhys Davids, p. 114.

[3] The text goes on to tell how "the Blessed One entered into the first stage of deep meditation, rising out of which he passed into the second, &c., for which see Rhys Davids, p. 115, fol. 634[b]. The venerable Ananda asked the venerable Aniruddha, "Has the Blessed One utterly passed away?" "Nay, the Blessed One has entered into that state in which sensations (*hdu-shes*) and ideas (*ts'or-ba*) have ceased," &c. f. 652[b]. See the Pâli version. We are told that 18,000 bhikshus died at the same time as the Buddha.

Then he thought, "If Vaidehiputra Adjatasatru, who has such infinite faith, suddenly heard that the Blessed One has died, he would die of a hemorrhage. I must devise some means of informing him of it." So he told the brahman Varshakâra, the great noble of Magadha, of the danger to Adjatasatru of suddenly hearing of this event, and he added, "Go quickly, Varshakâra, into the park and have made representations (*ri-mo*) (1.) of the Blessed One having examined the five subjects while living as a bodhisttava in the Tushita heaven (see p. 15), and having three times expounded the truth to the six Kâmâvatcharas devas,[1] coming to enter his mother's womb as an elephant; (2.) acquiring perfect and unsurpassable enlightenment at the foot of the Bo tree; . . . (6.) having converted different persons in many places, and having reached the end of a buddha's career, (represent him) in his last wrappings (*gzims-mal-du*), in the town of Kusinârâ. Then get ready seven tubs full of fresh butter, and one with pieces of goçirsha sandal-wood. When the king shall come to the gate of the park, you must ask him if he would not like to see it; and when he shall come to the pictures, you will explain them to him, commencing with the first. When he shall have heard that the Blessed One is dead, he will fall to the ground; then you must put him into one of the tubs of fresh butter, and when the butter shall have melted, you must put him into another, and so successively in the seven (f. 637[a]); after which you must put him into the tub with the pieces of goçirsha sandal-wood, and he will recover." After giving these instructions, Mahâkâçyapa started for Kusinârâ, and Varshakâra did as he had told him, and Adjatasatru's life was saved.

On the morrow after the Buddha's death, Aniruddha sent Ananda to the Mallas of Kusinârâ (f. 639[a]). "Go, Ananda," he said, "and say to the Mallas of Kusinârâ, 'O Vasishtas, to-day at midnight the Master left behind

[1] *Hdod-pa-na spyod-pai-lha.* See Lalita Vistara (Foucaux's translation), p. 37.

every particle of the skandhas, and has utterly passed away; do whatever you see fit, so that hereafter you may not have to reproach yourselves, saying; "Our Master left behind every particle of the skandhas, and utterly passed away within our district, and we did not show him proper honours and attention."' "[1]

Ananda went and did as he was bid (f. 640), and explained to the Mallas that the Buddha's remains must be treated as those of a king of kings. Then the Mallas asked that seven days be allowed them to get everything ready for the funeral (f. 641).

On the seventh day, having prepared a golden bier, and got together all the perfumes, garlands, and musical instruments within twelve yojanas, from Kusinârâ to the Hiranyavati river, from the twin sala grove to the crested tchaitya of the Mallas[2] (*Makuta bandhana tchaitya*), they went out of the town to the twin sala tree grove to honour the Buddha's remains (f. 641ᵇ). When they came there, the principal Mallas of Kusinârâ said, "O Vasishtas, let the Mallas women and maidens make a canopy of their garments over the Blessed One; then when we have honoured his remains with perfumes and garlands, they will carry his body to the western gate of the city, which we will traverse and leave by the eastern gate; then after having crossed the Hiranyavati, we will go to the Makuta bandhana tchaitya of the Mallas, and there we will burn the body" (f. 642). But when the Mallas women tried to move the body, they were unable to do so; and Aniruddha told Ananda that the will of the gods was that the Mallas and their sons should carry the bier. So Ananda told the Mallas, and they lifted up the bier and carried it to the Makuta bandhana tchaitya (f. 643).

Now at that moment there fell in the town of Kusinârâ

[1] Csoma's translation of this passage, Asiat. Res., vol. xx. p. 309–317, and Foucaux, Rgya-tcher-rol-pa, ii. p. 417 *et seq.*, is incorrect in several places, notably in this and parallel passages. Moreover, it omits several important facts.

[2] In Bigandet, vol. ii. p. 81, it is called Matulabandana.

such a quantity of mandârava flowers (*Erythrina fulgens*), that they were knee-deep. There was an ajivaka [1] (*hts'o-ba-chan*), who was going to the Pâvâ country on business, and this man picked up a quantity of these divine flowers. Mahâkâçyapa, with five hundred disciples, was going to Kusinârâ, and was passing through the Pâvâ country when he met this man, and from him he heard that the Buddha had been dead seven days. Among Kâçyapa's disciples there was an old man, who, when he heard of the Buddha's death, spoke these unseemly words: "Why should we thus lament? for now the old mendicants (*rgan-dzugs*) are freed from being told, 'This may be done, this may not be done;' now we may do what we want to do and not do what we do not want to do" (f. 644[a]). But Kâçyapa rebuked him and spoke to his followers of the impermanency of all created things.[2]

When the Mallas tried to light the funeral pile, they were unable to do so, and Aniruddha told Ananda that it was because Mahâkâçyapa had not arrived; then he repeated this to the Mallas (f. 645).

When the people saw Mahâkâçyapa coming from afar off, they took perfumes and wreaths, &c., and went out to meet him;[3] then they bowed down at his feet and followed after him to the place where the Blessed One's body was. He uncovered the body and worshipped it. At that time there were in the world four great sthaviras—Adjnata Kaundinya, Tchunandana (*Skul-byed tchen-po*), Daçabala Kâçyapa, and Mahâkâçyapa; and as Mahâkâçyapa was the greatest among them through his knowledge and virtue, he had a store of robes, alms, bedding, medicines, and other necessaries (*yo-byad*); so he changed the garments which enshrouded the Blessed One for others from his

[1] Bigandet, vol. ii. p. 83, says that the man who was carrying the flowers was "a heretic Rahan," called Thoubat (Subhadra), and that he it was who rejoiced at the Buddha's death, and spoke the words of our text.

[2] Cf. Rhys Davids, *op. cit.*, p. 127. Beal, Four Lectures, p. 68, gives the bhikshu's name as Balanda.

[3] This passage is incorrectly translated by Csoma (at least in Foucaux's translation of it, p. 422, the only one I have at my disposal).

store; and having replaced the cover of the coffin, the fire burst forth from the pile and consumed the body (f. 645[b]).

When the body had been consumed, the Mallas put out the fire with milk, and putting the remains (*sku-gdung*) in a golden vase, they placed it on a golden bier, and having honoured it with perfumes and the sound of music, &c., they took it to Kusinârâ, to the centre of the town, where they again paid it honours. Now the Mallas of Pâvâ heard that, seven days previously, the Blessed One had expired in the town of Kusinârâ, and that his relics had received the relic-honours; so they assembled their troops and marched to where were the Mallas of Kusinârâ, to whom they said, "All ye Mallas of Kusinârâ assembled, hearken, sirs. The Blessed One has lived and has been honoured in our country for a long time, but while stopping in your country he has expired (f. 647); give us a portion of his relics (*çariras*), which we will carry to Pâvâ, where we will erect a tchaitya of his relics, which we will honour, worship, and revere, &c., and (where) we will institute a great periodical feast."—"Vasishtas" (the Mallas of Kusinârâ replied), "the Blessed One was honoured and loved by us, and as he died while near our city, we will not relinquish a portion of his relics."—"If you give us a portion, it is well; but if you will not give it, we will carry it off by force." Then, when the Mallas of Kusinârâ heard this, they consented.

The kshatriya Buluka of Rtogs-pa gyo-ba (the Bulis of Allakappa?), the kshatriya Krodtya of Roruka (*Sgra-sgrogs*, the Koliyas of Ramagrama?),[1] the brahman of Vethadvipa (*Khyab-hjug gling-na gnas*), the kshatriya Çakyas of Kapilavastu, the kshatriyas Licchavis of Vaisali,[2] also heard of this event, and they also went to Kusinârâ with their troops and made the same request. Vaidehiputra Adjatasatru, king of Magadha, heard what

[1] The same as the Çakyas of Devadaha. See Fah-Hian, p. 88–89.

[2] Cf. Rhys Davids, *op. cit.*, p. 131 *et seq.*

had happened, and also that the above-mentioned tribes had gone to Kusinârâ; so he told it to the brahman Varshakâra, and ordered him to assemble his troops, so that he also might go there and get a portion of the relics of the Blessed One (f. 648). When the troops were ready, Adjatasatru mounted his elephant, but the recollection of the virtues of the Blessed One made him faint, so that he fell to the ground; so likewise when he tried to mount his horse he fainted. "Varshakâra," he then said, "I cannot go; take you the army and salute the Mallas of Kusinârâ in my name, and ask them for a portion of the Buddha's relics."

Varshakâra did as he had been told, and the Mallas gave him the same answer as they had given to the Mallas of Pâvâ; but when they saw the great multitude of the king's men,[1] they taught their wives and children how to use bows, and when the united forces of the Buluka, of the Mallas of Pâvâ, &c., advanced toward the town to fight, they assembled all their forces, with their wives and young men, and sallied forth to resist them (f. 649).

Now there was a brahman called Droṇa[2] who had come with the troops, and when he perceived that there was going to be blood shed, he put on his skin robe (*gyang-gdzi*), and going to the Mallas of Kusinârâ he said, "The Blessed Gautama was long-suffering, and greatly praised patience; why then would you slaughter each other over his remains? I will divide his relics into eight parts, and you will give me the vase wherewith I shall have divided them, and I will build in the town of Droṇasama (?) a tchaitya of the relics of the Blessed Gautama,"

[1] Csoma adds, "who had come to carry off by force the Blessed One's relics;" but I have not found this in my text. At all events, it is difficult to see why they prepare to fight, for they had consented to divide the relics.

[2] The text has *Bre-bo dang mnyam-pa*. The latter portion of this expression is generally rendered in Sanskrit by *sama*, "even, level." The brahman's name would thus be Dronasama (?); but I have thought it advisable to drop the second part and to follow the Southern version. (Fol. 650[b]) the brahman calls his native place "the town of *Bre-bo dang mnyan-pa*."

&c. (as above). The Mallas accepted his proposal; then he went successively to each of the other parties, and having also obtained their consent, he divided the relics among them, and he took as his share the vase which the Mallas of Kusinârâ had given him to make the division with (f. 651).

Then a young brahman who had also come with the troops said to the Mallas of Kusinârâ, "Hearken to me, all ye assembled Mallas of Kusinârâ. For a long time I have honoured and loved the Blessed Gautama, and now that he has expired in your town, I beg you to give me the embers of the cremation fire, so that I may build in the Nyagrodhika country (= Pipphalivana)[1] a tchaitya of the relics of the Blessed One," &c. So the Mallas gave the brahman Nyagrodha the embers . . . (f. 652).

At that time there existed in Jambudvipa eight tchaityas of the body relics of the Blessed One; the tchaitya of the vase made nine, and that of the embers ten. Of the eight measures of relics of the Seer (*Spyan-ldan*), seven remained the object of honours in Jambudvipa; the other measure of the relics of the Greatest of men is honoured in the city of Roruka (?)[2] by a king of nâgas. Of the four eye-teeth of the Greatest of men, one is honoured in the heaven of the Thirty-three; the second is in the town of Anumana (? *Yid-ong-ldan*); the third is in the country of the king of Kalinga, and the fourth eye-tooth of the Greatest of men is honoured by a nâga king in the city of Roruka[3] (f. 652^b).

[1] Cf. Rhys Davids, p. 134: "And the Moriyas of Pipphalivana heard the news . . ." Also Fah-Hian, chap. xxiv.

[2] *Sgra-sgrogs*, which may be a translation of Râmâgama of the Pâli text.

[3] Cf. Rhys Davids, p. 135, and his note on same page; also Bigandet, vol. ii. p. 95.

CHAPTER V.

HISTORY OF THE CHURCH DURING THE HUNDRED AND TEN YEARS WHICH FOLLOWED THE BUDDHA'S DEATH.

THE following account of the councils of Râjagriha and Vaisali, and of the spread of Buddhism in Kachmere, is taken from the eleventh volume of the Dulva, and is the only canonical version of these events to be met with in Tibetan works. Before giving an analysis of these passages, I must call attention to the difficulties which the text presents. These difficulties are so real that a learned Tibetan lama from the monastery of Snar-Thang, near Tachilunpo, has said of this volume that "this translation is not felicitous; it is full of obsolete expressions, is badly written, and in the latter part of the volume the correctors' minds appear tired and their other faculties worn out; and all this is a source of much incertitude."[1] The translators of this volume were the well-known Indian pundits Vidyakaraprabha[2] and Dharmaçriprabha.

Mahâkâçyapa, whom we have seen (p. 144) acknowledged as the head of the order on account of his wisdom and virtues, heard, after the death of the Buddha, people remark that whereas 80,000 bhikshus had died at the same time as Çariputra, 70,000 on Maudgalyayana's death, and 18,000 more when the Buddha had died, the words of the Blessed One had vanished like smoke; and that as all the mighty bhikshus had utterly passed away, the Sûtranta, the Vinaya, and the Mâtrikâ of the Blessed One were no longer taught. When he heard people thus censuring,

[1] See Dulva xi. f. 706.

[2] See Udânavarga, p. xi.

blaming, and slandering (f. 652), he told what he had heard to the bhikshus, and concluded by saying that they must assemble in that place[1] (*i.e.*, at Kusinârâ). The bhikshus assented to his proposition. "Who shall convoke the clergy?" "Let it be the venerable Purṇa." Then the venerable Mahâkâçyapa said to the venerable Purṇa, "Purṇa, strike the gaṇṭa and assemble the bhikshus;" and Purṇa consented; and after having entered into the state of abstraction of the fourth dhyana of perfect freedom, and having acquired the sight of knowledge, he arose and commenced striking the gaṇṭa. Then from all parts assembled the congregation of bhikshus[2] (among whom were) five hundred arhats. When these were assembled Mahâkâçyapa said to them, "Venerable sirs, what member of the congregation of bhikshus has not come?" and they discovered that the venerable Gavampati was not there. Now at that time Gavampati was in the hermitage of the çiriçaka tree (*shing shi-ri-sha-kai gdzal-med khang-stong*). Then Kâçyapa said to Purṇa, "Go, Purṇa" (f. 654), "to where Gavampati is, and tell him, 'Kâçyapa and all the other members of the sangha greet you, and request that you will come to them in all haste for business of the order.'" The venerable Purṇa consented; so he left Kusinârâ and transported himself to the hermitage of the çiriçaka tree, and having bowed down at Gavampati's feet, he delivered Kâçyapa's message. Then Gavampati considered within himself what could be the matter, and when he discovered that "the lamp of wisdom had been blown out by the wind of impermanency," that the Blessed One had passed away (f. 655), he told Purṇa that he could

[1] The other accounts of the first synod are Mahawanso, chap. iii.; Dipawanso, chap. iv.; Fah-Hian, chap. xxx.; Hiuen Thsang, B. ix. p. 33 (St. Julien's trans.); Beal, Four Lectures, p. 69 *et seq.*

[2] According to Hiuen Thsang, B. ix. p. 36, all those of the congregation who did not take part in the council of Râjagriha, from which originated the Sthavira school, held a separate synod, in which they formed another collection of the canonical works and founded the school of the "great assembly" or the Mahâsanghikanikâya. Bhavya, in his Kayabhetrovibhanga, says that the Mahâsanghika school only commenced 160 years after the Buddha's death. See p. 182.

not go, for his end was nigh; so he gave him his alms-bowl and his three robes, and told him to present them to the sangha; then, by means of his magical powers, he was consumed and passed into the state of parinirvâṇa (f. 656). Then Purṇa, having honoured his remains, returned to the twin sala tree grove, where the five hundred bhikshus and Kâçyapa were, and presenting them with the bowl and robes, he told them what had occurred.

Kâçyapa told the bhikshus that he thought it would be advisable to assemble in Magadha, where the Blessed One had acquired omniscience, and he consulted the bhikshus as to the proper spot to choose. One of their number proposed to go to the Bodhi tree (and there hold the synod), but Kâçyapa said that as Adjatasatru was a very firm believer, he would provide the sangha with all the necessaries, and that they must consequently go to Râjagriha. The bhikshus consented, and then asked if Ananda, who had been the Master's attendant, and to whom several of the sûtras had been addressed, would not be admitted into the synod. Kâçyapa said that if they made an exception in Ananda's favour, the other bhikshus who had had something to do with the Blessed One would be angered; however, if they were willing that he (Ananda) should be appointed to supply the sangha with water when they required it, he would be admitted, otherwise he would have to be excluded. The bhikshus having shown their willingness, Kâçyapa asked Ananda, "Venerable Ananda, if you are sent to get water for the assembly?"—"I will go." Then Kâçyapa having repeated the question, said, "Hear me, venerable sirs. This venerable Ananda, the personal attendant of the Blessed One, who has been in close attendance on the Blessed One, and to whom he spoke several of his sûtras, is to be appointed to bring water to the assembly. Now I ask you if you approve of the appointment of the venerable Ananda. If it appears proper, remain silent. It is approved. Now hear me. The venerable Ananda, the attendant of the Blessed One, who stayed near his person, and to whom the Blessed One spoke several of his sermons, has for these reasons been appointed to supply the sangha with water. If the sangha requires water, the venerable Ananda, having been appointed to the office of supplying it with water, must supply it with water. If the sangha approves (these arrangements), let all remain silent. The assembly is silent, therefore the venerable Ananda is appointed water-provider of the assembly (*dge-hdun*)."

Then Kâçyapa said to Ananda, "Go along to Râjagriha with the congregation of bhikshus by the way which suits you best; I am going directly there (through the air)." So Kâçyapa went to Râjagriha, and when first Adjatasatru, king of Magadha, saw him, the recollection of the Buddha made him fall senseless to the ground (f. 658). When Kâçyapa had told him of the intention of the five hundred bhikshus well versed in the Sûtranta, the Vinaya, and the Abhidharma, he gave orders to supply them with everything which they might require, and he had the city decorated as if for a feast.

When the elders[1] (with Ananda) arrived, they asked Kâçyapa where they could reside (and hold the council). Neither the Kalantaka-nivasa bamboo grove nor the Vulture's Peak could answer their purpose, but the Nyagrodha cave[2] was sufficiently secluded if it had bedding in it (or seats, *mal-stan*). So when the king heard that this place suited them, he had it provided with beds (f. 659).

As soon as the bhikshus had assembled, Kâçyapa requested Aniruddha to examine if any one out of the five hundred was still subject to passions, anger, ignorance, desire, or attachment.

[1] *Rgan-rims*, which I take throughout these pages to be the same as *gnas-brtan* or *sthavira*.

[2] Or the Pippala cave. See Fah-Hian, p. 117, and Hiuen Thsang, B. ix. p. 22. Our text is wrong, for the Sattapani cave by the side of the Webhâra mountain was the place where the synod was held. See Mahawanso, p. 12.

Aniruddha discovered that there was only one out of their number in this case, and that it was Ananda; so Kâçyapa excluded him from the assembly (f. 661).

"Bear with me, venerable Kâçyapa," said Ananda; "I have neither sinned against morality, the doctrine, nor against good behaviour, neither have I done aught unseemly or detrimental to the congregation. Be forbearing then, O Kâçyapa!"

"Ananda, thou wast the Blessed One's close attendant, what wonder then that thou didst not commit any of the sins thou hast mentioned; but if thou sayest that thou hast done no wrong to the congregation (f. 661[b]), how comes it that when the Blessed One said that women were as dangerous as snakes, and that it would be wrong to admit them into the order, thou didst ask that they might be allowed to enter it?"[1]

"Bear with me a while, Kâçyapa," replied Ananda. "I thought of all that Mahâprajâpatî Gautamî had endured, and how it was she who had nursed the Blessed One when his mother died. I only asked that women who were (my) relatives and friends might enter the order. 'Twas surely no wonder, no subject of shame!"

Then Kâçyapa said, "When the Buddha (shortly before his death) explained to thee how it was possible for a buddha to prolong at his will his life, why didst thou not ask him to deign to remain in the world during the rest of the present age for the weal of mankind?"

"Kâçyapa," Ananda replied, "'twas no wonder, nor is there aught to be ashamed of, if I did not do so, for I was then possessed by the Evil one."[2]

"Moreover, thou didst commit another sin," rejoined Kâçyapa, "for thou didst rest thy feet for a whole day on the golden-coloured raiment of the Blessed One."

"I did so," replied Ananda, "because at the time there was no friendly bhikshu anywhere about" (f. 663).

[1] See p. 61.

[2] See the Book of the Great Decease. Sacred Books of the East, vol. xi. p. 40, 48.

"There is yet another sin which thou hast committed, for when the Blessed One was nigh unto death between the twin sala trees, and he did ask thee for some clear water, (how came it that thou didst not get it for him?")

"Kâçyapa, I have nought to reproach myself therein; nor was it surprising, for five hundred waggons had just crossed the Kakusthana river, and had made it muddy."

"But why didst thou not hold up thy bowl towards heaven, for the devas would have filled it? Moreover, when the Blessed One, having ordained that at the half-monthly recitations of the Prâtimoksha Sûtra, when the portion appertaining to the minor moral precepts (*ts'ul-khrims phra mo*) and the minutiæ (*phran-ts'egs*) was reached, the bhikshusangha might stop the recitation or go on with it, why didst thou not ask the Blessed One what was to be understood by the terms 'minor moral precepts and minutiæ'?[1] Now (as a consequence of thy negligence), I say that all which is not in the four pârâjika, the thirteen sanghâdisesa, the two aniyata, the thirty nirsaggiyâ pachittiya, the ninety pachittiya, the four pratidesaniya, and all the many sekhiyâ dharmas are minor moral precepts and minutiæ. Others again say that all which is not in the four pârâjika, the thirteen sanghâdisesa, the two aniyata, the thirty nirsaggiya pachittiya, the ninety pachittiya, and the four pratidesaniya are minor moral precepts and minutiæ (f. 664). But others say that all which is not in the four pârâjika, the thirteen sanghâdisesa, the two aniyata, the thirty nirsaggiya pachittiya, and the ninety pachittiya, are minor moral precepts and minutiæ. Again, others say that, with the exception of the four pârâjika, the thirteen sanghâdisesa, the two aniyata, and the thirty nirsaggiya pachittiya, all are minor moral precepts and minutiæ. Others say that, with the exception of the four pârâjika,

[1] This omission of Ananda's seems to have been one of the chief causes put forward for the convocation of the first council.

the thirteen sanghâdisesa, and the two aniyata, all are minor moral precepts and minutiæ. Now if a tirthika should discover that some bhikshus adhere to the four pârâjika, while others keep to the thirteen sanghâdisesa, (he would say), 'The doctrine of the Çramaṇa Gautama has vanished like smoke; while the Çramaṇa Gautama was yet alive, his disciples strictly kept his ordinances, but now they allow themselves all the indulgences they see fit. They do what they want to do, and do not do what they do not want to do.' Therefore, in not questioning the Blessed One for the sake of future generations, thou didst wrong."

Ananda replied, "When the Blessed One spoke these words, I was overcome with grief (at the prospect) of losing the Tathâgata."

"There again thou wert in the wrong; for if the attendant of the Tathâgata had (borne in mind) that all created things are of their nature impermanent, he would not have felt sorrow. Moreover, why didst thou show to men and women of low habits the Tathâgata's hidden privy parts?"[1]

"Venerable Kâçyapa," replied Ananda, "'twas no wonder nor source of shame to me, for I thought that women, being naturally sensual, if they but saw the privy parts of the Blessed One, would they not cease being so?" (f. 665).

"Moreover, thou didst show to corrupt women the golden body of the Blessed One, which was then sullied by their tears."[2]

"I thought," replied Ananda, "that if they then but saw the Blessed One, many of them would conceive a longing to become like him."

"Ananda," said Kâçyapa, "thou art still under the rule of passions; none may enter here who have not put

[1] F. 664b. *Khyim-pai hkhor dang bud-med spyod pa pan-pa-rnams-la de-bdzin-gshegs-pai hdoms-kyi sba-ba-sbubsu nub-pa bstan-pa. . . . mo-mts'an dang bral-bar ma gyur-tam.*

[2] This alludes to the woman who, worshipping the body of the Buddha after his death, let her tears fall on his feet. See Beal, Four Lectures, p. 75.

away all passions; so depart thence; thou canst not be among pure-speaking men."

Great was Ananda's grief, but he called to mind what the Blessed One had said to him shortly before his death. "Ananda," he had said, "sorrow not, neither be distressed nor afflicted. Thou must turn (*ġtod*) to the bhikshu Mahâkâçyapa (as to the head of the order). Be patient and do as he shall tell thee. Weep not, Ananda; thou shalt magnify the law of virtue; thou shalt not bring it low."

Then Aniruddha said to Ananda, "Go, Ananda, and destroy every particle of the passions, become an arhat, and then, but only then, thou mayest enter the synod."

Ananda thought of his Master who was dead; his eyes filled with tears, and he was sorrowful; but he departed for the city of Vriji (*sic*—Vaisali ?), and arranged himself as was the rule during summer (f. 666[b]). Now Ananda's attendant at that time was the venerable Vrijiputra (or an ayuchmat of Vrijian descent),[1] and he expounded the law to the fourfold assembly while Ananda diligently applied himself (to cast off all sin). But when Vrijiputra looked, by means of the mental abstraction of samadhi, he found out that Ananda was not yet freed from all passions, so he went to him and said—

> "Gautama, be thou not heedless;
> Keep near a tree in the dark, and on nirvâṇa
> Fix thy mind; transport thyself into ḍhyana,
> And ere long thou shalt find the abode of peace."

When Ananda heard the advice of the venerable Vrijiputra, day was waning; then he went and seated himself (near a tree) and fixed his mind on the five obscurations (*i.e.*, sin), and in the first watch of the night he had thoroughly freed his mind of them. In the middle watch, after having washed his feet outside the vihar, he entered it and laid himself down on his right side, and just as he

[1] Cf. Beal, *op. cit.*, p. 71.

was putting one foot on the other, lo! he acquired the notion of the visible, of memory, of self-consciousness (*shes-bdzin-dang-ldan pai hdu-shes*). As he was putting his head on his pillow, his mind became detached and freed from all asravas (f. 667). Then Ananda in the enjoyment of bliss and peace was free, and having become an arhat, he went to Râjagriha and entered the Nyagrodha (Sattapani) cave, where Kâçyapa and the five hundred arhats were compiling (or about to compile) the dharma.

Kâçyapa said to the bhikshus, "Sirs, whereas hereafter bhikshus may be oblivious and ignorant (or weak, *lus nyam tchung-bas*), and not able to understand the Sûtranta, the Vinaya, and the Abhidharma, because there are no gâthâs of the sûtras, therefore in the forenoon the gâthâs of the sûtras will be recited,[1] and in the afternoon the Sûtranta, the Vinaya, and the Abhidharma will be taken into consideration (discussed or recited)." Then the bhikshus asked Kâçyapa which of the Sûtranta, the Vinaya, or the Abhidharma would be collated first, and Kâçyapa decided that the Sûtranta should first receive their attention.

Then the five hundred arhats requested Mahâkâçyapa to preside over the assembly, and he therefore sat down in the lion's seat (presidential chair or pulpit). Then he asked the assembly if they would allow Ananda to commence with the compilation of the Sûtranta of the Tathâgata. They consented by remaining silent (f. 668ᵇ), and then the five hundred arhats spread their cloaks over the pulpit.

Ananda, after having circumambulated the pulpit, keeping it to his right side, bowed down to the elders and sat

[1] *Snga-droi dus-su mdoi ts'igsu-bchad-pas brjod-par byao.* This is a remarkable phrase, which can hardly admit of any other translation than the one I have given, but I do not see to what part of the canon it refers. It may be rendered literally, "in the forenoon—of sûtra—with gâthâs—it will be spoken." No further mention is made of this forenoon occupation of the council, which was probably to collect short verses of the sacred discourses which would enlighten the bhikshus who might be unable to learn long passages of the sacred works. Perhaps this refers to the composition of the *udânas.*

down in the pulpit. Then he thought, "If I have understood the whole of the Sûtranta as spoken by the Blessed One, there is the sûtranta spoken by the Blessed One in the abode of the nâgas, that which he spoke in the abode of the gods, and that which he spoke to (before) me. I will explain (recite) each one of them as they took place (*i.e.*, chronologically), as I heard and understood them."

Then Kâçyapa said to Ananda, "Where did the Master, desiring the good of the world and having conquered (the Evil one), explain the chief dogmas? Ayuchmat, recite (*gsungs*) the sûtranta (which he then spoke)." Then, having collected himself, Ananda recited in a loud voice and with clasped hands the sermon (sûtranta) of the Establishment of the Kingdom of Righteousness, or *Dharma chakrapravartana Sûtra* (f. 669).

When he had finished, Adjnata Kaundinya said to Mahâkâçyapa, "Venerable Mahâkâçyapa, I heard this sermon; it was spoken for my benefit. It dried my blood and the ocean of my tears. I left behind the mountain of bones; it closed the door of perdition, and opened (for me) the door of heaven and of freedom. When that precious jewel of a sûtra was spoken, I and 80,000 devas acquired the clear eye of truth, and became free from sin (*dri-ma*). Now that I hear that sermon of long ago, (I see) that there is nothing which is not transitory!" and he fell senseless to the ground. Great also was the agitation of Ananda and of all those present as they thought of their dead Lord, and that even he had not escaped the universal law of decay.

Then Kâçyapa asked Ananda which was the second sûtra. "It was also spoken at Benares for the sake of the five bhikshus"[1] . . . (f. 671). When Ananda had finished reciting the second sûtra, Adjnata Kaundinya said that it had made an arhat of him, and had converted his four companions, &c., &c., and again he fell senseless to the ground, &c. (f. 671^{b}); and when Ananda had finished re-

[1] See p. 37.

citing each sûtra, Kâçyapa and the assembly cried aloud, "This, then, is the dharma; this is the vinaya (rule)!"

In this way Ananda recited all the sûtranta which the Blessed One had spoken, and he mentioned in which villages, towns, countries, and kingdoms they had been uttered; and when it was a sûtra concerning a skandha, he put it in a compilation relating to the skandhas; when it related to an ayatana, he compiled it with the six ayatanas. All that had been explained by the çravakas he compiled in the "explanations by the çravakas." All the explanations (*bshad*) of the Buddha he gathered together in the "explanations of the Buddha." All which related to acquiring memory, abstraction, to real change, to the bases of supernatural power (*irrdhipada*), to the five faculties, to the branches of the bodhi, the branches of the way, he collected in the "branches of the way." All sûtras which had been rightly spoken he collected in the "rightly spoken sûtras." Those which had gâthâs with them he collected in the "well-named sûtras." When it was a long sûtra he placed it in the Dîrghâgama. The medium length sûtras he placed in the Majjimâgama, and those which were of one, two—ten words (f. 674) formed the Êkôttarâgama.[1]

(F. 674.) When he had finished, Kâçyapa asked him, "Venerable Ananda, is your exposition (*lung*) at an end?"

"Venerable Kâçyapa, that is all;" and with that he descended from the pulpit.

Then Kâçyapa said, "Venerable sirs, the whole of the Sûtranta of the Blessed One has been compiled, we will now pass to the Vinaya."

Now at that time there was the venerable Upali, a wise man, and one conversant with the origin of the rules and

[1] This passage would lead us to suppose that the canon was written down at this council, but this is not explicitly said, as the verb "to write," *hbri-ba*, does not once occur. The probable explanation is that certain bhikshus were appointed custodians of one section and others of another, and that they only taught the section which they had been appointed to learn by heart.

their history; so Kâçyapa ascended the pulpit and proposed to the assembly that Upali should compile the Vinaya section. When the assembly had consented, Kâçyapa said to Upali, "Venerable Upali, if you (recite the vinaya), will you repeat every particle of the Tathâgata's vinaya?" "I will," he replied.

When Upali had taken his place in the pulpit, Kâçyapa asked him to narrate where and for what reason the first ordinance had been laid down by the Blessed One. "It was at Benares," Upali replied; "it was on account of the five bhikshus, and he ordained that cloaks (*sham-thabs*) should be circular (*zlum-por*)"[1] (f. 674[b]).

Kâçyapa then asked him where and for what reason the second ordinance had been made. "It was at Benares," Upali replied; "it was on account of the five bhikshus, and he ordained that (bhikshus) should wear circular sanghâtî (*ţchos-gos*). . . . The third rule was promulgated in the village of Kalandaka, on account of the man from Kalanďaka called Sudatta (*Bzang-sbyin*)," &c., &c. (f. 675); and in this way he narrated each of the ordinances laid down by the Buddha, and the 499 arhats listened attentively; and as he finished with each rule they said, "This is the teaching of the Master; this is the law; this is the rule, &c., &c.; these are the pârâjika, these the sanghâdisesa, these the two aniyata, the thirty nirsaggiya pacittiya, the ninety pacittiya dharmâ, the four pratidesaniya, the many sekhiyâ dharmâ, the seven adhikarana samatha dharmâ. These (things) are to be put away, these to be conceded. Having entered the order, this is the way to be ordained (to receive the *upasampada* ordination). This is the way to ask, and the (proper) act to perform. . . . Such and such persons may enter the order, such others may not enter it. This is the way to confess (one's sins) (*gso-sbyong*). This is the way to enter seclusion (for the *was* season). These are the habits, these the lesser moral

[1] Cf., however, Beal, *op. cit.*, p. 76, where Upali is said to have recited the rules as they are arranged in the Pratimoksha Sûtra. The chronological method appears more rational.

prescriptions (*phra-mo ni hdi*). This the index (*gleng-gdzi*). This the way to worship (*mos-pa*)."[1]

Then Mahâkâçyapa thought, "For the sake of those men who will hereafter wish for wisdom and who will follow whatever letters there be, for the sake of those who will delight in the essence of the doctrine (lit. the profound signification), why, I myself will expound the Mâtṛikâ to preserve the sense of the Sûtranta and Vinaya as it was spoken."[2] So he mounted the pulpit and said to the bhikshus, "Venerable sirs, in what does the Mâtṛikâ consist?"

"The Mâtṛikâ (they replied) is that which makes perfectly lucid the distinguishing points of that which ought to be known. Thus it comprises (explanations of) the four smrityupasthâna, the four right renunciations, the four irrdhipada, the five faculties, the five forces, the seven branches of bodhi, the holy eightfold way, the four kinds of analytical knowledge, the four fruits (rewards) of the virtuous man (çramana),[3] the four words of the dharma (*tchos-kyi ts'ig-bdzi*),[4] absence of kleça, the knowledge of what is desirable, perfection, the very void of very void (*stong-pa-nyid stong-pa-nyid*), the uncharacteristic of the uncharacteristic (*mts'an-ma-med-pa nyid mts'an-pa-med-pa*), the samadhi by means of mixing (? *hdres-pa bsgo-nas-pai bsam-gtan*), the emancipation of perfect understanding, subjective knowledge, the abode of peace (*i.e.*, *nirvâṇa*), supernatural sight, the correct way to compile and put together all the dharma,[5] this is in what consists the Mâtṛikâ (*i.e.*, the *Abhidharma*, or metaphysics). . . ."

[1] These are the different headings of sections of the vinaya in the Tibetan translation.

[2] This phrase is obscure. The text (f. 676a) says, "*Ma-ongs-pai-dus-na mi-rnams shes-rab dzen-pa yi-ge tsam-gyis rjesu hbrang-la, zab-moi don-la mos-par-gyur-pa, de rnams-la, mala bdag-kho-nas . . . bshad-par-byao.*" Beal's version of the origin of the Abhidharma Piṭaka, *op. cit.*, p. 79, substantially agrees with our text, although it says that it was Ananda who recited it.

[3] See the Çramana phala Sutra, p. 105, Grimblot, Sept Suttas Pâlis.

[4] Or *tchos-kyi ts'ig-gdzi*, the root words or fundamental dogmas of the dharma.

[5] *Tchos-kyi rnam-grangs-kyi-phung-po yang-dag-par bsdus-pa dang btags pa ste*, says the text. It must be noticed that the text does not say that Kâçyapa delivered these metaphysical doctrines of the Buddha as a separate part of the canon. They are only considered as a commentary on those subjects laid down in the preceding sections of *sûtra* and *vinaya*.

When Kâçyapa had finished compiling the metaphysical parts of the doctrine, then the yakshas above the earth cried out, "Bravo! the venerable Mahâkâçyapa and the five hundred other arhats have compiled the Three Baskets (*Tripiṭaka*) of the Tathâgata; the devas will swell in number, and the asuras will diminish! . . ."

When the work of the council was over, Kâçyapa thought that as he had done all that was necessary for the preservation of the doctrine to future generations, his time had come to pass away; so he went to Ananda and said to him, "Ananda, the Blessed One committed to my care the keeping of the doctrine, and passed away. Now, when I shall have passed away, thou shalt take care of the doctrine (*i.e.*, be patriarch). Moreover, there shall be born in Râjagriha a son of a merchant, who, from the fact that he will be covered with a linen garment, will be called Çânâvasika (*Sha-nai gos-chan*). Returning from a sea-voyage, he will entertain the Buddhist sangha for five years, (after which) he will enter the order, and thou shalt confide the doctrine to him" (f. 678).

Then Mahâkâçyapa went and worshipped the four great chaityas and the eight chaityas of the relics, after which he went to the realm of the nâgas and revered the eye-tooth of the Buddha, and also to the Trayastrimcat devas' heaven, where was another tooth of the Buddha (see p. 147). Vanishing from the summit of Sumeru (where is the Trayastrimcats abode), he came to Râjagriha, and decided to tell King Adjatasatru that he was about to die. He went to the king's palace, and said to the doorkeeper, "Go and tell King Adjatasatru that Kâçyapa is standing at his gate, and would like to see him." "The king is asleep," answered the porter. Kâçyapa insisted that he should go and tell him; but the porter replied, "Venerable sir, the king is violent; (if I awaken him), he would have me put to death." "Tell him, then, when he awakens, that Kâçyapa has passed away." Kâçyapa then climbed the southern peak of Kukutupada (*lho-phyogs-kyi-ri bya-gag-*

rkang) mountain, and having arranged a grass mat in the centre of the three peaks,[1] he went through the marvellous manifestations customary on such occasions, and entered parinirvâṇa (f. 680).

Adjatasatru was greatly distressed on hearing of Kâçyapa's death. He ascended the Kukutupada mountain in company with Ananda (f. 681), and having told him that he had not been able to see the Buddha after his death, and now could not see Mahâkâçyapa after his nirvâṇa (f. 682), the sthavira promised him that he should see him.[2] Moreover, the king had a chaitya built on the spot where Kâçyapa had passed away, and he honoured it.

When Çânâvasika had happily returned from sea,[3] and had stored away his wealth in his treasury, he entertained the congregation for five years. At the expiration of that time he went to the Bamboo grove, and having saluted Ananda, who was standing in the door of the gandhakuta, he said to him, "Where is the Buddha?" "My son," the sthavira replied, "the Blessed One has passed away." When Çânâvasika heard this he fell senseless to the ground. He was revived with water, and having recovered his senses, he asked where was the sthavira Çariputra? "He also is dead, and so is Mahâmaudgalyayana and Mahâkâçyapa. My son," added Ananda, "now that thou hast finished laying up goods for the disciples of the Blessed One, lay up stores of the Dharma and enter the order of the Blessed One's doctrine." "So be it," replied Çânâvasika, and he was ordained, and in a little while he acquired the triple knowledge, and learnt (by heart) the Tripiṭaka, for he remembered whatever he heard Ananda say (f. 682).

[1] Cf. Hiuen Thsang, B. ix. 6. He also says, p. 7, that it was twenty years after the Buddha's nirvâṇa that Kâçyapa died. See also Edkins, *op. cit.*, p. 64.

[2] The text does not tell us that Ananda fulfilled his promise, but we know from other sources that Adjatasatru was able to look at the body of Kâçyapa, over which the mountain had closed.

[3] The text here is so corrupt that it is impossible to follow it closely. I have only reproduced the outlines of it.

One day at the Bamboo grove a bhikshu spoke the following gâtha:—

"In whom life is of (but) an hundred years,
It is as the footprint of a bird on water;
Like the appearance of the footprint of a bird on water
Is the virtue of the life of each separate one."[1]

When Ananda heard this, he went to where these (*sic*) bhikshus were and said, "My son, the Blessed One did not say that, but he did say—

'In whom life is of an hundred years,
There is therefore birth and decay;
By teaching to both classes of men
That here on earth exists permanency,
The unbeliever will have angry thoughts,
The believer perverted ideas.
Having wrongly understood the Sûtranta,
They go like cattle in a swamp.
When they are nigh unto dissolution,
Their minds have no knowledge of their own death;
When one understands not what he has heard, 'tis fruitless;
To understand what is erroneous is as smoke.
To hear, and of correct understanding
To be deprived, is to have intelligence with(out) fruit.'"[2]

Then (that bhikshu) said to his master, "Ananda has grown old, and his memory is impaired; he has become broken down by old age. This man's (*lus-chan-de*) memory is bad; he does not remember well; his mind is impaired through old age." His master told him, "Go and say, 'Sthavira Ananda, (you are) again wrong;'" and the bhikshu went and repeated these words. "My son," the sthavira replied, "I did not say that the Blessed One did not say

[1] This verse is extremely obscure. It reads, *Gang-na lo-brgya hts'o-ba ni, des-par tchu-la bya kar bdzin, tchu-la bya kar mthong-ba ltar, bdag-nyid gchig-pui hts'o-ba dge.* I propose reading in the second and third lines *bya rkang*, instead of *bya kar*. The two words are graphically alike. This, however, does not make the fourth line very clear.

[2] Here again the text appears incorrect; the last two lines are *thos-pa yang-dag nyid-shes-pa, bral-ba hbras-bu blo ldam yin.* Or is this intentional to set forth Ananda's failing memory?

that."[1] The bhikshu repeated the words of his master, to which Ananda replied (f. 683b), "If I should speak to the bhikshu (your master), it would occasion a quarrel. It is not my duty to go to where he is; he has not come to where I am."

Then he thought, "Çariputra, Mahâmaudgalyayana, &c., have passed away, and when I shall have passed away the doctrine of the Blessed One will still be followed for a thousand years. The men of the old times have ere now passed away, and the young men and I do not agree; I stand alone; I am like an outcast, for all my associates and friends have long since departed. . . ." So he said to Çânâvasika, "My son, the Blessed One, having confided the doctrine to Mahâkâçyapa, passed away. He confided it to me, and now I intrust it to thee, and when I shall have passed away thou shalt protect it. Moreover, in the city of Mathura (*Bchom-brlag*), the two sons of a merchant of that country, whose names will be Nata and Phata (*sic*), will build a vihara at Rimurundha[2] (*sic*), and will become the patrons of the vihara; this has been foretold by the Blessed One. He has also predicted that after the building of the vihara of Rimurunda (*sic*) there will be a son of a perfume-seller called Gupta (*Sbas-pa*) whose name will be Upagupta (*Nyer-sbas-pa*). He will enter the order one hundred years after the nirvâṇa of the Blessed One; and, having become a buddha without the characteristic signs,[3] he will accomplish all the acts of a buddha." . . . Then the venerable Ananda said, "The time for my passing away has come." Then he thought, "If I should die here (in the Bamboo grove), King Adjatasatru and the Vrijians being on bad terms with each other (f. 685b), the

[1] The text appears incorrect here. The negation appears out of place, or perhaps here again Ananda had forgotten what he had previously said.

[2] Conf. Târanâtha, p. 11 of the text.

[3] That is to say, he will have an enlightened mind, but will not have the thirty-two signs of the great man, or the eighty peculiarities which characterised the Buddha Gautama. The legend of Upagupta of the 47th chapter of the Hdsang-blun (Der Weise und der Thor) says that he was a native of Benares, and was converted by Yasheska or Yaças.

Licchavis of Vaisâli would not get a portion of (my) relics. If I should pass away in Vaisâli, they would not relinquish (a portion to Adjatasatru). I will pass away in the middle of the Ganges river." So he went there.

Now King Adjatasatru saw in a dream the staff of the standard that was borne above him broken, and he was frightened and awoke, and then he heard from the porter that the sthavira Ananda was about to pass away. Hearing this, he fell senseless to the ground, and when, revived by water, he had regained his senses, he asked, "Where has the venerable Ananda passed away?" "Mahârâja," replied the venerable Çânâvasika, "he who had been created to follow after the Blessed One, the mighty lord who has guarded the treasure of the Dharma, he whose intellect enables him to arrest existence (in himself), has gone towards Vaisâli." So Adjatasatru assembled his fourfold army and set out for the bank of the Ganges.

(F. 686.) The devas told the men of Vaisâli, "The venerable Ananda, the lamp of mankind, the lover of all humanity, this mighty one, having dispelled the shades of sorrow, is about to attain perfect peace (to die)." Then the Licchavis of Vaisâli got together their army, and when they reached the banks of the Ganges, the venerable Ananda entered a boat and went to the middle of the Ganges. Then King Adjatasatru bowed his head at the feet of the sthavira Ananda and said, "The wide eye of a buddha is open like a hundred-leaved flower (*hdab-ma brgya-pa lta-bur*); thou who hast been a lamp to three existences and who hast reached peace, we go to thee for a refuge; if (of a truth) thou hast reached peace, for our sakes cast down thy body here from the water where thou hast gone!" The men of Vaisâli said the same thing. But Ananda reflected, "If I cast my body in the Magadha country, the Licchavis will certainly be distressed; if I cast it in the Vriji country,[1] the ruler of

[1] The text is obscure; it reads, *magadhai grong-du* and *grong-khyer skaso* (?) *byed dag-tu*. I don't understand this last expression at all.

Magadha will be displeased. Therefore, I will give half of my body to the sovereign and half to the people (*ts'ogs*), and by this means both of them (*i.e.*, both parts of my relics) will receive proper and lasting honours."

As Ananda was dying the earth shook in six ways. Just then a rishi who had a retinue of five hundred followers came to the sthavira Ananda by magical means and with clasped hands said, "I beg thee to receive us into the order of the well-spoken law, and that we be ordained and receive the requisites of bhikshus." Then Ananda said, "Come hither with your disciples;" and hardly had he conceived the wish but the five hundred disciples were there. The sthavira Ananda created dry land in the middle of the river, and having made it inaccessible, he admitted into the order the rishi and his five hundred followers; and having conferred on them the desired upasampada ordination, they obtained the reward of anagamin. He explained the three acts,[1] and they cast off all kleça and obtained the reward of arhatship. As they had entered the order in the middle of the river Ganges and in the middle of the day, to some they became known as Madhyantika (*Tchu-dbus*), to others as Madhyanika (*Nyi-mai-gung*) (f. 687).

Then they bowed their heads at Ananda's feet and said, "The Blessed One allowed Subhadra, the last of his converts, to enter nirvâṇa before him;[2] now we beg the master to allow us to enter nirvâṇa before him, so that we may not see him die."

The sthavira replied, "The Blessed One confided the doctrine to Mahâkâçyapa and died; the sthavira Mahâkâçyapa intrusted it to me (and said:) 'When I shall have passed away, I intrust this doctrine to you.' The Blessed One has said of Kachmere, 'The country of Kachmere is the best place for dhyana that can be wished for. One

[1] Probably "right acts, right thoughts, right speech." See Feer, Introduction du Bouddhisme dans le Kachmir, p. 9. Our text says that all the five hundred were called by the name of Madhyantika or Madhyanika, and Târanâtha, p. 7, agrees with this.

[2] See p. 138.

hundred years after the death of the Blessed One[1] (the Buddha went on to say) there will be a bhikshu called Madhyantika; he will introduce the teaching into this country.' Therefore, my son, introduce the doctrine (there)."

"I will act accordingly," (Madhyantika the rishi) replied.

(F. 687^b.) Then the venerable Ananda commenced showing all kinds of miracles. A Magadha man with tears of love cried, "Master, come here." A Vrijian with tears of love cried, "Master, come here." Hearing these words spoken on the banks of the river by the two men, he wisely divided in two his worn-out body. Then Ananda gave his blessing, and having shown different miracles, he became like water thrown on fire (*i.e.*, steam) and entered parinirvâṇa. Half of his body was taken by the men of Vaisâli and the other half by King Adjatasatru. So it was said—

> "By the sagacious diamond of wisdom,
> Who had subdued the mountain of his own body,
> A half was given to the sovereign,
> A half the mighty one gave to a nation."

After that the Licchavis had a chaitya built in Vaisâli and placed (the half of the body therein). Likewise King Adjatasatru, having built a chaitya in the city of Paṭaliputra, placed (the other half in it).

Madhyantika thought, "My master ordered me to introduce the doctrine into Kachmere, (for) the Blessed One has predicted that there would be a bhikshu called Madhyantika who, having conquered the malicious nâga Hulunta[2] in Kachmere, would introduce the doctrine. I will accomplish the purpose of the teacher." So the venerable Madhyantika went to the Kachmere country

[1] This is extraordinary, for either Ananda's life must have been much longer than all other legends say, or else Madhyantika only carried out Ananda's command some seventy years after his master's death. This would allow sufficient time for Çâṇavasika's patriarchate. See Târanâtha's remark, *op. cit.*, p. 10.

[2] Conf. p. 238, where he is called the nâga-king Hu-lor.

and sat down cross-legged. Then he thought, "To conquer the nâgas of Kachmere, if I can but trouble them, I will be able to subdue them." So he composed his mind in deep meditation, and the Kachmere country trembled in six ways. The nâgas were troubled, they panted violently, and having caused rain to fall in torrents, they tried to injure the sthavira, but he remained deep in the perfect composure of the profound meditation of mercy; so these nâgas were not able to move even the hem of his garment. Then these nâgas rained down arrows, but the sthavira made them reach the ground as beautiful flowers, ulvas, padmas, kumudas, and white lilies. The nâgas commenced to throw at him a string of thunderbolts [1] and of great arrows, a continuous stream of swords and axes; but as they all fell on the sthavira in a rain of blue lotus flowers, they said, "As one sees those summits of a glacier remain unchanged though struck by the rays of the sun, those summits of mountains on which all is harmless, so the drenching rain fell as a shower of various flowers, and the rain of arrows falling from the sky has become garlands of flowers!"

As he (Madhyantika) was in the state of perfect composure of the profound meditation of mercy, the fire (of the thunderbolts) did not burn his body, nor did the weapons or poison harm it; so the nâgas were astonished. Then the nâgas went nigh unto the sthavira and spake to him, saying, "Venerable one, what would you?"

The sthavira said, "Give me this place."

"A stone is not much of an offering!" the nâgas replied.[2]

"The Blessed One has predicted," the sthavira rejoined, "that this place would be mine. This Kachmere country, being a good place for meditation, henceforth it is mine."

[1] This passage has embarrassed M. Feer, who reads the text *rtseg-chig rdo-rtse*, "une quantité de pointes de rochers." I think it better to read *rtse-gchig rdo-rje*, lit. "a stream of thunderbolts." There is no doubt about *rdo-rje* in my copy of the text. The word *rtse gchig* occurs farther on in connection with swords, axes, &c.

[2] The sthavira was probably seated on a stone when he made this request.

The nâgas said, "Did the Blessed One say so?"

"He did," answered the sthavira.

"Sthavira," said the nâgas, "how much (land) shall be offered (to you)?"

"As much as I cover when seated cross-legged."

"So be it, Venerable One," the nâgas replied.

Then the sthavira sat down cross-legged (f. 689[a]), and (down to) the lower ends of the nine valleys (all the land) was covered by (him) sitting cross-legged.[1]

The nâgas asked him, "Sthavira, how many followers have you?"

The sthavira thought, "How many bhikshus shall I get together? I will have the five hundred arhats (who were converted with me)." So he said, "Five hundred arhats."

"So be it," the nâgas said; "but if a single arhat out of the number is wanting, then we[2] will take back the Kachmere country."

Madhyantika said to the nâgas of Kachmere, "Notwithstanding, there must be people who give when there are persons who (live on what they) receive, so I must introduce householders (here);" and to this the nâgas gave their consent.

When the sthavira had made by himself villages, towns, and provinces, he settled large numbers of people (in them), but they said to him, "Sthavira, how can we develop our prosperity?" Then the sthavira took the people with him to the Gandhamâdana (*sbos-kyis ngad-ldan*) mountain and said, "Pull up saffron!" (f. 689[b]). Then the nâgas of Mount Gandhamâdana were angered, but the sthavira having subdued them, they asked, "How long will the doctrine of the Blessed One endure?" "A thousand

[1] I think that my translation is justified by the text, and also by the remarks of Hiuen Thsang, B. iii. p. 168–169. *Non-pa* in the text means "to cover;" *sas non-pa*, "to cover with earth;" *lung-pa dgni-mdo*, "the lower ends of the nine valleys;" *skyil-mo-grung-gis*, "by the action of being seated cross-legged;" *non-pa*, "be covered."

[2] *Bdag-gis* is used as well for the singular as the plural throughout the Bkah-hgyur.

years," answered the sthavira. Then they made him this promise, "As long as the teaching of the Blessed One endures, so long will we allow you (to take saffron plants from here)."[1] So when the sthavira had planted the saffron in Kachmere, he blessed it (and it prospered).

When the sthavira Madhyantika had introduced the doctrine of the Blessed One into Kachmere, he spread it abroad, and having gladdened the hearts of the charitable and virtuous, and having shown different miracles, he passed away as water when thrown on fire. After that his body had been burnt with the best of sandal-wood, aloe-wood, and other kinds of wood, it was placed in a chaitya which was built (for that purpose).

Now the venerable Çânâvasika received into the order the venerable Upagupta, by whom the doctrine was greatly spread. He (Çânâvasika) said to the venerable Upagupta, "Venerable Upagupta, be attentive. The Blessed One, having intrusted the keeping of the doctrine to the venerable Mahâkâçyapa, passed away. The venerable Mahâkâçyapa intrusted it to (my) master; (my) master (intrusted it) to me, and passed away. My son, now when I also shall have entered nirvâṇa, you must defend the doctrine and devote all your energy to telling every one, 'Thus spoke the Blessed One.'" Then the venerable Çânâvasika having gladdened the hearts of the charitable and virtuous, having performed different miracles, such as producing sparks, fire, rain, lightning (from out his body), utterly passed away into the middle where there is no particle of corporality.

The sthavira Upagupta (taught) the venerable Dhîtika, and the venerable Dhîtika having accomplished the requirements of the doctrine, (taught) the venerable Kâla (*Nag-po*), and he the venerable Sudarçana (*Legs-mthong*), and in this order the mighty ones (lit. the elephants[2]) passed away (f. 690^b).

[1] Conf. Târanâtha, p. 9–10 (12–13 of the trans.)

[2] *Glang-po*, "elephant," may imply here that these first patriarchs were the mightiest of their order, and were not succeeded by as great ones.

One hundred and ten years after the death of the Blessed Buddha the sun of the Conqueror was obscured, and the bhikshus of Vaisâli imagined ten false propositions which transgressed the law and the rules, which were not of the Master's teaching, which were not comprised in the Sûtranta, nor to be found in the Vinaya, which transgressed the Dharma; and the bhikshus of Vaisâli taught that these evil things were right. These ten practices were: the bhikshus of Vaisâli practised as lawful the exclamation *alala;* (those who) did not agree were heterodox; (those who were) assembled (elsewhere than at Vaisâli) were heterodox; those who did agree were orthodox.[1] This was the first proposition which transgressed the doctrine, which was not the Master's teaching, which was not in the sûtras, nor to be found in the Vinaya, which transgressed the Dharma, which the bhikshus of Vaisâli carried into practice, teaching that what was unlawful was lawful.

Moreover, the bhikshus of Vaisâli (said), "Venerable sirs, enjoy yourselves;" and indulging in enjoyment in the congregation of bhikshus, they made enjoyment lawful; and those who did not agree were heterodox; those who were assembled (elsewhere than at Vaisâli) were heterodox; those who did agree were orthodox. This was the second proposition, &c.

Moreover, the bhikshus of Vaisâli held as lawful that (a bhikshu) might dig the earth with his own hand, or have it dug, &c. This was the third proposition, &c.

Moreover, the bhikshus of Vaisâli held as lawful the practice of keeping salt as long as one lived, if he added to

[1] This phrase, which recurs many times in the same words, is exceedingly difficult. The text is, *Mi mthun -pas tchos-ma yin-pa dang, hthun pas tchos-ma yin-pa dang, mi mthun-pas tchos-kyi las byed-de.* I propose considering the second *mi-mthun-pas* = *mi-rnams mthun-pas*, and the first *mi-mthun-pas* as taken in its usual acceptation of "not agreeing." My translation, however, is very doubtful. From f. 690 to the end of the volume is extremely obscure, and, as I have remarked, severely criticised by the Tibetan lama. The general sense is, however, clear, the difficulties bearing on unimportant details.

(his supply) at the right time some consecrated salt,[1] &c. This was the fourth proposition, &c.

Moreover, the bhikshus of Vaisali practised as being lawful during journeys, going a yôjana or a half yôjana (away from their viharas), then meeting and eating. This was the fifth proposition, &c.

(F. 692ª.) Moreover, the bhikshus of Vaisâli having deemed it lawful to take food, hard or soft, that was not left-over food, with two fingers, did practise as lawful eating with two fingers. . . . This was the sixth proposition, &c.

Moreover, the bhikshus of Vasâli held it lawful to suck fermented drinks as would a leech (*srin-bu bad-pa bdzin-du*), though one was made ill by drinking (thus). . . . This was the seventh proposition, &c.

Moreover, the bhikshus of Vaisâli held it lawful to eat between times a mixture of half-milk and half-curds, &c. This was the eighth proposition, &c.

Moreover, the bhikshus of Vaisâli held it lawful to use a new mat (*gding-pa*) without patching it around the edge (the width of) a Sugata span,[2] &c. This was the ninth proposition, &c.

Moreover, the bhikshus of Vaisâli held it lawful to take a round alms-bowl and to besmear it with perfumes, to make it redolent with sweet burnt incense and adorn it with different kinds of sweet-smelling flowers. Then they put a mat on a çramana's head and on it (the bowl), and he went through the highroads, the lanes, the cross-

[1] The text is, *Ji-srid hts'oi bar-du byin-gyis brlabs-pai ts'wa dus su rung-ba dang lhan-chig bsres-nas kun-tu spyod-ching tswa rung-bai dzes byed pa-ste.* Conf. Târanâtha, p. 41 (trans.), note 3. In Dulva, x. 290, the Buddha allows salt to be kept in certain cases. It must be kept in a box with a cover. See also the Tibetan Prâtimoksha Sûtra, pâcittiya 67, where the Vinaya-vibhanga says that a bhikshu who hides another's alms-bowl, &c., &c., or his salt-horn (*tswa khug*); the text of the Prâtimoksha, however, reads, instead of this expression, *phor-bu*, "drinking-cup." Revue de l'Hist. des Religions, 1884.

[2] In the Bhikshuni Vinaya-vibhanga it is said that a Sugata span is equal to a cubit and a half. It moreover remarks that Sugata means "the Master."

roads, saying, "Hear me, all ye people who live in Vaisâli, ye town's people and ye strangers; this alms-bowl is a most excellent one; he who gives here, who gives very much, he who makes many offerings here, will receive a great reward; it will profit him much, it will avail him much." And in this way they got riches, gold, and other treasures, which they (the bhikshus of Vaisâli) made use of, thus holding it lawful to have gold and silver; and this was the tenth proposition, &c.[1] . . . (f. 693).

Now there was at Vaisâli a sthavira called Sarvakâma[2] (*Thams-chad hdod-pa*) known as an arhat contemplator of the eight perfect freedoms (*rnam-par thar-pa brgyad bsgom-pa dzas-bya-ba*), who had lived in Ananda's time. Moreover, in the town of Çonaka (*Nor-chan*) there lived an arhat called Yaças (*Grags-pa*), also an arhat contemplator of the eight perfect freedoms, and he, wandering about with a retinue of five hundred, came to Vaisâli when (the bhikshus of that place) were fixing (*i.e.*, dividing) their treasures (f. 694). The censor (*dge-skos*) having declared that the sthaviras of the community were at liberty to make use of the property, asked (Yaças), "Venerable sir, what will you take of the goods?" Then he explained (to Yaças) the whole thing (*i.e.*, the tenth indulgence?); and the sthavira thought, "Is this canker unique or are there others?"[3] And he saw that the relaxation of the rules was increasing by following the ten unlawful customs (*dngos*). Therefore, to preserve the doctrine, he went to where the venerable Sarvakâma was, and having bowed down at his feet, he said to him, "Is it lawful or not to say *alala?*"—"Venerable sir, what does that mean,

[1] The list of the ten indulgences varies greatly; see Mahâwanso, p. 15; Beal, Four Lectures, p. 83; and especially Rhys Davids, Buddhism, p. 216.

[2] In the Mahâwanso, p. 18–19, it is said that Sarvakâma was a Pâchîna priest, and that he was at that time high priest of the world, and had already attained a standing of 120 years since the ordination of Upasampada. The same work, p. 15, calls Yaso, son of Kakandako, the brâhman, versed in the six branches of doctrinal knowledge and powerful in his calling.

[3] Obscure: the text reads, *Nges tchu-bur hdi gchig-pu byung-bar zad-dam gdzan yang yod*, lit. "Truly this sore has it appeared alone, yet another is."

'Is it lawful to say *alala?*'" Then Yaças explained it in the same terms used above, and Sarvakâma answered, "Venerable sir, it is not lawful."—"Sthavira, when was it declared (unlawful)?"—"It was in the town of Çampa." —"On account of what?"—"On account of acts of the six bhikshus."—"What kind of a transgression was it?"—"They committed a dukkata offence."—"Sthavira (said Yaças), this is the first proposition which disregards the Sûtranta, the Vinaya, which is not the Master's teaching, which is not in the sûtras, which does not appear in the Vinaya, which transgresses the Dharma, which the bhikshus of Vaisâli teach as lawful when it is unlawful. If they practise it will you remain quiet?" (Sarvakâma) remained without ever saying a word. Then (Yaças) said, "Then, sthavira, I will ask you if it be lawful to amuse oneself?"—"Venerable sir, what does that mean, 'Is it lawful to amuse oneself?'" Yaças having explained what it meant, he replied, "Venerable sir, it is not lawful. It was declared unlawful in the town of Çampa in consequence of acts of the six bhikshus, and it was pronounced a dukkata offence."—"Sthavira, this is the second proposition which disregards the Sûtranta, &c. If they practise it will you remain quiet?" (Sarvakâma) remained without ever saying a word.

Then (Yaças) said, "Then, sthavira, I will ask you if it be lawful to use one's strength (to dig the earth[1])?" . . . "Venerable sir, it is not lawful. It was declared unlawful at Çravâsti, in consequence of the acts of the six, and it was pronounced a pâcittiya."—"Sthavira, this is the third proposition," &c., &c.

"Sthavira, I will ask you then this question, Is it lawful to use (kept) salt?" . . . "Venerable sir, it is not lawful. It was declared unlawful at Râjagriha on account of an act of Çariputra, and it was pronounced a pâcittiya." —"Sthavira, this is the fourth proposition," &c., &c.

[1] See 73d pâcittiya of the Bhikshu Prâtimoksha, 56th of the Bhikshuni Prât.

"Sthavira, I will ask you then this question, Is it compatible with (the rules) of journeying (to go a league or a half league and then eat)?"—"Venerable sir, it is not lawful. It was declared unlawful at Râjagriha on account of what Devadatta had done, and it was pronounced a pâcittiya." . . . "Sthavira, this is the fifth proposition," &c., &c.

"Sthavira, I will ask you then this question, Is the practice of using two fingers lawful?" . . . (f. 696[b]). "Venerable sir, it is not lawful. It was declared unlawful at Çravasti on account of what a great number of bhikshus had done, and it was pronounced a pâcittiya."—"Sthavira, this is the sixth proposition," &c., &c.

"Sthavira, then I will ask you this question, Is it lawful to get sick (from sucking wine)?"—"Venerable sir, it is not lawful. It was declared unlawful at Çravasti on account of an act of the ayuchmat Suratha (*? Legs-ongs*), and it was pronounced a pâcittiya," &c., &c.

"Sthavira, then I will ask you this question, Is the practising (of drinking) a mixture[1] (of milk and curds) lawful?"—"Venerable sir, it is not lawful. It was declared unlawful at Çravasti on account of an act of a number of bhikshus, and it was pronounced a pâcittiya," &c., &c.

"Sthavira, then I will ask you this question, Is the mat practice lawful?" . . . "Venerable sir, it is not lawful. It was declared unlawful at Çravasti on account of an act of a number of bhikshus, and it was pronounced a pâcittiya," &c., &c.

"Sthavira, then I will ask you this question, Is the gold and silver practice lawful?"—"Venerable sir, it is not lawful. It is a nissaggiya pâcittiya according to the Vinaya, . . . the Dirghâgama, the Majjimâgama, . . . the Kathina section of the (Prâtimoksha) Sûtra, . . . the Ekottarâgama," &c., &c.

"Sthavira, this is the tenth proposition which disregards

[1] See 37th–39th pâcittiyas of the Bhikshus, 25th–27th of the Bhikshuni Prâtimoksha.

the Sûtranta, the Vinaya, which is not the Master's teaching, &c., &c. If they practise it will you remain quiet?" "Venerable sir," replied Sarvakâma, "wherever you choose to go I will be your adherent in following the Dharma."[1]

Then he composed his mind in the dhyana of perfect perfection, and remained in it.

Now at that time there lived in the city of Çoṇaka a venerable sthavira called Sâlha (*Gyo-ldan*), who had lived with Ananda. He was an arhat contemplator of the eight perfect freedoms. Then Yaças went to the venerable Sâlha, and having bowed down at his feet (he asked him the same questions and received the same answers), and he also agreed to be his adherent.

After that Yaças went to the city of Samkâcya, where lived the venerable sthavira Vâsabhagâmi (*Nor-chan*), an arhat like the two preceding ones, and also a contemporary of Ananda's. From him also he received the same answers to his questions.

(F. 700.) Then Yaças went to Pâṭaliputra (*Dmar-bu-chan*), where lived the venerable Kuyyasobhito (*Zla-sgrur*),[2] &c., &c. (F. 700.) After that he went to Çrughna, where lived the venerable Adjita (*Ma-pham-pa*), to whom he also explained the ten indulgences, &c., &c.

Then he went to Mahismati (*Ma-he-ldan*), where lived the venerable Sambhûta (*Yang-dag skyes*); . . . after that to Sahadsha (*? Lhan-chig skyes*), where lived the venerable

[1] This oft-recurring phrase is obscure, but I see no other way of translating it. *Des song-la phyogs ts'ol-chig dang, ngas tchos bdzin-du phyogs byao.*

[2] This name is variously written *zla-sgur*, *zla-rgur*, or *zla-sgrur*. I have adopted the last form, which is also followed by Schiefner, Târanâtha, p. 290. The word *çrughna* is also transcribed by *srug-na* or *sug-na*. See Schiefner, *loc. cit.* The Mahawanso, p. 19, says, "Sabbakâmi, Sâlho, Rêvato, Kujjasôbhito, Yaso son of Kâkandako, and Sambûto, a native of Sâna, these six theros were the disciples of the thero Ananda. Vasabhagâmiko and Sumano, these two theros were the disciples of the thero Anuradho. . . . They repaired to the Vâlukarâma vihara, a situation so secluded (that not even the note of a bird was heard), and free from the strife of men. The high priest Rêvato, the chief of the interrogating party, questioned the thero Sabbakâmi in due order on the ten indulgences, one by one."

Revata (*Nam-gru*), to whom he also explained the ten indulgences in the same terms used in conversing with Sarvakâma. When Revata heard of all his journeying, he told Yaças to take some rest, after which he would accompany him as his partisan.

While these things were taking place, the bhikshus of Vaisâli went to where the bhikshus of Yaças' company were and asked them where was their master, and then they learnt that he had gone to seek partisans. "Why did he want partisans?" they asked.

"Sirs, on account of the schism in the order."

"Venerable sirs, what have we done to cause a schism in the order?"

Then (Yaças' disciples) told them; but they replied, "This is not right; why oppose us because we seek different interpretations (*rnam-pa*) for the commandments of the departed Master?"

Then one of their number (*i.e.*, of Yaças' disciples?), whose mind was straight, and whose harsh words were well meant,[1] said to them, "Venerable sirs, you are doing what is not done (by all the rest of the order), what is not lawful, what is not becoming in çramaṇas. You have formerly heard that the doctrine of the Blessed One will last a thousand years, but you will be the cause that in days to come the doctrine will be obscure; so it is that those who disregard any of the commandments create a cancer (which will go on spreading). To help to maintain the doctrine, what are you then doing but bringing about schisms?" They were terrified on hearing this, but remained silent under his harsh words (*sbogs-pa*).

(F. 702.) Then (the bhikshus of Vaisâli) commenced talking to one another. "The venerable Yaças has gone to get partisans; if we have caused a schism in the order, why remain pondering over it? Say what must be done." Then one of their number said to another, "Let us do what (Yaças) has done. He has gone to get partisans; let

[1] The text is *phan-pai brlang ts'ig-gis*, "with words of useful abuse."

us also seek partisans who will uphold us." Another said, "Sirs, they are going to fight us; we must flee." Another said, "Where can we go? wherever we may go we will be thought badly of. We must sue for pardon; we are, as it were, in a trap." Another said, "Let us get all (the bhikshus) who are in the neighbourhood together (by giving them) alms-bowls, robes, nets, drinking-cups, girdles, and all will be arranged (? *phyir gang rigs par byao*)." This course being approved, they decided to act accordingly; so they gave to some (bhikshus) robes, to some mantles, to some nether garments, to some sweat-cloths, to some cushions, to some alms-bowls, to some water-strainers, and in this way they got them all together and remained in their midst.[1]

When Yaças had little by little got together his partisans he came back to Vaisâli, and his disciples asked him, "Master, have you found your partisans?" "My sons," he replied, "they will shortly be here."

When his disciples had told him of the right claimed by the Vaisâli bhikshus to interpret diversely the commandments, and that they were using terms not formerly spoken by (the Buddha), he said, "As the partisans for relaxing the rules will rapidly increase, (we) must do everything for the true doctrine; for the gâthâ says—

'He who instantly does a thing to be postponed, who postpones (a thing to be done) instantly,
Who follows not the right way of doing, a fool he, trouble is his share;
Cut off by associating with obscure and unworthy friends,
His prosperity will decrease like the waning moon.
He who swiftly does what is useful has not forsaken wisdom.
He who has not put away the right way of doing wise, happines will be his,
Not cut off by associating with worthy, virtuous friends,
His prosperity will go on increasing like the waxing moon.'"

Then Yaças sat down in the hall (*hkhor-kyi khamsu*);

[1] Conf. Beal, *op. cit.*, p. 90, where the goods are given to Revata. The Tibetan text is not very clear, and my translation is open to correction.

having composed his mind in the fourth dhyana of perfection, and having discerned the proper course (to follow), he beat the gaṇṭhâ and assembled 700 arhats less one, all contemporaries of Ananda. Now at that time the venerable Kuyyasobhito was deep in the samadhi of arresting (*hgog*), and he did not hear the gaṇṭhâ. When all the arhats had assembled, the venerable Yaças thought, "If I should salute each one by name it would cause great confusion" (? lit. if I should call them by name there would be much wrangling). "I will not call them by name." So he bowed to those who were well stricken in years, and having saluted by raising his hands to his forehead those who were verging on old age, he took his seat.[1]

Just then Kuyyasobhito came out of his meditation, and a deva came and asked him, "Venerable Kuyyasobhito, why stand you there thinking? Go quickly to Vaisâli, where the 699 arhats are assembled to maintain the doctrine, thou who art the first master (*khyod dang mkhan-po gchig-pa*)."[2] Then he vanished from Paṭaliputra, and coming to Vaisâli, he stood before the door of the hall and asked admission, for it was closed.

After having told those within who he was in several verses (f. 703–704), he was admitted and took his seat.

Then the venerable Yaças informed them of the ten indulgences in the same terms which he had previously used in speaking to Sarvakâma and the other arhats, and they gave the same answers we have seen given above, after which they said, "These bhikshus of Vaisâli who proclaim that which is unlawful lawful, and who act accordingly, we condemn them!" And this formula they repeated after each indulgence had been condemned.

(F. 705.) When they had examined and condemned the ten indulgences, they beat the gaṇṭhâ, and having assem-

[1] This passage is obscure. The first part of it, which is the most embarrassing, is, *De-dag-gis ming-nas phyung-ste brjod-na ni, hkhrug-pa tchen-por hgyur-bas, ma-la bdag-gis ming-nas mi dbyung-bar brjod-par byao.* . . .

[2] Which may also be, "Thou art the one master (missing to complete the 700)."

bled all the bhikshus at Vaisâli, Yaças informed them of the proceedings and decision of the council (f. 705^{b}).

The text of the Vinayaksudraka ends abruptly here, and I have not been able to find in any canonical text any mention of the subsequent work which the Mahâwanso says the council performed in settling the whole canon; nor does the Chinese version of the council of Vaisâli [1] mention anything beyond the condemnation of the ten indulgences. It will, however, be seen, by referring to Bhavya's work (p. 187), that the Northern authors do not disagree with the Southern ones as regards the history of these events.

[1] See Beal, Four Lectures, p. 83 *et seq.*

CHAPTER VI.

HISTORY OF THE SCHOOLS OF BUDDHISM.

THE 90th volume of the sûtra of the Bstan-hgyur contains three works on the schismatic schools of Bhuddism, one of which, the *Samavadhoparacha chakra*, by Vasumitra (f. 157–163), has been translated by Professor Wassilief in his work on Bhuddism. I have endeavoured in the following pages to condense the information contained in the work of Bhavya, the *Kayabhetro vibhanga* [1] (f. 163–172), in that of Vinitadeva, the *Samayabhedo parachanachakra*,[2] and in a curious little work called the *Bhikshu varshagrapritsha* (f. 284–296), the author of which is unknown. The theories of the different schools are unfortunately given by both Vasumitra and Bhavya in about the same words, and so concisely, that it is a very difficult if not an impossible task, to give a satisfactory translation of them. I have, however, attempted to translate the greater part of Bhavya's remarks, and by means of Vinitadeva's work, which is a compilation of that of Vasumitra, I hope that I have been able to elucidate a few of the latter's observations which I think are rather obscure in Professor Wassilief's translation. I have deemed it prudent to retain in the translation the greater part of the technical Sanskrit

[1] In Tibetan, *Sde-ba tha-dad-par byed-pa dang rnam-par bshad-pa*, or "The thorough explanation of the differences of the schools."

[2] In Tibetan, *Gdzung tha-dad-pa rim-par glag-pai hkhor-lo-las sde-pa tha-dad-pa bstan-pa bsdus-pa*. "Compilation teaching the differences of the schools from the Samavadhoparacha chakra (by Vasumitra)." With the present account conf. Mahâwanso, p. 20–21, where we are told that the seventeen schisms arose in the second century after the death of the Buddha.

terms in their original form, for by translating them mistakes might be made which would entirely alter the sense of the original, whereas the Sanskrit term will enable the reader to reconstrue more easily what may have been the original text.

The first twelve pages only of Bhavya's work are translated, for the last five present but little interest, and add nothing to our knowledge of the doctrines of these schools :—

Adoration to the triratna!

How came about the eighteen schools and their peculiar features? This is the way in which they are all said to proceed from (the teaching of) the one highest Lord.

One hundred and sixty years[1] after the utter passing away of the Blessed Buddha, when King Dharmâçoka (*i.e.*, Kâlâsoka) was reigning in Kusumapura (*Me-tog-gis rgyas-pa*, *i.e.*, Paṭaliputra), there arose a great schism in the congregation on account of some controverted questions, and it divided into two schools, the Mahâsânghika and the Sthavira. Of these, the Mahâsânghika school gradually divided into eight fractions (to wit), the Mahâsânghika school, the Ekavyavahârika, the Lokottaravâdina, the Bahuçrutîya, the Pradshnaptivâdina, the Tchaityika, the Pûrvaçaila, and the Avaraçaila.

The Sthavira school gradually divided into ten fractions —(1) the Sthavira proper, also called the Haimavata; (2) the Sarvâstivâdina; (3) the Vaibâdyavâdina; (4) the Hetuvidya, which is also called by some persons Muduntaka (or Muruntaka); (5) the Vatsîputrîya; (6) the Dharmottarîya; (7) the Bhadrâyanîya; (8) the Sammatîya, which is also called by some persons Avantaka, and by others Kurukullaka; (9) the Mahîçâsaka; (10) the Dharmaguptaka; (11) the Saddharmavarshaka (or properly Suvar-

[1] The two Açokas are generally confounded in Northern Buddhist works. See, however, p. 233, where we find the correct date for Açoka the Great's reign. The Annals of Khoten appear, however, to have derived some of their statements from Southern Buddhist works not known to, or, at all events, not mentioned by Northern writers.

shaka), which some persons call the Kâçyapîya; (12) the Uttarîya, called also by some the Samkrântivâdina. These are the eighteen schools.[1]

The Mahâsânghika received this name on account of the great number of its followers, which made it a great assembly or *Mahâ sangîti.*

Some persons contending that all the doctrines are thoroughly understood by an unique and immediate wisdom (*skad chig gchig-dang-ldan-pai-shes-rab*), for all doctrines of the blessed Buddhas are comprehended by the intellect (*thugs-gis* instead of *thugs-gi*), are for this reason called "Disciples of the dispute on one subject," or *Eka vyavahara.*

Those who say that the blessed Buddhas have passed beyond all worlds (*i.e.*, existences), that the Tathâgata was not subject to worldly laws, are called, "Who has passed beyond all worlds," or *Lokottaravadina.*

Those who were taught by the master Bahuçrutiya are called *Bahuçrutîya.*

Those who contend that misery (*dukha*) is mixed with all compound things are called *Pradshnaptivâdina.*

Those who live on the Tchaitya mountain are called the *Tchaityika.*

[1] By referring to Vasumitra, f. 158, we learn that the Sarvâstivâdina was the same as the Hetuvidya or Muduntaka. With this exception, and by supposing that the Vaibâdyavâdina of our list is the same as the Shaṇnagarika of Vasumitra, the two lists agree. The *Bhikshu varhhagrapritsha*, f. 295, has as follows: There are four schools (*sde, nikaya*), which are—(1) the Aryâsarvâstivâdina, (2) the Mahâsânghika, (3) Aryâsammatiya, (4) Aryâsthavira. There are eighteen divisions, of these four come from the Aryâsarvâstivâdina—(1) the Kâçyapiya, (2) Mahîçâsaka (the text has by mistake *Sa-srung*), (3) the Dharmaguptaka, (4) Mûlasarvâstivâdina. Six divisions come from the Mahâsânghika school—(1) Pûrvaçaila, (2) Avaraçaila, (3) Vaibâdyavâdina, (4) Pradshnaptivâdina (*Btags-par-smra*), (5) Lokottavavâdina (the original school makes up the six). Five divisions come from the Sammatîyas—(1) Tamraçâṭiya, (2) Guptaka, (3) Kurukullaka, (4) Bahuçrutîya, (5) Vatsîputrîya. Three divisions proceed from the Sthaviras—(1) Jetavanîya, (2) Abhayagiriya, (3) Mahâvihâravâsina. It appears difficult to reduce Bhavya's list to ten sects, as his text prescribes. The list of schools given in the Mahavyutpatti is substantially the same as that of the Bhikshu Varshagrapritcha. The Mahawanso tells us that the Abhayagiri schism occurred in the 453d year after the Buddha's death. See Turnour, p. 207.

Those who live on the Purva mountain (*çaila*) and on the Avara mountain are respectively called *Pûrvaçaila* and *Avaraçaila.*

Those who teach that the sthaviras belong to the body of the elect (*ariyas*) are called *Sthavira.* They are also called *Haimavatas* because (f. 164^b) they live on Mount Himavata.

Those who say that all exists, the past, the future, and the present, are called in consequence, "They who say that all exists," or *Sarvâstivâdina.*

Those who say that some things exist, (such as) past actions of which the result has not matured, and that some do not exist, (such as) those deeds of which the consequences have occurred, and the things of the future; making categories (or divisions), they are called in consequence, "They who speak of divisions," or *Vaibâdya-vâdina.*

They who say that things which have been, which are, and those which will be, have a cause (*hetu*), are called, "They who speak of a cause," or *Hetuvidya.*[1]

They who live on Mount Muruntaka are for that reason called *Muruntaka.*

They who, teaching of man's birth, say that, womankind being the dwelling-place (*vâsa*) of the family, man, being born of her, is a son of the dwelling-place or *vâsa-putra*, are for this reason called *Vâtsiputriya.*[2]

Those who were taught by the master Dharmottara are the *Dharmottariya.*

The disciples of Bhadrayana are the *Bhadrayaniya.*

They whose teacher was Sammata are the *Sammatiya.*

They who congregated in the city of Avanta were consequently called the *Avantaka.*

[1] The text says, "They who speak of wind," *rlung smra-bai.* This is of course a mistake, as *rgyu* and *rlung* are graphically similar.

[2] Correctly we should have Vâsaputriyas ; but we know that this was not the name of the sect. Conf. Stan. Julien, Listes divers des Noms des dix-huit Ecoles schismatiques; Journal Asiatique, 5th series, No. xiv. pp. 353 and 356.

They who live on the Kurukula mountain are for that reason (called) *Kurukula(ka)*.

They who declaring in their teaching, from the properties of the word "earth," that all the great mass of human beings will have no other existence, are the *Mahîçasaka*, or "Those who teach much" (?).[1]

They whose master (founder) was Dharmagupta are the *Dharmaguptaka*.

They who have caused the rain of the law of laudable ideas to fall are called "(The school of) the good rain," or *Suvarshaka*.

They whose master was Kaçyapa are the *Kaçyapiya*.

In like manner, they whose master was Uttara are the *Uttariya*.

They who say that the pudgala (individuality) passes from this world (*i.e.*, life) into another are called, "They who speak of passing," or *Samkrantivadina*.

Of these (f. 165[a]), the Mahâsânghika and seven others, for *a priori* reasons, and the Sthavira, Sarvâstivâdina, Mahîçâsaka, Dharmottariya, and Kaçyapiya, for *a posteriori* reasons, are believers in the non-existence of the soul (*anâtmavâdinas*), and say that all things are without atman. They say that those who teach of self are in conformity of views with the tirthikas, and that all things (*dharma*) are without atman.

All the other (sects), the Vâtsiputriya, &c., five (in all), believe in (the existence of) the pudgala.[2] They say that when the six senses have discerned that the pudgala (passes) from (one set) of skandhas to another, one is perfectly freed from transmigration.[3] These are the differences of the eighteen schools.

[1] The text is difficult, "*Sa sui* (?) *skad-kyi dbyings-las rjesu ston-du bsgyur-te, skye-boi ts'ogs tchen-po-la yang srid-pai mi hbyung-bar rjesu ston-par byed-pa-ni, mang-ston-pao.*" The difficulty rests on the first words, and I do not feel sure of having overcome it. *Mahîçasaka* is generally translated *sa-ston-pa* or *sa-ston-gyi-sde*, "the school of the teaching of the earth;" probably this means "the school which derives its teaching from a comparison with the earth," in which case it would agree with Bhavya. Conf. Stan. Julien, p. 352, No. 44, p. 355, No. 68, 69.

[2] Are we to understand by this that *pudgala* = *atman*?

[3] We are not told whether we are

Other people say that it is not so. They say that there were three original divisions (lit. root-divisions, *rtsa-bai dbye-ba*), to wit, the Sthavira, the Mahâsâṅghika, and the Vaibadyavâdina. Moreover, there are two (sub)divisions of the Sthavira—the Sarvâstivâdina and the Vâtsiputriya. Again, the Sarvâstivâdina are divided into two—the Sarvâstivâdina (or Mûla Sarvâstivâdina ?) and the Sautrantika. There are four (sub)divisions of the Vâtsiputriya—the Sammatiya, the Dharmottariya, the Bhadrayaniya, and the Shaṇnagarika. In this way are the Sthavira divided into six schools.

Moreover, the Mahâsânghika school has eight divisions (according to their theory)—the Mahâsânghika, the Pûrvaçaila, the Avaraçaila, the Râjagiriya, the Haimavata, the Tchaityika, the Samkrântivâdina,[1] and the Gokulika. This is the way in which they divide the Mahâsânghika.

The Vaibadyavâdina (they say) comprise four divisions—the Mahîçâsaka, the Kâçyapiya, the Dharmaguptaka, and the Tamraçâṭiya (f. 165[b]).

This is the way in which they give the eighteen divisions of the schools of the Ariyas.

Again, others say that 137 years after the death of the Blessed One, King Nanda and Mahâpadma convened in the city of Pâṭaliputra all the different Ariyas. Mahâkâçyapa, a man who had attained to unassailable composure, and the venerable Mahâloma (*spu tchen-po*), Mahâtyâga (*gtang-ba tchen-po*), Uttara (*bla-ma*), &c., arhats, with correct analytical knowledge, there assembled to bring round the wicked to agree with the good.[2]

to understand by this that this knowledge itself is *nirvâṇa*, or whether it only shows the way to liberation.

[1] The text has *bden drug-pa* = Shattasatyika (?), but it is undoubtedly a mistake for *don-grub-pa* or Samkrântivâdina. The two Tibetan expressions may easily be mistaken in writing.

[2] This passage, which appears to me very important, is not without difficulties. The word *rgyal-po*, "king," is in the singular, whereas we might expect the plural, although Nanda and Mahâpadma reigning together might be spoken of in the singular. See Wassilief, Târanâtha, p. 291, where he gives this passage from the work of Tshantsha Khutuktu. This relates to the events which followed the second council, that of Vasâila, which we have seen (p. 171) the Vinaya places 110 years after the Buddha's death.

Having settled the habits (? *tcha-byad*) of the bhikshus (*i.e.*, the ten indulgences? see p. 171), and having exhibited different miracles, there occurred, on account of five propositions, a great schism in the congregation (*sangha*). The Sthaviras called Nâga, Sthiramati (*Yid brtanpa*), and Bahuçrutiya advocated the five propositions and taught accordingly. They said that (the doctrines concerning) answer to another (or advice to another, *gdzanla lan-gdab*), ignorance (*mi shes-pa*), doubt (lit. doublemindedness, *yid gnyis-pa*), complete demonstration (*yongsu btags-pa*), restoration of self (*bdag-nyid gso-bar byed-pa*), were the way, and that they were taught (lit. the doctrine of) by the Buddha.[1] Then they (the congregation) became divided into two schools, the Sthavira and the Mahâsânghika, and for sixty-three years after the division of the congregation they obstinately quarrelled (*hkhrug long-gio gnas-so*).

One hundred and two years later, the Sthavira and the Vâtsiputriya rightly collected the doctrine (*bstan-pa yangdag-par badus-so*). After they had rightly collected it, there arose two divisions of the Mahâsânghika, the Ekavyaharika and the Gokulika. The Ekavyaharika considered as fundamental doctrines that the blessed Buddhas (f. 66[a]) having passed beyond the world, the Tathâgata is not subject to worldly laws; that the *dharmachakras* of all the Tathâgatas do not agree;[2] that the words of all the Tathâ-

[1] Vasumitra, *op. cit.*, 175[a], says, "It is asserted that a little more than a century after the death of the Blessed Buddha, after the setting of the radiant sun, in the city of Paṭaliputra, during the reign of King Açoka, the one ruler of the (whole) land (of India), occurred the schism of the Mahâsânghika. It took place on account of the conception and promulgation of five propositions: influence by another (*gdzan-gyis nye-bar bsgrub-pa*), ignorance (*mi shes-pa*), doubt (*som-nyi*), investigation of another (*gdzan-gyi rnam-par spyod-pa*), the production of the way (by) words (*lam sgra* (*yis*) *hbyin-pa*)." Vinitadeva, *op. cit.*, f. 173[a], has, "There is no intuitive knowledge (*rang rig ma yin-no*); to even arhats are doubt and ignorance (*dgra-bchom-pa-rnams-la yang somnyi dang mi-shes-pa yod-de*); the explanations of another are useful in (acquiring) the fruit (*hbras-bu-la gdzan-gyi brda-sprad dgos-so*); to speak of misery, to explain misery (to another), will produce the way (*sdug-bsngal smos-shing, sdug bsngal ts'ig-tu brjod-pas lam skye-bar hgyurro*)." Conf. also Târanâtha, p. 41, line 20.

[2] So I understand the text, which is, *De-bdzin-gshegs-pa thams-chad-kyi tchos-kyi hkhor-lo bskor-bai rjesu gsungs-pa ni mi hjug-go;* lit. of all the Tathâgatas, the wheel of the law has been spoken in agreement (it) does

gatas are revered in their spirit (*snying-po-la*). (They say) that all the Tathâgatas here (in this world) are without longing for rûpa; that the bôdhisattva does not pass through the successive stages of embryonic development [lit. does not receive the condition of *kalala* (*nur-nur*), *arbuda* (*mer-mer*), *pechi* (*nar-nar*), and *gana* (*gor-gor*)], (but that), after having entered his mother's side as an elephant, he appears (*i.e.*, is born) (by) his own (will?). (They say) that a bôdhisattva has no *kamasandjna* (*hdod-pai hdu shes*); he is born at his will among inferior beings for the salvation of mankind (lit. to bring people to maturity). (They say) that with one wisdom (*djana*, *ye shes*) the four truths are perfectly understood; that the six vidjnânas are subject to passions (*hdod-tchags-dang-bchas*) and free from passions. (According to their theories) the eye sees forms; arhats acquire the doctrine by others; and, moreover, there is a way to cast off ignorance, uncertainty; complete demonstration, and misery (exist).[1] There are words (spoken while) in a state of perfect abstraction; there is (such a thing as) to cast off impurity; he who has perfectly acquired right restraint has cast off all yoga (attachment). Tathâgatas have not the right view (of the rest of) humanity. The mind (*sems*) being of its nature radiant, it must not be said that anuçayas (*bag-la nyal*, thoughts) participate of

not exist. Wassilief, however (Buddhisme, p. 235, note 6), translates it, "The predication of the Tathâgata does not enter (*mi hjug-go*) into the wheel of the doctrine." The text of the Tibetan translation of Bhavya must be incorrect, for both Vasumitra (f. 158b) and Vinitadeva (f. 172b) agree in saying just the opposite. The first says, "All the words of the Tathâgata turn with the wheel of the law" (*i.e.*, are true); the latter, "The turning the wheel of the law is of the word" (*tchos-kyi hkhor-lo bskor-ba ni ts'ig-gi yin-no*); which I suppose means that the wheel of the law is in agreement—is part of the words spoken by the Buddha; but the phrase is curiously constructed, and, to me, ungrammatical. By changing the order of the words in Bhavya it would be easy to arrive at the same sense as that of the other texts, but the negation would have to be suppressed.

[1] The text is, *Dgra-bchom-pa-rnams kyang gdzan-dag-gis bstan-pa sgrub-par-byed-do. Mi-shes-pa dang yid gnyis dang yonsu brtags-pa dang sdug-bsngal spong-pai lam yang yod-do.* Vasumitra, *op. cit.*, f. 159a, refers to the same theories, but his words are very obscure. See Wassilief, Buddh., p. 228.

the mind or that they do not participate of it. Anuçayas are one, the completely spread out (*kun-nas ldang-ba, i.e.,* the mind) is another. The past and the future do not exist (in the present). The çrotapatti (f. 166[b]) can acquire dhyana. These are the fundamental doctrines of the Ekavyaharika.

(As to) the (sub)divisions of the Gokulika, the Bahuçrûtiya and the Pradjnaptivâdina, the Bahuçrûtiya hold as fundamental doctrines that there is no mode of life leading to real salvation (*niryanika*); that the truth of suffering, subjective truth (*? kun rdsob-kyi bden-pa*), and the venerable truth (*aryasatya, hphags-pai bden*) (constitute) the truth. To perceive the suffering of the sanskâra is to enter perfect purity. There is no (way) to see the misery of suffering and the misery of change. The sangha has passed beyond the world (*i.e.,* is not subject to worldly laws or conditions). Arhats acquire the doctrine by others. There is a rightly preached way (*yang-dag-par bsgrags-pai-lam yang yod-do*). There is a right entry into perfect composure (*samâpatti*). Of this description are the fundamental doctrines of the Bahuçrutiya.

The Pradjnaptivâdina say that suffering is no skandha; that there are no perfect âyatanas; that (all) sanskâras are bound together; that suffering is absolute (*paramârtha, sdug-bsngal-ni don-dam-por-ro*); that what proceeds from the mind is not the way; that there is no untimely death (*dus-ma yin-par htchi-ba ni medo*); that there is no human agency (*skyes-bu-byed-pa yang med-do*); that all suffering comes from *karma* (deeds). Of this description are the fundamental doctrines of the Pradjnaptivâdina.

The Sthavira Tchaityika are yet another division of the Gokulika. A paṛivradjaka by the name of Mahâdeva, who had entered the (Buddhist) order, lived on a mountain with a tchaitya. He rejected the fundamental laws of the Mahâsânghika, and established a school which was called Tchaityika; and these are the six sects derived from the Mahâsânghika.

There are two divisions of the Sthavira, the Old Sthavira (*sngar-gyi gnas-brtan*) (f. 167ª) and the Haimavata.

The fundamental doctrines of the Old Sthavira are as follows: Arhats are not perfected by the teaching of another, so likewise the remainder of the five propositions are denied; the pudgala exists; there is an intermediary state (between two successive existences); arhatship is parinirvâṇa (*dgra-bchom-pa yongsu mya-ngan-las-hdas-pa ni yod-do*); the past and the future exist (in the present); there is a sense (? *don=artha*) of nirvâṇa. These are the fundamental doctrines of the (Old) Sthaviras.

The fundamental doctrines of the Haimavata are that a bodhisattva is not an ordinary mortal; that even a tirthika has the five abhidjnanas; that the pudgala is separate from the skandhas, because in the (state of) nirvâṇa in which the skandhas are arrested the pudgala exists. Words enter into samâpatti (*i.e.*, words are spoken in that state); suffering is removed by the marga. These are the fundamental doctrines of the Haimavata.

Moreover, the first Sthavira (*dang-poi gnas-brtan*) divided into two sects, the Sarvâstivâdina and the Vâtsiputriya.

The fundamental doctrines of the Sarvâstivâdina are all comprised in two (propositions ?). The compound and the elementary exist. What is the consequence of this (theory)? That there is no pudgala; therefore if this body without âtman comes into existence, there being no agent (*byed-pa med-ching*), no right-doer, one consequently drops into the stream of existence.[1] This is the way they speak. These are the fundamental doctrines of the Sarvâstivâdina. Their fundamental doctrines are all comprised in *nâma-*

[1] This passage on the theories of the Sarvâstivâdina is difficult: *Hdus-byas dang hdus-ma byas-so. De skad smras-pas-chir hgyur. Gang-zag ni med ches bya-ba ste, ji skad-du bdag-med-pa-yi lus hdi hbyung-na, byed-pa med ching, rigs-pa-po-yang med, ji-ltar hkhor-bai tchu-klung hjug-hgyur-ba.* It is not contrary to what Vasumitra tells us, f. 160. See also Vinitadeva, f. 173ᵇ, who has that they believed it very meritorious to honour tchaityas; that they distinguished three kinds of elementary, &c., &c.

rûpa. The past and the future exist (at the present time); the çrotapatti is not subject to degeneracy. There are three characteristics (f. 167[b]) of compound things. The four holy truths are gradually understood. The void, the undesired, and the uncharacteristic lead to the unblemished (state, *skyon-med-pa-la*). With fifteen seconds one has attained the fruit of çrotapaṇṇa.[1] The çrotapatti finds dhyana. Even the arhat has an imperfect existence.[2] Ordinary mortals can cast off râga or evil-mindedness. Even a tirthika has the five abhidjanas. There are means for even a deva to lead a virtuous life (*brahmâchariya*). All the sûtras have a straight (*drang-po, ṛichu*) sense. He who has entered the unblemished (truth), has (passed) beyond the kâmadhatu. There is a right view of the kâmaloka (*i.e.*, inherent to persons inhabiting the kâmaloka?). All the five vidjnanas are not under the rule of the passions, (but) they are not also free from passions. These are the fundamental doctrines of the Sarvâstivâdina. There is, moreover, a sect (*bye-brag*) of the Sarvâstivâdina which is the Vaibâdhyavâdina.

The divisions of the Vaibâdhyavâdina are the Mahîçâsaka, the Dharmaguptaka, the Tamraçatiya, and the Kâçyapiya.

The fundamental doctrines of the Mahîçâsaka are: The past and the future do not exist; present compound things exist. To distinguish misery is to see into the parts of the four truths. Anuçayas are one and the evident cause (*mngon du rgyu = sems?*) is another (*i.e.*, they must be distinguished). There is no intermediary existence (between two successive regenerations); there is (such a thing as) a life of virtue (*brahmâchariya*) in the abode of devas;[3] even

[1] Wassilief, *op. cit.*, p. 248, note 3, tells us that there are sixteen periods or moments through which one must pass before he becomes an ariya. Conf. Vasumitra, f. 160[b], "Having entered the unblemished reality, the mind's development (*sems bskyed-pa*) in fifteen (moments) is called çrotâpanna."

[2] The text has *dgra-bchom-pa yang nyam pa sring-ngo.* I read the last words *nyams-pa srid-do.*

[3] Vasumitra, *op. cit.*, f. 162[b], says the contrary, and Vinitadeva, f. 173[b], also. Vasumitra, *loc. cit.*, also says that they deny an intermediary existence, but Vinitadeva does not agree with him.

an arhat accumulates merit.[1] All the five vidjnânas are (subject to) the passions and without passion (*râga*). The pudgala pervades all the individual;[2] the çrotapatti acquires dyana. Ordinary beings (can) cast off passions and wickedness. The Buddha is comprised in the sangha. The emancipation (lit. perfect freedom) of the (or a) Buddha and of the çravakas is one. There is no such thing as to perceive (*mthong*) the pudgala. Neither the mind nor its manifestations, nor anything which participates in the least of the conditions of birth, passes from this life into another. All compound things are momentary. If birth is through an extension of the sanskâra, the sanskâra do not (however) exist permanently. Karma is as is the mind. There is no liberty of body or speech;[3] there is no condition not subject to degeneracy; there is no reward for honouring a tchaitya. (Any) present event is always an anuçaya (*da-ltar byung-ba rtag-tu ni bag-la-nyal-ba yin-no*). To distinguish compound things is to enter the unblemished (truth).

These are the fundamental doctrines of the Mahîçâsaka.

The fundamental doctrines of the Dharmaguptaka are as follows: The Buddha is not comprised in the sangha.[4] There is a great reward from (offerings made to) the Buddha, but none from (those made to) the sangha. There is (such a thing as) a life of virtue (*brahmâchariya*) in the abode of the devas. There are worldly laws (*hjig-rten-pai-tchos-ni yod-do*). These are the fundamental doctrines of the Dharmaguptaka.[5]

[1] Vasumitra, *loc. cit.*, says the contrary, but Vinitadeva agrees with our text.

[2] The text is, *Gang-zag ni mgo la-sogs-pa lus dang mnyam-pa yin-no*, lit. "the pudgala is equal to the head and all the rest of the body." Vasumitra, f. 162[b], says, "The pudgala is even with the head" (*mgo mnyam-pa yod-do*).

[3] That is to say, if I understand rightly the text (*sems ji-ltar-ba de-ltar las-yin-gyi-lus dang ngag-gi las ni med-do*), the mind is the only faculty with freedom of action.

[4] But Vasumitra, f. 163[a], says, "The Buddha is represented in the sangha." Vinitadeva agrees with our text. In the following clause the words in brackets are supplied from Vasumitra's work; our text is evidently imperfect.

[5] Vasumitra, *loc. cit.*, adds that "the body of an arhat is without asrava. All the rest (of their theories) are like those of the Mahâsânghika."

The fundamental doctrines of the Kâçyapiya are as follows: Requital, and subjection to the laws of requital, as also the law of coming to pass (*i.e.*, the *pratityasamudpada*) exist. To a person who has cast off (all sin?) is perfect knowledge.[1] All the other assertions (*hdod*) of the Kâçyapiya are (like) those of the Dharmaguptaka.

The fundamental theory of the Tamraçaitya is that there is no pudgala.

Furthermore, the fundamental doctrines of the Samkrântivâdina, a sect of the Sarvâstivâdina (f. 168[b]), whose chief doctrines are (due to) the master Uttara, are that the five skandhas pass (*hpho, samkrânti*) from this life to another. There is no arresting the skandhas when the way has not been discovered.[2] There is a skandha which has inborn sin (*? rtsa-bai ltung-ba dang-bchas-pai-phung-po yod-do*). The pudgala is not to be considered subjectively (*don-dam-par*). All is impermanent. These are the fundamental doctrines of the Samkrânti (school). These are the fundamental doctrines of the seven divisions of the Sarvâstivâdina.

The fundamental doctrines of the Vatsîputrîya are: The possession of what one was attached to and upadana are solidary (*? nye-bar blangs-pa nye-bar-len pa dang-ldan-pa ni btags-so*). There are no properties (*? dharma*) which pass from this life into another.[3] When one has been attached to the five skandhas, the pudgala transmigrates. There are compound things (*sanskâra*) which are mo-

[1] The text says, "To one who has cast off (sin) is imperfect knowledge" (*spangs-la yongsu ma shes-pa yod-do*), but this cannot be correct. Vasumitra (f. 163[a]) has, *Spangs-pa yongsu shes-pa yod-do, ma spangs-pa yongsu spang dzes-pa med do.* It appears, moreover, to me that Bhavya's phrase shows us that *spangs-pa* in Vasumitra ought to be translated by, "He who has cast off (sin)," not, "What is cast off," as Wassilief has it, *op. cit.*, p. 257. Vinitadeva (f. 173[b]) has, *Yongsu shes-la-ma-spangs-pa . . . medo.* "To one who is perfectly wise there is nothing which has not been cast off," which confirms our translation of Bhavya.

[2] Vasumitra, *op. cit.*, 163[b], says the contrary, and Vinitadeva does not mention the doctrines of this school.

[3] Conf. what Vasumitra says, f. 162, "With the exception of the pudgala, there is nothing which passes from this life (into another)." Vinitadeva says about the same thing.

mentary, and also (some) which are not momentary. One must not say that the pudgala is either an *upadana-skandha*, or that it is not. They do not say that nirvâṇa is in the unification of all conditions, or that it is in the disruption (of them).[1] They do not say that nirvâṇa is real existence (*yod-pa nyid*), or that it is not real existence. (They say that) the five vidjnânas are not subject to passions; that there are none without râga. These are the fundamental doctrines of the Vatsîputrîya. There are yet two divisions of the Vatsîputrîya, the Mahâgiriya and the Sammatiya.

The fundamental doctrines of the Sammatiya are: (The belief in) the existence of what shall be (*i.e.*, future things), of what is, of what shall be arrested; (the belief in the existence of) birth and death (as well) as of the thing which shall die, of the agent, of the thing which shall decay (as well as of) decay, of what shall go (as well as) in going, of what must be perceived (as well as) in perception (*vidjnana*).[2]

There are two kinds of Mahâgiriya (*ri-tchen-po*), the Dharmottarîya and the Bhadrâyanîya.

(F. 169[a].) The fundamental doctrines of the Dharmottarîya is: In birth is ignorance; in the arresting of birth is the arresting of ignorance. The Bhadrâyanîya are like unto them. Some say that the Shaṇnagarika school is a division of the Mahâgiriya; others that it is a division of the Sammatîya, thus making four divisions of the Vatsîputrîya school.

The eighteen divisions (*rnam-pa*) came into existence gradually through following (the theories of) certain doctors who are the originators of them.[3] There is much

[1] This clause is obscure; it runs, *Mya-ngan-las-hdas-pa ni tchos thams-chad dang gchig-pa-nyid-du dam tha-dad-pa-nyid-du mi brjod-do.* Neither Vasumitra nor Vinitadeva mention this doctrine.

[2] In other words, they believe in subjective and objective existence. The passage is certainly obscure, and I offer my translation as tentative. Conf. what Vasumitra (f. 162) and Vinitadeva (f. 174[b]) say of this school. The latter classes it with the Kaurukullaka, Guptaka, and Vatsîputrîya schools.

[3] Bhavya gives this as the theory of another class of historians.

more to be said about another separation. Here is how (arose) the diversity of doctrines and the four divisions of the Sarvâstivâdina, which was caused by the diversity (of opinions) on substance (*bhava*, *dngos-po*), characteristics (*lakshana*, *mts'an-nyid*), condition (*gnas-skabs*), and change (*gdzan gdzan-du hgyur-ba-nyid*).

Concerning primary substance and its change, the Bhadanta Dharmatrâta said that, according to circumstances (*tchos-rnams*) and time, there is (no) changing of substance and no transmutation into another substance (*bhava*). If a gold vase has been destroyed and (afterwards) made into something else, made into another shape, it will not however be another substance (*rdsas*). Likewise milk, if it become curds, though it has acquired a different taste, property (*nus-pa*), another shape (*smin-pa*), (yet) it is the same substance.[1] In like manner, if past conditions (*dharma*) exist in the present, (they retain) the substance (*dngos-po*) of the past. There is no destructible matter therefore, he said, if the present (condition) exists in the future; the present substance (*dngos-po*) is not of a destructible nature (*i.e.*, it will be the same in the future).

(The theory of) the change of characteristics is (the work) of the Bhadanta Ghoshaka. He said that all things under the influence of time cannot but have in the future and in the present the characteristics which they had in the past. The future and the future characteristics of a thing cannot but be the past and present ones. For example, if men loved one woman, they are not without affection for all the rest (of womankind).[2]

(The theory of) the change of condition is (the work) of the Bhadanta Vasumitra. He said that things under the influence of time which are said to change do not

[1] The text is *kha-dog ni ma yin-pa*, "it is not the colour," which I suppose must imply that the new qualities acquired by milk in becoming curds do not depend on the colour, &c., but on the circumstances and time.

[2] *Dper-na skyes-bu-dag bud-med gchig-la tchags-par-gyur-pa-na, lhag-ma rnams-la tchags-pa-dang-bral-ba ni ma yin-no.*

alter their condition (*gnas-skabs*). For example, in a single vegetable one speaks of one life, in a series of an hundred it is an hundred lives, in a thousand it is a thousand existences. That is what he said.[1]

(The theory of) passing from one (condition) into another (*i.e.*, of change) is (the work) of the Bhadanta Buddhadeva. He said that when one looks at the remote (*sngon*) and the proximate (*phyi-ma*) in the work of time on things, one says that they (have passed) from one (condition) into another. For example, one speaks of a woman as "*ma*" (or mother); she is also called "*bu-mo*," (or girl). So it is that these (four) men say that all things exist, and they are Sarvâstivâdinas.

Likewise some (teachers) said that there are seven *pratitya* (*rkyen*),—cause (*hetu*), thought (*âlambana*), proximity (*? de-ma-thag-pa*), the âtman (*bdag-po*), karma, food (*zas*), dependency (*rten*). Some said that there being four ways of mental perception, truth was various (*bden-pa so-soo*). Others say that as there are eight (kinds) of religious knowledge (*tchos-shes-pa*) and knowledge derived from experience (lit. example, *rjesu shes-pa*), there is no analytical knowledge. . . .

Here we will leave Bhavya, for the remaining pages of his treatise only recapitulate the opinions of the Sarvâstivâdina school, and we know enough of these from Vasumitra. Although it is not within the scope of this work to examine in detail the doctrines of the Mahâyâna schools of Buddhism which superseded those of which Bhavya and Vasumitra speak, and which were called by their opponents Hinâyâna schools, yet I cannot refrain from giving the following extract from a very interesting Vaipulya sûtra called Angulimaliya sûtra (*Bkah-hgyur*, Mdo xvi., f. 208 *et seq.*) (f. 273[a]): "All sentient beings exist in the essence (*garbha*) of the Tathâgata;" this is the teaching of the Mahâyâna, whereas the Çravakayâna

[1] *Sngon-bu gchig-bu bgrangs-pai-ts'e dzes-bya, grangs stong-du bgrang-ni gchig ches brjod-par-gyur-pa-la, paits'e-ni stong dzes-bya-ba dang grangs brgyar gtogs-pai-ts'e ni brgya hdrao.*

(*i.e.*, the Hinâyâna) says, "All sentient beings exist by eating" (*zas-la gnas-so*).

The words *nâma* and *rûpa* originate in the Çravakayâna; they are not in the Mahâyâna (doctrine). *Nâmarûpa* are as follows and nothing more: the freedom (*moksha*) of the Çravakas and the Pratyikabuddhas is only a name (*nâma*), so they do not understand either form or space. The freedom of the blessed Buddhas is something else than a myrobolan in the palm of the hand.

The three *vedanâ* originate in the Çravakayâna; they are not in the Mahâyâna. These three notions (*vedanâ*): to have been so fortunate as to have heard that the Tathâgata will never cease from being the most exalted, that is, a *vedanâ*. To have been so fortunate as to have heard that the blessed law will vanish, that is a *vedanâ*. To have been so fortunate as to have heard that the sangha will disappear, that is a *vedanâ*. These are the three *vedanâ* of the Mahâyâna.

The four holy truths are chief dogmas (*grags-pai-ts'ig*) in the Çravakayâna; but a similar collection is not in the Mahâyâna. The Tathâgata is eternal; that is a great truth in the Mahâyâna; but suffering is not a truth. The Tathâgata is everlasting; that is a great truth in the Mahâyâna, (but) the origin (of suffering) is not a truth. The Tathâgata is the most exalted of everlasting (things); that is a great truth in the Mahâyâna, (but) the cessation (of suffering) is not a truth. The Tathâgata is passionless (*dzi-bao*); that is a great truth in the Mahâyâna, (but) the way (to arrest suffering) is not a truth. These are the four holy truths in the Mahâyâna. The action of suffering is not a truth, for if the action of suffering was a truth, it would be true for the four (classes) of suffering (beings);[1] then the four holy truths would apply to those of the worlds of brutes, pretas, asuras, and of Yama.

[1] So I understand the text, *Sdug-bsngal-gyi-bya-ba bden-du lags-na, sdug-bsngal-ma bdzi bden-par hjyur-te*, &c.

The five organs of sense are a chief dogma in the Çravakayâna, but it is not so in the Mahâyâna. (Here) the five organs of sense are: To see the Tathâgata as eternally visible (*gsal bar*) in all one's meditation, this is the (organ of the) eye. Having heard "the Tathâgata is eternal," always to meditate this way is the (organ of the) ear. Always to reflect that the Tathâgata exhales the fragrance of eternity is the (organ of the) nose. Always to reflect that the essence of the Tathâgata is in nirvâṇa (the freedom from sorrow)[1] is the (organ) of the tongue. Always to reflect when one has heard and felt that the *dharmakâya* of the Tathâgata is the most exalted body, that is the body.

The six senses (*âyatana*) are a chief dogma in the Çravakayâna, but there is no such series of six senses in the Mahâyâna. (With it) what is called the six âyatana are: To reflect, as a means for arriving at perfection, that the Tathâgata must be considered (seen) as eternally visible, that is the âyatana of the eye. To reflect, as a means for arriving at perfection, that one has heard "the Tathâgata is eternal," that is the âyatana of the ear. To reflect, as a means for arriving at perfection, that one has heard the essence (*garbha*) of the Tathâgata is the odour of eternity (or is an eternal fragrance), that is the âyatana of the nose. To reflect, as a means for arriving at perfection, that the essence of the Tathagâta is the doctrine (*bstan-pa*), is the âyatana of the tongue. To reflect, as a means for arriving at perfection, that one has heard and felt that the dharmakâya of the Tathâgata is the most exalted mind of that body (*sku dei blo-dam-pa*), that is the âyatana of the body. To perfectly believe with unwavering heart in the manifest doctrine of the Tathâgata, that is the âyatana of the door of entering (*i.e.*, this sense of the way of truth), is the âyatana of the mind (*manas*).

The seven branches of the Bodhi is a chief dogma in

[1] *De-bdzin-gshegs-pai snying-pai nas ma-ts'ang-ba-med-par sgan-pa de mya-ngas-nas* (=*mya-ngan-las hdas*) *ni lcheo.*

the Çravakayâna. Even in the Mahâyâna those seven (branches) are difficult terms to find, like the blooming flower of the fig-tree (*udumbara*). Those seven branches of the Bodhi, the seven full-blown flowers, are the eternity of the Tathâgata.

The holy eightfold way is a chief dogma in the Çravakayâna. This Mahâyâna has another holy eightfold way than right views, &c. Furthermore, the teaching that the Tathâgata is the chief eternity (*rtag-pai mtchog*) is an holy eightfold way. To have heard and fully appreciated the greatness of the Tathâgata is to have found the right way to pass beyond sorrow (nirvâṇa). (To know that) the Tathâgata's eternity, everlastingness, is the highest blessing, is to become cool.[1] Enlightenment (*bodhi*) is bliss (*shis-pa ni sangs-rgyas-te*). The Dharmakâya is the Tathâgata. The essence of the Tathâgata is without old age (*i.e.*, knows no decay). These are what one must know as the eight branches of the way. The nine branches of the *sûtra nikaya* are a chief dogma in the Çravakayâna. This Mahâyâna says that there is but one mode of conveyance (*yana*) in all penetrating (f. 275[a]) wisdom. The ten forces of the Tathâgata are a chief dogma in the Çravakâyana; in this Mahâyâna there are not ten forces of the Tathâgata, but an unlimited force. Whereas the Blessed Buddha is incomprehensible and cannot enter the mind, therefore his might is infinite. The Blessed Buddha taught infinite parables (in the) sûtra nikaya (*mdo-sde mthah-yas-pa ldem-po-ngad-tu ston-pao*).[2] This is the only way. The Tathâ-

[1] *De-bdzin-gshegs-pai-rtag-pa ther-zug gyung-drung-gi mtchog bsil-bar-gyur-pa.*

[2] Which might perhaps be rendered, "The Blessed Buddha expounded in parables the infinite of the *sûtra nikaya.*" Made manifest by parables the doctrine of the infinite as it was contained in the sûtras in obscure terms. However, it may simply imply that the Mahâyâna taught that the doctrines in the sûtras were to be understood allegorically, a theory which we know to have been held by some of the earlier schools. See Vasumitra's Samayabedhoparachanachakra, f. 161[a]. "(The Sarvâstivâdina school teaches that) there are doctrines which have not been taught in the precepts (*lung-du mi ston-pai tchos-rnams yod-do.*) Conf. however, Wassilief's translation of this phrase. Buddh., p. 249, where I cannot follow him.

gata is the only vehicle (*yana*), the one refuge, the one truth to follow after, the one realm (*khams*), the one being, the one colour (? *kha-dog*); therefore there is but one *yana*, the others are but expedients."

I would like to examine more in detail the characteristics of the Mahâyâna doctrine, which gave a new impetus to Buddhism, and perhaps made it acceptable to races which would have refused it in its primitive purity; but enough has been said to show how pervaded its teachings were with mysticism and ideas antagonistic to Gautama's teaching. I will only give a short text concerning a very interesting feature of the Mahâyâna theory, namely, that of the three bodies or *kayatrâya*, in which we find an important link in the chain of doctrinal evolution, which finally led to the theory of the Adi Buddhas or "divine essence," and to that of the Dhyâni Buddhas.

"Once I heard the following discourse (said Ananda), while the Blessed One was stopping at Râjagriha, on the Vulture's Peak, together with an innumerable number of bodhisattvas, dêvas, and nâgas who were doing him homage. Then from out this company, the Bodhisattva Kshitigarbha (*Sai-snying-po*), who was (also) there, arose from his seat and spoke as follows to the Blessed One: 'Has the Blessed One a body?' The Blessed One said, 'Kshitigarbha, the Blessed One, the Tathâgata, has three bodies: the body of the law (*Dharmakâya*), the body of perfect enjoyment (*Sambhôgakâya*), the apparitional body (*Nirmanakâya*). Noble sir (*Kûlaputra*), of the three bodies of the Tathâgata, the Dharmakâya is a perfectly pure nature (*svabhâva*), the Sambhôgakâya is a perfectly pure samadhi; a perfectly pure life is the Nirmanakâya of all Buddhas. Noble sir, the Dharmakâya of the Tathâgata is the prerogative of being without *svabhâva*[1] like space; the Sambhôgakâya is the prerogative of being visible like

[1] I think that *svabhâva* is here used to express "absence of all characteristics." In Angulimaliya Sûtra, f. 250, "The Blessed Buddha is like space, and space is without characteristics." Dr. Edkins, J. R. A. S., 1881, p. 63, renders the expression Dharmakâya by "doctrinal self."

a cloud; the Nirmanakâya being the object of all Buddhas, is the prerogative of permeating all things as does a rain.'

"The Bodhisattva Kshitigarbha said to the Blessed One, 'Make visible these definitions of the true bodies of the Blessed One.' Then the Blessed One said to the Bodhisattva Kshitigarbha: 'Noble sir, the three bodies of the Tathâgata will be discerned thus: the Dharmakâya is discernible in the whole air of the Tathâgata; the Sambhôgakâya is discernible in the whole air of a bodhisattva; the Nirmanakâya is discernible in the air of different pious men. Noble sir, the Dharmakâya is the nature inherent to all buddhas; the Sambhôgakâya is the samadhi inherent to all buddhas; the Nirmanakâya is the object of all buddhas. Noble sir, purity in the abode of the soul,[1] the science like a mirror (*adarçadjnâna*), is the Dharmakâya; purity in the abode of the sinful mind is the science of equality (*samatadjnâna*); purity in the perceptions of the mind, the science of thoroughly analysing, is the Sambhôgakâya; purity in the abode of the perceptions of the five doors,[2] the science of the achievement of what must be done, is the Nirmanakâya.'[3]

"Then the Bodhisattva Kshitigarbha said to the Blessed One, 'I have heard the blessed truth from the Blessed One; it is exceeding good; Sugata, it is exceeding good!'

"The Blessed One said, 'Noble sir, he who has understood this exposition of the truth from the Blessed One has acquired an inexpressible, incalculable amount of merit.'

"When the Blessed One had thus spoken, the Bodhi-

[1] *Kun-gdzi gnas-su dag-pa. Kun-gdzi* appears to be used here for "the seat of the passions." See Jaschke, Dict., s.v. *kun.*

[2] *Sgo lnga* is here used for *âyatana*, "the senses," the science of the achievement of what must be done = Sansk. *Krantyânuchdhanadjnâna.* See Buddh. Trig., f. 9.

[3] The Chinese Buddhist dictionary, San thsang fa su (B. viii. f. 13, Stan. Julien, *l. c.*) defines this body "the body gifted with the faculty of transforming itself. The buddhas having a divine power which escapes the human mind, can transform themselves and appear in all places to explain the law," &c.

sattva Kshitigarbha, the dêvas, nâgas, yakshas, gandharbas, and men were delighted, and lauded greatly what the Blessed One had said." [1]

If we refer to the work of the Chinese Buddhist Jin Ch'an, we find that Dharmakâya has become Vairojana (*i.e.*, the omnipresent), Sambhôgakâya is called Rajana (*i.e.*, the infinitely pure or glorious), and Nirmanakâya is Çakyamuni. "Now these three Tathâgatas are all included in one substantial essence. The three are the same as one; not one, and yet not different; without parts or composition. When regarded as one, the three persons are spoken of as Tathâgata. But it may be asked, if the persons are one substance, how is it that this one substance is differently manifested? In reply we say there is no real difference; these manifestations are only different views of the same unchanging substance." [2]

[1] See Bkah-hgyur, Mdo xxii. f. 81. Conf. Stan. Julien, Mem. sur les Contrées Occidentales, i. p. 240. In the Karandavyuha (Burnouf, Intr. à l'Hist., p. 200) the preceding interpretation of Dharmakâya is unknown. "In each of the pores of the Bodhisattva Avalokitesvara rise mountains and woods where live gods and sages, exclusively devoted to the practice of religion. It is for this reason, said Çâkya, that he is called Dharmakâya "who has for body the law." See also J. Edkins, J. R. A. S., 1881, p. 63; Wassilief, Buddh., p. 127; Beal, Catena, p. 124, 373.

[2] Beal, Catena, p. 124.

CHAPTER VII.

THE EARLY HISTORY OF BOD-YUL (TIBET).

THE early history of Tibet or Bod-yul can only be said to commence with the introduction of Buddhism, or perhaps rather of Chinese influence, into that country, and it appears highly probable that all the events chronicled as anterior to that epoch must be considered in great part as legendary. It is, moreover, worthy of remark that these legends seem to be a rather clumsy adaptation of the Chinese ones relative to their first sovereigns, which are recorded in the Bamboo books.

Another consideration, however, exercised great influence with Tibetan historians when, in the reign of Ral-pa-chan, they commenced writing their national history, and that was to make the genealogy of their monarchs ascend, if not to the Buddha himself, at least to one of his friends and protectors. And as we have in Europe families who are proud to claim descent from the Virgin Mary or from the wise men of the east, so likewise the first Tibetan monarch claims descent from Prasenadjit, king of Koçala, one of the early converts and the life-long friend of the Buddha Gautama.[1]

What information is derivable from early Chinese

[1] Sanang Setsen, in his history of the Eastern Mongols, p. 21, says that the Çakya race (to which the Buddha belonged) was divided into three parts, whose most celebrated representatives were Çakya the great (the Buddha), Çakya the Licchavi, and Çakya the mountaineer. Gnya Khri bstan po, the first Tibetan king, belonged to the family of Çakya the Licchavi. Many other Buddhist sovereigns of India and elsewhere claimed the same descent. See Huen Thsang, Si-yu-ki (Julien), i. p. 179, ii. p. 107, &c.

authors, such as Sse-ma-tsien, or from the later compilation of Ma-twan-lin relative to the Tibetans, may not be applicable to those tribes which founded the kingdom of Tibet, for the early Chinese were only acquainted with the eastern and north-eastern Tibetan tribes which have always been wilder than those situated farther west. Nevertheless, as all these tribes belonged to the same stock, it may prove interesting to note what few particulars I have been able to collect from the works at my disposal.

The Chinese name for the early Tibetans is *K'iang* (羌) (Sse-ma-tsien, Kh. 123, p. 6), or "shepherds," and even to the present day a large part of the Tibetan nation are pastors. They were divided into small clans, which were continually at war with one another, and were considered by the Chinese as an assemblage of ferocious tribes still barbarians. Each year they took "a little oath" to their chiefs, who were called Than-phu (*Btsan-po*, "noble"), when they sacrificed sheep, dogs, and monkeys. Every three years they took "the great oath," and sacrificed men, horses, oxen, and asses. They had no written characters, but made use of notched pieces of wood and of knotted cordelets.[1] In short, the degree of civilisation of the early Tibetans may unquestionably be compared with that of the Lo-lo tribes of our days, who inhabit Yunan, and who are most likely of the same stock as their eastern neighbours. The Tibetans pretend that their first parents were a monkey-king who had been sent to the snowy kingdom by Avalokitesvara and a rakshasi or female demon. They had six children, and as soon as they were weaned the father took them into a forest of fruit trees and abandoned them. When, after a few years, he came back, he found to his great surprise that their number had increased to five hundred. They had eaten all the fruit in the forest, and so, pressed by hunger, they came clamouring piteously around him. The monkey-king had recourse to his patron

[1] Abel Remusat, Recherches sur les Langues Tartares, p. 384; and Bushell, J. R. A. S., New Series, xii. p. 440 *et seq.*

Avalokitesvara; he cried to him for help from the top of the Potala mountain, and the god declared that he would be the guardian of his race. So he went to Mount Sumeru and cast down a great quantity of the five kinds of grain, so that the famished apes filled themselves, and a great quantity which was left over sprung up and supplied stores for their future wants. Wonderful were the results which followed their eating of this grain; the monkeys' tails and the hair on their bodies grew shorter and shorter until they finally disappeared. The monkeys commenced to speak; they were men; and as soon as they noticed this change in their nature they clothed themselves with leaves.[1]

As a consequence of the first parents of the Tibetans being a monkey and a rakshasi, the people of Tibet show peculiarities of both their ancestors. From their father, the holy monkey, they get their gentleness, considerateness, piety, charitableness, and abstemiousness; moreover, they derive from him their love for good works, their gentle speech, and their eloquence. From their mother, the rakshasi, they get their sensuality, lasciviousness, and their love for trade, their trickiness, and their deceitfulness. From this side they get greediness, enviousness, stubbornness, and mischievousness, and, when provoked, violence and cruelty.[2]

We cannot consider this picture of the character of the Tibetans as flattering, but since they are responsible for this description of themselves, we can accept it as probably correct, and in reality it does not differ much from what we have heard of them from European travellers.

The early religion of Tibet is known as the *Bon* or

[1] J. J. Schmidt, Forschungen im Gebiete der älteren Religionen der Völker Mittel-Asiens, p. 212. See also Markham's Tibet, p. 341; and Buddaguhya's epistle to Khri srang lde btsan, f. 387 (Bstan-hygur, Mdo xciv.); E. B. Tylor, Primitive Culture, 2d edit., p. 376–378; Gust. Kreitner, Im fernen Osten, p. 834, gives a Tibetan legend concerning the origin of Chinese, Mongols, and Tibetans different from that of our text. See also Huc's Souvenirs de Voyage.

[2] Schmidt, *op. cit.*, p. 214.

Gyung-drung-gi-bon,[1] and this creed is still followed by part of the Tibetans and the barbarous tribes of the Himalayas. Mr. Brian Hodgson connects it with the primitive Turanian superstitions and the doctrines of Çaivism; "but," he adds, "in the Himalayas even the Bon-pa priests themselves can tell nothing of the origin of their belief."[2] The word Bon-pa is unquestionably derived (as General Cunningham was first to point out, Yule's Marco Polo, i. p. 287) from *Punya,* one of the names of the *Svastikas* or worshippers of the mystic cross swasti, which in Tibetan is called "*gyung-drung.*"

The only work of the Bon-pa which has been made accessible to Western scholars is a sûtra translated by A. Schiefner;[3] but Buddhist influence is so manifest in it that it is impossible to consider it as giving us very correct ideas of what this religion was before it came in contact with Buddhism. The Bon-pa religion has repeatedly been said to be the same as that of the Tao-sse,[4] and it is remarkable that these two religions have drawn so largely from Buddhist ideas that they have nearly identified themselves with it.

I fancy that the following description of the religious ideas of the Lo-los of Sse-tchuen will give us some idea of what was the early Tibetan national religion. "The religion of the Lo-los is sorcery; it almost entirely consists in exorcising evil spirits, which are, they say, the sole authors of evil. They fear the devil and devilish imprecations; therefore to get away from their evil influences they wear on their persons amulets as talismans, and hang

[1] See Schiefner, Ueber das Bon-po Sutra, p. 6.

[2] J. R. A. S., vol. xvii. p. 396–399. See also his notice "On the Tribes of Northern Tibet," in his Essays, p. 80, *note.*

[3] The Tibetan title of this work is *Gtsang-ma klu hbum dkar-po,* or "The holy white nâga hundred thousand." Mem. de l'Acad. de St. Peters., xxviii., No. 1. See also E. Schlaginweit, Ueber der Bon-po Secte in Tibet.

[4] Klaproth, Description de Tibet, p. 97, 148. Sutra in 42 Sections, Intr., "The Bon-pa of China," &c. See on the influence of Buddhism on Taoism, Dr. Legge's Lectures on the Religions of China, p. 166–170 *et seq.*

on the walls of their houses branches of trees or skulls of animals." [1]

From the work translated by M. Schiefner we learn that the founder of the Bon-pa religion was Gshen-rabs, or Gshen-rabs mi-bo, called also excellent Mahâpurusha, glorious Mahâpurusha, "whose compassion shines forth like the rays of the sun. In his right hand he holds the iron hook of mercy, and in his left the mudra of equality. On his head is the mitra jewel." It may possibly be that this "iron hook of mercy," with which Gshen-rabs fishes people out of the ocean of transmigration, has something to do with the swastika cross, which is also a hooked cross. "In former times, as a bodhisattva," he says (f. 28[b]), "I have obtained perfect freedom by walking in the way of perfect charity." He took upon himself the task of teaching the holy law to all humanity in the ten regions of the thousand millions of continents, and for that purpose he took the form of the holy white nâga Hundred-thousand. He taught the four truths of Gshen-rabs, the five perfections—charity, morality, patience, steadfastness, and meditation. The five exoteric perfections—virtue, charity, prayer, means, and wisdom. The nine branches of the *gyung-drung* (cf. the nine *Bodhyanga*), &c.; in all the 142 rules of deliverance which "are the foundation and root for humanity." "Any one who masters them possesses all knowledge. For him who has faith this doctrine is the foundation of all knowledge. Shun evil, and learn to know this excellent law" (f. 9[b]).

"Form is the cause of transmigration, of desire, of misery, and by walking in the way of the five perfections, of charity, morality, patience, steadfastness, and meditation (the five Buddhist *paramitas*), one will leave behind the torrent of the misery of lust and subjection to transmigration."

"If any one lives in the perfection of charity, it is

[1] See Vivien de St. Martin, Année Geographique, 1873, p. 99, from a letter of M. Crabouiller to the *Missions Catholiques*.

happiness; if he enters the perfection of charity, it is happiness; if he abides in the perfection of charity, it is happiness; if he remains steadfastly in the perfection of charity, it is happiness. If any one is in possession of this idea, it is the heaven of Bon (*Bon-nyid*). If any one is in possession of this idea, it is the *gyung-drung* (*svasti*) of Bon. If any one is in possession of this idea, it is the wisdom of Bon. So it is in like manner with the perfection of morality, patience,[1] &c.

The first king of Tibet was *Gnya-khri btsan-po* (in Mongolian Seger Sandalitu), a son of King Prasenadjit of Kosala. He was elected by the twelve chiefs of the tribes of Southern and Central Tibet, who hoped by this means to put an end to the internecine wars which were ravaging the country. He took up his residence in the Yar-lung country[2] (*i.e.*, the Sanpu valley, south of Lhasa), and built a castle at Phyi-dbang-stag-stse, which became known as the U-bu bla-sgang or Ombo-blang-gang. He ruled according to law, and the kingdom was in happiness. He organised an army to protect his person, to quell troubles in the country, and to keep off foreign enemies. The five principal sages glorified (the king) in records in gold and turquoises (E. Schlaginweit, Könige von Tibet, p. 332–834). This last remark seems to confirm what the Chinese say about the Tibetans making use of a species of *quippus*. According to Sanang Setsen (p. 23),

[1] See Schiefner, *op. cit. passim.*

[2] The Yar-lung river empties into the Yaru Tsang-po a little east of Dhamda, and takes its rise in the Dalatang Tchukhang glaciers. Its course has been explored by Europeans. "*Yar-lung*," says Jaschke, Dict., *s. v.*, p. 508, "a large tributary of the Yang-tse-kyang, coming from the north, in Western China, east of the town of Bathang. Nevertheless Tibetan historians, from a partiality to old legends, describe it as flowing near the mountain of Yarlhasampo, which is a snowy mountain between Lhasa and the frontier of Bhotan, near which, according to tradition, the first king of Tibet, coming from India, first entered the country." Sarat Chandra Das, *op. cit.*, p. 214, says "that he erected the great palace of Yambu Lagari, on the site of which Lhasa was built in later days." This can hardly be made to agree with the statement that Srong btsan-sgam-po moved his capital to Lhasa. Though it is true that he says "my great-grandfather Totori snyan-shal resided in Lhasa, on the red mountain (Dmar-po-ri = Potala)." Sanang Setsen p. 325.

this king ascended the throne 313 B.C., but the *Grub-mthah sel-kyi me-long* (Sarat Chandra Das, J. B. A. S., vol. l. p. 213) says that he was born in the year 416 B.C.

This king and his six successors are known as the "seven celestial *Khri*." When they died their corpses were carried off to heaven. I think that we may find some analogy between these celestial rulers and the "twelve celestial sovereigns" of the *San hwang* of the Chinese, just as the next series of six Tibetan kings, who are known as the "six terrestrial *Legs*," resemble the Chinese "eleven terrestrial sovereigns."[1]

The fourth king among the six terrestrial Legs was *Spu-de gung-rgyal*, or "the tiger-haired king," in whose reign charcoal and wells were first made, iron, copper, and silver ore were smelted, and ploughs were introduced into the country (Schlaginweit, p. 835). We can imagine from this in what a savage state the Tibetans must have lived prior to this reign; and from the nature of these discoveries, as well as that of others appertaining to agriculture, it appears probable that they resulted from intercourse with the Chinese.

The eight kings who successively ruled after the six preceding ones are called "the eight terrestrial *Lde*," with which compare the nine human sovereigns of the third august line of the Chinese.

The next sovereign in succession was *Tho-tho-ri long-btsan*, who was born between 252 A.D. (Csoma) and 348 (Sanang Setsen).

His third successor was *Lha-tho-tho-ri snyen-bshal*, who was born about 347 A.D.[2] During this king's reign Buddhism first made its appearance in Tibet, and it is probable

[1] See "Annals of the Bamboo Books," i. 6. Shu-King, pt. v. bk. xxiii. p. 3 of Legge's edition.

[2] Csoma, Tib. Gram., p. 194, says "The Rgyal-rabs gsal-bai me-long puts Thothori's birth five hundred years after Gnya khri-btsan-po." This would place his birth towards the middle of the third century A.D. But as Tibetan history only counts four kings between him and Srong-btsan sgam-po's reign, which certainly commenced in the early part of the seventh century, this early date for Thothori's birth seems untenable. This Thothori is probably the

O

that the first missionaries in Tibet came from Nepal. This prince ascended the throne at the age of twenty in 367 A.D. (Sanang Setsen). While he was at Ombu in his eightieth year (427 A.D.), there fell from heaven into his palace a casket which contained a copy of the *Za-ma-thog bkod-pai mdo* (*Karandavyuha sûtra*), an almsbowl (*patra*), the six essential syllables (*Om maṇi padme hum*), a golden *tchaitya* and a clay image of the *chintamaṇi.* It is remarkable that the Karandavyuha sûtra, which does not appear to have been especially venerated in China or in India, was one of the favourite books of the Nepalese, and an object of great veneration in their country. This is one of the reasons which has led me to suggest that Buddhism first came to Tibet from Nepal. Another one is that when King Srong-btsan sgam-po wanted to propagate this religion in Tibet, he sent for religious works to Nepal, and, as we shall have occasion to relate farther on, he made his envoy translate this sûtra before returning to Tibet.

A few years after the apparition in Tibet of these objects of Buddhist worship, five strangers came to the king and explained their use and power; but this first attempt at conversion proved unsuccessful. The king, most likely imbued with national superstition too deep-set to be easily dispelled, had all kinds of honours and offerings made to the precious casket, as if it were a fetish, but did not embrace the religious ideas of the strangers, who departed from the country. Lhathothori lived a hundred and twenty years, dying consequently in 467 A.D. (Sanang Setsen).[1]

The fourth successor of Lhathothori was *Gnam-ri srong btsan*, who ascended the throne in the latter part of the

Fanni, son of Thufa Liluku of the Southern Liang dynasty (A.D. 397). See Bushell, *op. cit.*, p. 439.

[1] Csoma, *op. cit.*, p. 182, says that he died 371 A.D., and Sarat Chandra Das, *op. cit.*, p. 217, in 561 A.D. This last date is perhaps nearer the truth than the one I have adopted, but it is very difficult with the materials we have at our disposal to fix any date in Tibetan chronology. Csoma, Sanang Setsen, and Sarat Chandra Das, our chief authorities, do not agree on any one date. According

sixth century. During his reign the Tibetans got their first knowledge of medicine and mathematics (arithmetic) from China. The great salt-mine north of Lhasa, called the "great northern salt (mine"), or *Byang-gi tswa tchen-po,* which still supplies the greater part of Tibet, was discovered in his reign (Chandra Das, p. 217). Some of the tribes between Tibet and Nepal were also subdued. His son was the famous *Srong-btsan-sgam-po,* or, as he was called prior to the commencement of his reign, *Khri-ldan srong-btsan,* who was born about A.D. 600.[1]

This prince is known in Chinese history as *Ki-tsung-lun-tsan,* which appears to be a transcription of his name prior to his accession. Srong-btsan ascended the throne of Tibet in his thirteenth year, and the neighbouring states recognised him as their sovereign, so that his rule extended over the whole of Tibet, to the north as far as Khoten, which during his reign became subject to China, and to the east to China. To the south the frontiers were less well defined, and for several centuries the sovereigns of Tibet carried on a desultory warfare with the mountaineers who lived on the southern borders. One of Srong-btsan's first preoccupations appears to have been to form an alphabet for the Tibetan language. He dispatched a mission composed of seven nobles to India for that purpose; but they were unable to find a route, and so returned without having accomplished his design.[2] The king, however, did not relinquish his purpose, and in the third year of his reign (616 A.D.) he sent *Thoumi Sambhota,* son of Toumi Anu, together with sixteen companions, who, after having had to overcome great difficulties on their road, reached India. Thoumi Sambhota

to the Bodhimur (Sanang Setsen, p. 322), eighty-one years elapsed between the death of Thothori and the commencement of the reign of Gnam-ri. This puts the beginning of the latter's reign at A.D. 548.

[1] Csoma, *op. cit.*, p. 183, says that he was born 627 A.D. Sanang Setsen, p. 29, says 617 A.D. I have followed the indications furnished by the *Thang chu* which places Srong-btsan's first mission to China in 634.

[2] See Bodhimur in Sanang Setsen, p. 327.

went to Southern India, where he learnt the Indian characters from a brahman called *Li-byin* [1] and the pundit *Sinhaghosha*. He also made himself acquainted with the *nagari* characters then in use in Kachmere. He took twenty-four of these characters, with only slight alterations, and invented six new ones for sounds which did not exist in the Indian language, viz.: ཙ *tsa*, ཚ *t'sa*, ཛ *dza*, ཞ *zha*, ཟ *za*, and འ *ha*,[2] and with these he formed the Tibetan capital alphabet, or *Ka-phreng dbu-chan*.

Moreover, before returning to Tibet he translated the Karandavyuha sûtra, the Avalokitesvara sûtra, and a number of other works. He also carried back to Tibet a large collection of religious works.[3] In the Bstan-hygur, Mdo, vol. cxxiii., there is a work called *Sku-gzugs-kyi-mts'an-nyid*, by Aneibu (*i.e.*, son of Anu), and in vol. cxxiv. (*ngo*), two grammatical works attributed to *Thoumi Anu*(*i-bu* ?) or *Sambhota*, the *Sgrai bstan-bchos sum-chu-pa*; in Sanskrit, *Vyakaraṇamûla trinçadnâma* (f. 37–38), and the *Lung-du ston-pa stags-kyi hjug-pa*, or *Vyakaraṇa lingâvatara* (f. 38–40).

King Srong-btsan sgam-po soon became proficient in writing, and is credited with having translated several Buddhist works, among others the Karandavyuha sûtra, and with having composed instructions on horse-raising, verses and stories; but the chief work to which his name has remained attached is the *Maṇi bkhah-hbum*, or "The hundred thousand precious commandments,"[4] a glorification of Avalokitesvara and a history of his own life. I

[1] See E. Schlaginweit, *op. cit.*, p. 47, note 4. This name may be a corruption of *Lipikara*, "a scribe." The Bodhimur, *op. cit.*, p. 327, says that it was in Southern India. The same work, p. 49, says that the two teachers came to Tibet.

[2] They were made by differentiation of other Tibetan characters, the last one being, probably, a modification of the character *'a*. This sixth character denotes the pure vowel. See Jaschke, Tibetan Dictionary, *s. v.*

[3] See Bodhimur, *op. cit.*, p. 328.

[4] For an analysis of this work see E. Schlaginweit, Buddhism in Thibet, p. 84 *et seq.* I have not been able to examine this work, although we know of at least two copies of it in Europe, one in St. Petersburg, the other in the library of the French Institute, No. 58 of the Catalogue of Tibetan works.

have, however, been informed by Professor Wassilieff that this work is undoubtedly modern, and was written by order of the Dalaï lamas to maintain their authority.

In his twenty-second year the king married a Nepalese princess, a daughter of King Devala. She is known in Tibetan history as "the white Târa," and is said to have brought to Tibet many Buddhist images; but, if we refer to the Thang chu, and read of the innumerable raids which Srong-btsan made against China and the other neighbouring states, we may doubt whether he found much time to give to the study of Buddhism or to aid in spreading it within his domains.

Thai-tsung, the second emperor of the great Thang dynasty of China, who ascended the throne in 626 A.D., desiring doubtlessly to be on amicable terms with his warlike neighbour, sent a friendly mission to Srong-btsan, who in 634 sent a return mission and requested that the emperor would give him in marriage a princess of his family.[1] The emperor having refused, Srong-btsan got together a great army and advanced into Sse-tchuen, subduing all the tribes which opposed him, and which were allies of the Chinese. In 641 Thai-tsung granted Srong-btsan's request and gave him in marriage the princess *Wen-ch'eng*, of the imperial house, who is known in Tibetan history as *Za-kong*, or more generally *Kong-cho* (*i.e.*, *Kung-chu*, or "princess").

Although Tibetan works are unanimous in affirming that Buddhism was established in the country before the advent of Wen-ch'eng, her influence was unquestionably very great in helping to spread it; and we have the word of the Tibetan historian Buston for it that "in the commencement the Chinese *kechana* were the guides of the

[1] See Bushell, *op. cit.*, p. 443. The Tibetan account, as it has been preserved to us in the Bodhimur (p. 338) and the Maṇi bkah-hbum (Csoma, Tib. Gram., p. 196), although greatly distorted, is substantially the same as the Chinese. It speaks of three pretenders to the princess's hand,—the king of Magadha, the prince of the Stag-gzig (Persians), and the ruler of the Hur (Uigurs). See also Sarat Chandra Das, *op. cit.*, vol. I. p. 220.

Tibetans in Buddhism."[1] If these Chinese missionaries translated many Buddhist works into Tibetan, they must have been eliminated when the Indian pundits revised the translations in the ninth century, for there remain very few works in the Bkah-hgyur or Bstan-hgyur which are translations by Chinese Buddhists; nearly all are the work of well-known Indian pundits of the ninth and succeeding centuries.[2] On the other hand, we may perhaps argue that but few works were translated by Chinese because Buddhism was in their time in its infancy in Tibet, and that it was only in the eighth and ninth centuries that it became popular in that country; and I am inclined to think that this is the correct view of the question.

According to the Thang chu,[3] it was after Srong-btsan's marriage with the Chinese princess that he built a walled city and erected inside its walls a palace for her residence; which event I take to be the same as that chronicled by the Tibetans of his removing his capital to Lhasa and building the palace on Mount Dmar-po-ri.[4] "As the princess (Wen-ch'eng) disliked their custom of painting their faces red, Lung-tsan (Srong-btsan) ordered his people to put a stop to the practice, and it was no longer done.[5] He also discarded his felt and skins, put on brocade and silk, and gradually copied Chinese civilisation. He, moreover, sent the children of his chiefs and rich men to request admittance into the national schools

[1] See Wassilieff, Buddhism, p. 320.

[2] The Rgyal-rabs (E. Schlagintweit's edit., p. 49) says that the principal Buddhist teachers who came to Tibet in this reign were Kumâra from India, Çilamanju from Nepal, Tabuta and Ganuta from Kachmere, and Ha-chang (or Hwa-chang) Mahâdeva from China, and the *lotsavas* Thou-mi, Dharmagosha, and Çrivadjra.

[3] Bushell, *op. cit.*, p. 445.

[4] In 1640 the mountain became known as the Potala, from the name of the town at the mouth of the Indus where the Çakyas first resided (see p. 9), and a favourite residence of Avalokitesvara, the patron saint of Tibet. For a description of this celebrated place, see Markham's Tibet, p. 255; also a sketch of it on p. 256.

[5] Thang chu in Bushell, *op. cit.*, p. 445; also Wei thang thu chi (Klaproth's trans.), p. 27. Conf. what Huc says in the 2d vol. of his Souvenirs de Voyage about the habit of Tibetan women of Lhasa of painting their faces black.

to be taught the classics, and invited learned scholars from China to compose his official reports to the emperor."

Furthermore, he introduced into Tibet from China silkworms and mulberry-trees (Bodhimur, p. 341), and asked the emperor for persons knowing how to make wine, water-mills, for paper and ink; all of which were sent him with the calendar.[1]

Srong-btsan sgam-po established commercial relations with the Chinese, the Minak[2] (Tanguts), with Hindustan, Nepal (Bal-po), with the Hor (the *Hui-ho* of the Chinese?), and Guge (the modern Mngari Korsum), and extended his rule over half of Jambudvipa. A high tribunal was established to see that all laws were respected, to keep under the arrogance of the mighty, and to protect the oppressed. The authors of quarrels were whipped, the murderer was put to death, the thief was made to restore eight times the value of the stolen property, the adulterer was mutilated and exiled, liars and perjurers had their tongues torn out.[3]

The Nepalese and Chinese princesses had no children, so the king married four other women, one of whom, called *Khri cham,* belonging to one of the Mon tribes which lived among the mountains between Tibet and India, bore him a son, whom he called *Gung-ri gung-btsan.* He died in his eighteenth year, leaving a son called *Mang-srong mang-btsan,* who succeeded his grandfather in 650.

It was in the reign of Srong-btsan sgam-po that Tibet first became known among the Chinese as *Thu-fan*

[1] See Wei thang thu chi, *loc. cit.* Tibetan historians add that the Chinese princess introduced *nas-ch'ang* or whisky. That milk was for the first time made into butter and cheese, clay into pottery, and that the art of weaving was introduced. See Schlaginweit, *op. cit.*, p. 49. The beginning of the first cycle of sixty years among the Tibetans is A.D. 1026. See Csoma, Tib. Gram., p. 148. According to Bushell, *op. cit.*, p. 446, silkworms were introduced into Tibet during Kao-tsung's reign (649–684).

[2] *Minak* is generally supposed to have designated the Tangutans or the tribes of the Koko-nor basin. It is also used to designate the Manyak of Hodgson (Essays, ii. p. 66), who extend south of Ta-chien-lu at the present day.

[3] Bodhimur, *op. cit.*, p. 329. Conf. Bushell, *op. cit.*, p. 441.

(土番) or, as it ought to be read in this case, *Thu-po*,[1] which appears to be the transcription of two Tibetan words, *Thub-phod*, both of which mean "able, capable;" the last has been softened into *bod*,[2] and the final *d* dropped in the pronunciation. The Mongolian *Tubed* reproduces the Tibetan pronunciation very closely. Klaproth, however, and several other Orientalists after him, pretend that *Tubet* or *Tibet* is a word unknown among the people of that country, and that it is of Turkish origin. Mr. E. Colborne Baber, in his interesting "Travels and Researches in the Interior of China,"[3] (p. 98), says: "A Tibetan arriving in Ta-chien-lu from Lhassa, on being asked from what country he has come, will often reply, 'From *Teu Peu*,' meaning from 'High' or 'Upper Tibet.' Perhaps 'Teu Peu' is the source of our Tibet. . . . A native employs the expression 'Peu Lombo' ('Tibet country') to designate *en bloc* all the Tibetan-speaking nationalities, without intending to convey the least insinuation that they are subject to Lhassa." As a general rule, however, Tibet is called *Bod-yul*, or the "country of Bod," and in one work I have found it called "The country of the red-faced men" or, *Gdong-dmar-gyi-yul*.[4]

Mang-srong mang-btsan, or, as he is called in the Thang chu, *Ki-li pa-pu*, being very young at the time of his accession, the prime minister of his grandfather, called *Mkhar* or *Gar* by the Tibetans,[5] and *Lutungtsan*, "whose surname (tribal name) was *Chüshih*," by the Chinese, was made regent. The Tibetan history called Grub-mthah sel-kyi me-long (Sarat Chandra Das' trans.) says (p. 222) that in this reign the Chinese attacked the Tibetans; that

[1] See Bushell, *op. cit.*, p. 435.

[2] See A. Schiefner, Tibetische Studien in Mel. Asiat. de St. Petersb., i. 332, note.

[3] J. R. G. S., Supplementary Papers, vol. i. pt. 1.

[4] See p. 242. It must not be forgotten that the *Li-yul lo-rgyus-pa* is a translation. Buddhaghuya in his epistle to Khri-srong, calls him *Mgo-nag yongs-kyi rje*, "Lord of all the black-heads," an expression very common in the Chinese *King*.

[5] See Sarat Chandra Das, *op. cit.*, p. 220; Sanang Setsen, p. 338.

they were at first repulsed, but finally took Lhasa and burnt the palace on the Dmar-po hill. The Thang chu does not allude to these events, and we may doubt their veracity or suspect them of being interpolated.[1] This king died at the early age of twenty-seven in 679, and was succeeded by his son, called *Dgung-srong hdam* (or *hdu*) *rja*, or *Du-srong mang-po*, known in the Thang chu as *Kinushilung*. The extent of the kingdom of Tibet in this reign is described as follows in Tibetan histories: "In the time of this king (all the country) from the Royal river (*Yang tze*) in the east, to Shing kham in Bal-po (*Nepal*) in the south, to the far-off Kra-krag (tribes) of the Hor[2] in the north, Lo-bo tchum-rings (probably in Nepal), Sbal-ti (*Balti*), the plains of Nang god (or kod, part of *Balti*), and the lowlands of Shi-dkar (?) in the west, was under the rule of Tibet." During this reign tea was (first) brought to Tibet from China.

The king was killed on an expedition against Nepal, and was succeeded in 705 by his son *Khri-lde gtsug bstan mes Ag-ts'oms*, called in the Thang chu *Kilisotsan*, which name gives a quite correct pronunciation of the four first syllables of his Tibetan name. The king, who was a minor, concluded a treaty with the Chinese, with whom his father and grandfather had waged war during their whole reigns. He married the adopted daughter of the Emperor Tchang tsong. She was the daughter of Shuli, prince of Yung, and bore the title of Princess of Chin-

[1] This same work, p. 221, makes out Mang-srong to be the son of Srong-btsan, but with this the Thang chu (Bushell, *op. cit.*, p. 446) does not agree, nor does the Bod-himur, *op. cit.*, p. 347, which says that this king was the uncle of Srong-btsan; but on p. 343 it calls him his grandson.

[2] This word is said by Csoma to be used to designate the Turks. Schmidt, on the contrary, says that it meant the Mongols. M. Brian Hodgson, in his "Essay on the Tribes of Northern Tibet," says that "the *Horpa* occupy the western half of the region lying beyond the *Nyenchhen-thangla* range of mountains, and between it and the *Kwan leun* or *Kuenlin* chain, or Northern Tibet, and also a deal of Little Bukharia and of Songaria, where they are denominated *Kao-tse* by the Chinese, and *Dghurs* (as would seem) by themselves." The word *Hor* may be derived from the Chinese *Hui-ho*, which the Thang chu uses for these tribes.

ch'eng,[1] or *Chin-ch'eng kung-chu*, but, like her predecessor, the wife of Srong-btsan, she is generally called in Tibetan works "the princess," or *Kong-cho* (A.D. 710). This monarch contributed very materially to propagating and encouraging Buddhism. He built several monasteries, and invited a number of monks from Khoten, with a view of introducing monachism into Tibet, but failed, as nobody would come forward to take the vows of monkhood.[2] The *Suvarna prabhasa* sûtra and the *Karma çataka* were translated into Tibetan, the text of the first work having been obtained from China. The translations of these works which are at present in the Bkah-hgyur are of a later date, having been made during the reign of Ral-pachan.[3] Some emissaries whom he had sent to India to invite to Tibet two Indian pundits, Buddhaguhya and Buddhaçanti, committed to memory while in India five volumes of the Mahâyâna sûtras, which they subsequently reproduced in their own language.[4] This statement of the Tibetan historian is very interesting, and may help to throw some light on the somewhat obscure question of the discrepancies which wé find in different translations of a Buddhist text, such as the Buddhacharita of Açvaghosha, for example, of which the Chinese version has been made accessible through Mr. Beal's translation of it in vol. xix. of the "Sacred Books of the East." I have had occasion to compare the greater part of the Tibetan translation of this work with Mr. Beal's version, and was astonished to find that even in the case of this work, which is not a canonical one, the two translations could not have been made from the same original. If, then, we

[1] See Bushell, *op. cit.*, p. 456; Wei thang-thu-chi, p. 28; Bodhimur, *op. cit.*, p. 348, &c. This last work gives dates for all the events of Tibetan history, which are perfectly unacceptable. I have consequently adopted those supplied by the Chinese annals. With this exception, the events told by the Mongol and the Tibetan historians agree very well with those related in the Chinese works.

[2] Sarat Chandra Das, *op. cit.*, p. 223.

[3] See Bkah-hgyur, Rgyud xii. f. 208 *et seq.*, and Mdo xxvii. xxviii.

[4] Sarat Chandra Das, p. 223. A letter of Buddhaguhya addressed to Ag-ts'oms' son, Khri-srong, is in the Bstan-hgyur, vol. xciv. See p. 221.

find that Tibetan translations were made, not from written originals, but from ones which had been preserved orally for a long period before they were taken down in writing, we can understand how the early texts have become so changed, and in some cases distorted, in the Tibetan translations.

Ag-ts'oms had also translated from Chinese several works on medicine, astrology, and other works concerning religious ceremonies (magic ?).

He died in 755, leaving the throne to his son by Chin-ch'eng, called *Khri-srong lde bstan*, or, as he is known in Chinese annals, *Ki-li-tsan*.[1] He availed himself of the disturbed condition of the Chinese empire during the first years of Su-tsong's reign, and "daily encroached on the borders, and the citizens were either carried off and massacred, or wandered about to die in ditches, till, after the lapse of some years, all the country to the west of Feng-hsiang and to the north of Pin-chu belonged to the Fan barbarians, and several tens of chou were lost."[2] Tibetan rule extended over the greater part of Sse-tchuen and Yun-nan, and their troops in 763 took Ch'angan, the capital of China.

This sovereign is especially celebrated for the aid and protection he afforded Buddhist missionaries, to favour whom he did not even hesitate to persecute the followers of the national religion of Bon-po,—a strange measure for a follower of the most tolerant creed in the world! He called from India Çantarakshita;[3] but the teachings of this doctor met with so much opposition—from the Chinese Yôgatchariyas most likely—that he departed from Tibet,

[1] In the Chinese annals (Bushell, *op. cit.*, p. 439) we find a king called *Sohsilungliehtsan* between Khi-li-so-tsan (Ag-ts'om) and Khi-li-tsan (Khri-srong), whereas all Tibetan histories are unanimous in affirming that Khri-srong was son of the Chinese Princess Chin-ch'eng, and succeeded his father on the throne.

[2] See Bushell, *op. cit.*, p. 475.

[3] The Bstan-hgyur contains many works by this Atcharya, among others a commentary on the *Saty-advayavibhanga* of Djnanagarbha; commentaries on the *Madhyamika* theories, *Vâdangâyavritti pakshitâr-thâ*, &c.

but advised the king to invite Padma Sambhava of Udyana, who belonged to the Madhyamika school of Buddhism.[1] This celebrated teacher superintended the building of the famous Hsam-yas (pr. *Samye*) monastery at Lhasa, which is supposed to be a copy of the Nalanda monastery in Magadha.[2] I have not met with any works of his in the Tibetan Tripiṭaka, but his treatise on the Dhâraṇi doctrine is still extant. Ânanda, a Buddhist of Kachmere, also came to Tibet, where he taught the theories of the ten virtues, the eighteen dhatûs, and of the twelve nidanas. He also largely contributed to the increase of Buddhist works by the translations he made. In the Bstan-hgyar his name is of frequent occurrence, and in the sûtra section of that work there are two treatises by a Djaya Ânanda, who may possibly have been the same person. He must not, however, be confounded with the famous Ânandaçri, who came to Tibet in the ninth century. But by far the most popular teacher in Tibet during this reign, after Sambhava's death, was Kamalaçila. He at first met with a great deal of opposition from the Chinese *Hwa-shang* or *Ho-shang*,[3] the most influential of which was called Mahâyâna or Mahâdeva, perhaps the same as the *Hwa-shang zab-mo*, the author of two works in the Bstan-hgyur (Mdo, xxx., xxxiii.) Kamalaçila defeated him in a grand controversy held in the king's presence,[4] and from that time the Madhyamika doctrines were generally followed. Besides translating a great many Buddhist works into Tibetan, he wrote a large

[1] The followers of Padma Sambhava are called *Urgyen-pa*, an abbreviation for "disciples of the man from Udyana or Urgyen." They are chiefly found in the present day in those parts of Tibet which border on Nepal and India. See E. Schlaginweit, Buddhism in Tibet, p. 73.

[2] The pundit Nain Sing resided in this monastery when at Lhasa in 1874. He says that the images in it were of pure gold, and that it contains a large Buddhist library. See Markham's Tibet, p. cxx. It is south-east of Lhasa, and near the famous Dgah-ldan monastery. See Wei thang thu chi, p. 130.

[3] A Chinese expression for Buddhist monk. The word was transferred from the language of Khoten to Chinese. It corresponds to the Sanskrit Upadhyâya or "Master." See Edkins, Chinese Buddh., page 143.

[4] For all the particulars see the Bodhimur, *op. cit.*, p. 356–357.

number of treatises which are still extant in the Bstan-hgyur. In the sûtra section alone of that collection I have found seventeen works written by him. Taranatha says that he was a contemporary of King Çrimant Dharmapala of India (p. 171).

It was also during this monarch's reign that the Buddhist clergy was regularly reorganised; it received a firm constitution and was divided into classes.[1] Unfortunately I have not been able to find any notice on the habits of the Buddhist order in Tibet prior to this reorganisation, but it appears probable that they were much the same as in India, with only such material differences as a colder climate and national peculiarities required.

That Buddhism had not flourished in Tibet prior to this reign is made quite evident by a document preserved to us in the sûtra section of the Bstan-hgyur, vol. xciv. f. 387–391, and entitled "Epistle of the Master Buddhaghuya to the king of Tibet, Khri srong lde btsan, to his subjects and nobles." It is unfortunately not possible to give a translation of this interesting work here. I will only quote a few lines at the commencement of it. Buddhaghuya, after saluting the king, says: "Thou didst dispatch to India Vairotchana, Ska-ba-dpal brtsegs, Klu-yi rgyal mts'an, Ye-shes sde, Armandju,[2] and others, to whom thou didst intrust much wealth of gold and silver, to get the Dharma, increase the little religion that was in thy realm, and open the window which would let in the light on the darkness of Bod, and bring in its midst the life-giving waters. . . ." This suffices to show us that in the middle of the eighth century Tibet was hardly recognised as a Buddhist country.

[1] Bodhimur, p. 356.

[2] These are well-known names of *lotsavas* or interpreters, but they are more especially connected with following reigns. Buddhaghuya had been requested by the king to come to Tibet, but appears from his epistle not to have done so. He tells the king that "my body is wrinkled and I have no strength;" but wishing to serve him, he gave his two messengers this epistle, in which he described the duties of a king, of his nobles, and of the priesthood.

One of the first things which the Indian pundits and their Tibetan aides or *lotsavas* appear to have done was to determine the Tibetan equivalents of the innumerable Sanskrit words which have a special sense in Buddhist works, and to this we owe two excellent Sanskrit-Tibetan dictionaries, the larger one known as the *Mahâvyutpatti* or *Sgrabye-brag-du stogs-byed tchen-po*, and an abridged edition with the same title; both of these works are in the 124th vol. of the Mdo section of the Bstan-hgyur.

It is quite beyond the scope of this work to give even a list of the principal works which were made known in Tibet at this time. Besides the numerous canonical works which are mentioned in the index of the Bkah-hgyur and Bstan-hgyur as having been translated in the latter part of this sovereign's reign or in that of his successors, we must mention two due to King Khri srong lde btsan himself, and which have been preserved to us in the Mdo section of the Bstan-hgyur. One in the 12th and 13th vols. is a commentary on a work by Danshtasena, the other in vol. 124, entitled "Fifteen chapters of perfectly measured commandments," or *Bkah yang-dag-pai ts'ad-ma len bcho-lnga-pa*. Khri srong died in 786,[1] and was succeeded by his son *Mu-kri btsan-po* (or *Muni btsan-po*), who is known in Chinese as *Tsu-chih-hien*.

This young prince, of great promise, was poisoned by his mother after a reign of a year and nine months, and was succeeded by his brother *Mu-khri btsan-po*, or *Sad-na-legs*, as he is also called. Schlaginweit's Rgyal-rabs, however, erroneously calls this sovereign the son of the preceding one. He induced Kamalaçila, who had left Tibet,

[1] See Csoma's Chronological Tables, Tib. Gram., p. 183. It is impossible to make the statements of the Thang chu agree with the succession of kings as given by Tibetan and Mongolian writers, at least there exists great confusion in the names. I remark, *en passant*, that all Chinese works do not agree about events in Tibetan history; thus in the Wei-thang thu-chi, p. 127, we hear of a treaty concluded between Te-tsung and Khri-srong. But Te-tsung only became emperor of China in 799. It, moreover, calls them the uncle and the nephew. We know, however, that Khri-srong's uncle was the Emperor Tchong tsong (684–716).

to return and reside permanently in that country. He had many Buddhist works translated, and devoted much time to forming good interpreters for that purpose. According to Tibetan historians, he had a long and prosperous reign, and died at a good old age. On the other hand, the Thang chu says that he only reigned for six years, viz., 798–804.[1] As, however, he commenced his reign at a very early age, it appears improbable that the Chinese chronicles can be perfectly correct. Moreover, they do not mention any sovereign between the time of Mu-khri's death and the commencement of the reign of Ral-pa chan (Kolikotsu) in 816. But even supposing that he reigned until this date, we would still be unable to make the Chinese chronology agree with the Tibetan, for the latter say that Ral-pa-chan, his son and successor, was born between 846 and 864. Notwithstanding these discrepancies, we prefer, as we have said before, the dates furnished us by the Chinese, for we have no reasons for doubting their accuracy in general, and a great many for suspecting those given by the Tibetans or Mongols, who, as is well known, attach no importance to dates. We accept, therefore, provisionally 816 A.D. as the date of the commencement of the reign of *Ral-pa-chan* or Khri-ral, the Chinese *Kolikotsu*, second son of Mu-khri btsan-po.[2]

A few years after the commencement of his reign he concluded peace with China, and at Gungu Meru the Chinese and Tibetan monarchs had a temple erected, in which was placed a great stone slab upon which the sun and moon were represented, and where it was written that "whereas the sun and moon moved in the heavens in friendship, so would the two kingdoms do," &c.[3] He

[1] See Bushell, *op. cit.*, p. 439.

[2] Another fact which shows that the reigns of the two sovereigns who succeeded Khri-srong was short is that the *lotsavas* who figure in Khri-srong's reign are known to have assisted pundits who only came to Tibet in Ral-pa-chan's reign. Cf. the names of *lotsavas* given in Buddhagoshya's epistle with the list of translators in Schlaginweit's Rgyal-rabs.

[3] See Bodhimur, *op. cit.*, p. 361. For more particulars concerning this treaty see Bushell, *op. cit.*, p. 521, and rubbings of the inscription in the same work. Cf. also Schlaginweit, *op. cit.*, p. 58.

was the first Tibetan sovereign who appears to have paid any attention to the annals of his country; he had all the events of his reign recorded according to the Chinese system of chronology, and he adopted Chinese weights and measures.

The Chinese tell us that the Btsan-po, during his reign of about thirty years, was sick and unable to attend to business, and the government was in the hands of the chief ministers.[1] Tibetan history, however, attributes the profound peace which the land enjoyed during this reign to the sovereign's love of religion. He called from India the Buddhist pundits Djinamitra, Çrilendrabodhi,[2] Danaçîla, Pradjnavarman, Surendrabodhi, &c., who, assisted by the Tibetan interpreters Dpal brtsegs, Ye-shes-sde, Tchos-kyi rgyal-mts'an, &c., added an immense number of works to the Tibetan collection of Buddhist literature. Besides the canonical works which they translated, they made known to the Tibetans the works of Vasubandhu, of Aryadeva, Tchandrakirti, Nâgarjuna, Açvaghosha, &c., also numerous commentaries on the sacred works, such as the Pradjnaparamita in 100,000 verses, &c.[3] Moreover, they corrected all the translations made previously, and doubtlessly substituted their own work in place of the older ones; for, as I have remarked, nearly all the translations which are in the Tripiṭaka date from this reign. "They thoroughly revised the two collections of precepts (*i.e.*, the Bkah-hgyur and Bstan-hgyur) and the works on knowledge, and rearranged them."[4] And the work of these masters has never been superseded by the succeeding generations of doctors, for we may safely assert that at least half of the "two collections," as we know them, is

[1] Thang chu in Bushell, *op. cit.*, p. 522.

[2] The two first were disciples of Sthiramati. See Wassilieff, Taranatha, p. 320.

[3] Among other works translate at this time into Tibetan I note in the sûtra of the Bstan-hgyur a *ṭika* on the Saddharmapundarika, by Prithivibandhu from Ceylon (*Singagling*).

[4] See E. Schlaginweit, *op. cit.*, p. 69. The two collections may mean the Vinaya and Sûtra; the works on knowledge, the Abhidharma.

the labour of their hands. The mass of works on tantrik subjects was not known in their days, and was mostly added by Atisha and his disciples in the eleventh century; but I do not believe that any of the older canonical works (*i.e.*, of the Bkah-hgyur) are due to any translators posterior to this reign.

Ral-pa chan is said to have done much toward giving the priesthood a regular organisation and hierarchy. It appears probable that he was aided by Buddhist priests from some Northern Buddhist country, perhaps Khoten, although we read in the Sel-kyi me-long[1] "that he enforced the canonical regulations of India for the discipline and guidance of the clergy. . . . Thinking that the propagation of religion depended much upon the predominance of the clergy, he organised many classes of the priesthood. To each monk he assigned a small revenue, derived from five tenants." He established in monasteries three orders of auditors, meditation, and practice, and classes of elocution, controversy, and exegesis.[2] Ral-pa chan's elder brother, *Gtsang-ma*, entered the priesthood, became a famous teacher, and wrote several çastras; his younger brother was *Glang dar-ma* or *Dharma dbyig-dur btsan-po*, who succeeded him on the throne.

Ral-pa chan was so strict in enforcing the clerical laws that he stirred up a revolt, which was encouraged underhand by his brother Glang dar-ma, who was heir to the throne, the king having no children. The king was assassinated at the age of forty-eight (in 838), by two men who strangled him.[3] Glang dharma or *Tamo*, as he is called by the Chinese, is represented in the Thang chu as

[1] Sarat Chandra Das, *op. cit.*, p. 228.

[2] Bodhimur, *op. cit.*, p. 358. The same work, p. 49, says that Ral-pa chan killed the Emperor Tchao-tchong of the Thang, and took much spoil from China. This gives a good idea of the accuracy of Tibetan and Mongolian records. Tchao-tchong was assassinated in 904. See Gaubil's Histoire de la Dynastie Tang, Mem. Concernant les Chinois, xvi. p. 353.

[3] See Bushell, *op. cit.*, p. 439 and 522. Csoma, Tib. Gram., p. 183, gives A.D. 899 for Dharma's accession, and Sanang Setsen, p. 49, A.D. 902.

a man "fond of wine, a lover of field-sports, devoted to women, and, besides, cruel, tyrannical, and ungracious."[1] He appears to have persecuted Buddhism so effectually that all the lamas had to flee from Tibet.[2] The Rgyal-rabs says "that in this reign priests were made to use meat and intoxicating drinks. Whoever did not give up the way of living of the priesthood was banished. Some left of themselves, but those who remained had to take the drum and horn, and with bow and arrows follow the hounds in the chase. Some even had to learn the butcher's trade."[3] Glang Dharma was murdered, after a few years' reign,[4] by a Buddhist priest called *Dpal-gyi rdo-rje* or *Çrivadjra*, of Lha-lung.

He was succeeded by his son *Od-srung*, who may have had a hand in his murder, for the Rgyal-rabs says that as soon as he became king he consulted with Çrivadjra on the best means of re-establishing Buddhism. With this, however, Sanang Setsen does not agree, for he tells us that this prince reigned fifty-three years without the Law (p. 51).

He was succeeded by his son *Lde dpal hkhor btsan*, in whose reign eight copies of the sacred works were restored to the monasteries of Upper Mngari, and many persons were intent on re-establishing the supremacy of Buddhism. Nevertheless, with Glang Dharma the glory of Tibet as a nation vanished, and we learn from Ma-twan-lin that in the year 928 no one could be found at the court of China who could read a letter written in Tibetan which had been brought there by four priests.[5] The same work adds

[1] See Bushell, *op. cit.*, p. 522.

[2] Cf. the chap. of this work on the early history of Khoten, p. 243.

[3] See Schlaginweit, Könige von Tibet, p. 60.

[4] Acc. to Csoma, *loc. cit.*, he died in A.D. 900. Sanang Setsen, p. 49, says that he reigned twenty-three years, and was killed in 925. The Tang chu (Bushell, p. 439) places his death at about 842, which answers the requirements, for it would be difficult to believe that he extirpated Buddhism from Central Tibet in a year.

[5] Ma twan lin, Wen hien tung-khao, Kiuen, 335, p. 1, and Remusat, Recherches sur les Langues Tartares, p. 386.

that in the commencement of the tenth century the Tibetan nation was disunited, and formed tribes of a hundred or a thousand families.

In A.D. 1013 the Indian pundit *Dharmapâla* came to Tibet with several of his disciples, and in 1042 the famous *Atisha*, a native of Bengal, who is known in Tibet as *Jo-vo rje* or *Jo-vo rtishe,* also came there. He wrote a great number of works which may be found in the Bstan-hgyur, and translated many others, relating principally to tantrik theories and practices.

His principal disciple was the Tibetan *Bu-ston,* whose historical work called "The Jewel of the Manifestation of the Dharma," or *Tchos-hbyung rin-tchen,* is one of the principal authorities in Tibetan history. The good work was continued by *Marpa* and his disciple *Milaraspa,* whose missionary labours appear from his works to have been confined to those parts of Tibet which border on Nepal, and to the north of the *Mon* or hill tribes on the southern slope of the Himalayas. We know of two works by this missionary, or rather by his disciples, one an "Autobiography of the Reverend Lord Milaraspa," the other "The Hundred Thousand Songs of the Venerable Milaraspa." This last work, of which I possess a copy—due to the kindness of Mr. Wherry of Ludiana—is written in a language which offers many difficulties for one accustomed to the classical language of the translators of the ninth century, and we cannot help thinking that such radical differences in works which were composed at the most at an interval of three hundred years from each other, help to show that the so-called classical language of Tibetan works was an artificial one, which differed in its vocabulary, its phraseology, and its grammatical structure from the spoken language of the same period. The Buddhist pundits translated literally, and observed, as far as possible, the peculiarities of style of the originals. This is clearly shown by examining works translated into Tibetan from Indian dialects on the one hand, and from the language of Khoten or China on the other. The same stock phrases are rendered in an entirely different way, which is easily explained, however, by referring to the peculiar genius of each of these languages.

It is not my intention to follow the history of Buddhism in Tibet later than what we may call its Augustine era, which ended with Ral-pa chan; but I must call attention to the literature of this country, which is not so thoroughly Buddhistic as has been generally supposed. Without mentioning the numerous works on grammar, logic, and polity (*nîti*), which are contained in the Bstan-hgyur, and were translated from Sanskrit, we know of traslations of Kalidasa's Meghaḍuta, the Çatagâthâ of Vararutchi, the Aryâkosha of Ravigupta, &c., &c. Professor Wassilief says, "We know that besides the *Gesser Khan* the Tibetans have other poems; that they possess dramatical works, and have even translations of the Ramayana and of Galien."[1] Mr. Colborne Baber says, "Savants have allowed us to suppose that the Tibetans possess no literature but their Buddhist classics. A number of written poems, however, exist, couched in an elevated and special style; and, besides, there are collections of fairy tales and fables. . . . The epic mentioned above is styled *Djiung ling* (Moso Division), and is only one of three parts of a very extensive work known as the *Djriung-yi*, or 'Story Book.' . . . They have never published it, and even the manuscript of the three divisions cannot be obtained in a united form. But every Tibetan, or at least every native of Kham, who possesses any education, is able to recite or to chant passages of great length."[2]

[1] Mel. Asiat. de St. Petersb., ii. 574. We may add that in the 1st vol. of the *Bstod-ts'ogs* of the Bstan-hgyur is a translation of the Mahâbhârata.

[2] E. Colborne Baber, *op. cit.*, p. 88. I refer my readers to the work itself; the whole passage is highly interesting, but too long to be reproduced here. The word *Djriung-yi* may possibly be for *Rgyus-yi dpe*, "Book of Tales."

The library of the Academy of Science of St. Petersburg contains a number of Tibetan works on geography, such as the "Wonderful Story, a Description of the World,"[1] "A Geography of Tibet," &c., &c.

[1] See Mel. Asiat. de St. Petersb., i. 415, n. 445^b. No. 25,228 of the library of the University of St. Petersburg is a MS. geography of Tibet.

CHAPTER VIII.

THE EARLY HISTORY OF LI-YUL (KHOTEN).

THE country called in Tibetan works *Li-yul* has been diversely identified by Orientalists. Csoma takes it to be "a part of the Mongols' country;" Schiefner (*Tib. Lebens Çakyam.*, p. 327,[1] and *Taranatha*, p. 78) thinks that it was the Na-kie of Fah-Hien, Vakula of the Buddhist works; Wassilieff (*Buddh.*, p. 74) says that it was "the Buddhist countries north of Tibet, and particularly Khoten;" Sarat Chandra Das (*J. B. A. S.*, vol. i. p. 223) says, "Li-yul is identified with Nepal by the translators of *Kahgyur*. I have been able to ascertain that the ancient name of Nepal was Li-yul."[2]

The following pages will superabundantly demonstrate, I think, that Wassilieff's opinion is correct, and that by Li-yul we must understand Eastern Turkestan, or that region surrounded by the Kuen-lun, the Tung-lin, and the Thien-chan mountains, but more especially Khoten.

The Tibetan name of Li-yul admits of no other translation than "country of Li,"[3] which one might be inclined to compare with the modern Chinese name for Khoten, Ilichi. As to "Khoten," it is (as Abel Remusat has pointed out) a corrupt form of the Sanskrit Kusthana, the name of the first sovereign of Li, and which was after-

[1] P. 290 Schiefner says that it was in his eightieth year, shortly before his death, that the Buddha went to Li-yul.

[2] The only passage in Tibetan writers which places Li-yul south of Tibet is in E. Schlaginweit's *Könige von Tibet*, p. 850, and f. 21[a], line 4 of the text.

[3] Cf. Li-thang, name of a district in Eastern Tibet, or "Plain of Li." *Li* in Tibetan means "bell-metal." See Capt. Gill, "River of Golden Sands," 2d ed., p. 206.

wards applied to the country. The same remark holds good for the Chinese *Yu-thien.*

Fah-Hien and Huen Thsang, who visited Khoten in the fifth and seventh centuries respectively, have given us a glowing account of the power and splendour of Buddhism in that country at the time of their visits,[1] and the legends preserved to us by Huen Thsang are substantially the same as some of those which are contained in the Tibetan works which I have consulted for this notice. The same may be said of several passages translated by Abel Remusat in his *Histoire de la Ville de Khotan,* which work has enabled me to complete to a certain extent the Tibetan texts at my disposal.

The following notes are derived from four Tibetan works which are probably translations from works written in the language of Khoten or Djagatai Turki ; but as they are not followed by any colophon (with the exception of the fourth and least important one) giving the names of the translators, &c., it is quite impossible to decide this question. The titles of these works are as follows, classing them by their respective value :—1st, The Annals of Li-yul (*Li-yul-gyi Lo-rgyus-pa*) Bstan-hgyur, vol. 94 (*u*), fol. 426–444 ; 2d, The Prediction (*vyakarana*) of Li-yul (*Li-yul lung-bstan-pa*), do., fol. 420–425 ; 3d, The Prediction of the Arhat Sanghavardhana (*Dgra-bchom-pa Dge-hdun-hphel-gyi lung-bstan-pa*),[2] do., fol. 412–420 ; 4th, Goçringa Vyakarana (*Ri-glang-ru lung-bstan*) Bkah-hgyur, vol. 30, fol. 336–354. This last work, we are told, was translated into Tibetan from the language of Li-yul.

To translate these works literally would have proved very unsatisfactory, and would have given but an imperfect idea of their general value. I have, therefore, deemed it

[1] From a passage of Hoei-li's *Life of Huen Thsang* (p. 288) one might think that at the time of Huen Thsang's visit Khoten was a vassal of the Kao-tchang (Uigurs). P. 278 he says that there were a hundred convents in Khoten.

[2] Taranatha (p. 62) speaks of Sanghavardhana as living in Li-yul at the time when the Mletscha doctrine (Islamism) first made its appearance in India (p. 63).

best to give their contents in chronological order, and to use the past tense instead of the future, which occurs throughout these predictions or revelations (*vyakaranas*). Li-yul, like Tibet and a great many other Buddhist countries,[1] on adopting Buddhism, saw fit to recast nearly all its national traditions, and to consider the first king of the country, if not a descendant of the Çakyas, at least a son of one of the illustrious Buddhist monarchs of India. In the present case we are told that the founder of the kingdom of Khoten was a son of King Dharmâçoka.

In the days of the Buddha Kâçyapa, Li-yul was frequented by some Rishis, but they were badly treated by the people of the country, so they departed. Then the Nâgas were vexed, and from a dry country they converted Li-yul into a lake.[2] When Çakyamuni was in the world he visited Li-yul in company with a great number of his disciples. Then the Buddha Çakyamuni enveloped the whole of Li-yul, which was then a lake, with rays of light, and from out these rays there came 363 water-lilies, in the centre of each one of which was a lamp. Then these rays of light united into one, which circled around the lake, three times, going to the right, and then disappeared in the water.

After that the Blessed One said to the Arya Çariputra and to Vaiçravana, "Cut open this lake which is as black as the Samangasarana Parvata (?)." Then the Arya Çariputra made an opening for the lake (lit. pierced) with the butt end of his staff, and Vaiçravana (did likewise) with the end of his pike (*mdung*). After this the Blessed One remained for seven days for the weal of mankind in the

[1] Cf. Huen Thsang, *Si-yu-ki*, vol. i. p. 179, vol. ii. p. 77–210, &c.; also *Sanang Setsen*, p. 21.

[2] Cf. with this tradition that of the Chinese about the *Yok-chui* (Kingmill, *J. R. A. S.*, N.S., vol. xiv. p. 81 note). Cf. the history of the conversion of Kachmere and also what the Teshu-lama says in the history of Bod-yul he prepared for Warren Hastings (Markham's *Tibet*, p. 341). "When the divine Saki Sinha went to Kásí, this country of Bhot was an expanse of water. About one hundred years after this divine personage left his kingdom the water ran out through Bengal and the land was left dry." Cf. D. Wright's *History of Nepal*, p. 94 *et seq.*

temple to the left-hand side of the great figure on the Goçircha mountain, where there is now a little tchaitya.[1]

While there, Ananda asked the Blessed One about what had just occurred. Then the Buddha replied, "From the fact that Çariputra has pierced the lake with the butt-end of his staff and Vaiçravana with the end of his pike, the lake will hereafter dry up, and after my death it will be a land called Li-yul. In days to come, within the space which the light encircled three times there will be built a great city with five towers (?) (called) U-then."[2]—(Lo-rgyur, f. 426.)

King Adjatasatru having become king, reigned thirty-two years; five years after his accession to the throne[3] the Buddha passed away, after which he reigned twenty-seven years. From Adjatasatru to Dharmâçoka there were ten generations (of kings). Dharmâçoka was king fifty-four years.[4]—(Do., f. 429[b].)

Two hundred and thirty-four years after the death of the Buddha there was a king of India called Dharmâçoka, who, in the first place, had put to death many beings, but who had later on become a righteous man through the Arya, the Arhat Yaço (Yâças); he had confessed his sins

[1] Huen Thsang (xii. p. 229, Julien) calls this mountain Goçringa. I am inclined to think that Goçircha must be considered throughout our texts as synonymous with Goçringa. H. T. mentions (*loc. cit.*) the Buddha's prediction. See also Schiefner's *Tib. Lebens*, p. 290, where we have an abstract of our text. The mountain is there called Goçringa. It adds that the three hundred and sixty-three lilies represented the number of Buddhist *vihâras* which would be built in this country. Our text, for some unaccountable reason, omitted the explanation of this prodigy. The Goçringa mountain was 20 li south-west of the capital, Remusat (*op. cit.*, p. 43).

[2] The text has *Khar-lnga-ldan*, which I have supposed = *Mkhar-lnga-ldan*. U-then is probably a modern corruption of Kusthana.

[3] See also *Mahawanso*, p. 22 and 122. Cf. *Mahawanso*, p. 10, which says that the Buddha died in the eighth year of his reign.

[4] Perhaps this date alludes to the year in which Kusthana was born. If so, it places the date of Dharmâçoka's becoming king at 203 A.B. This is the only passage I have ever met with in Northern Buddhist works which speaks of Dharmâçoka as living later than a hundred years after the Buddha. See *Goçrin.*, vy. f. 340; *Hdzangs-blun*, p. 174, &c. The *Dipawansa*, vi. 1, says, "Two hundred and eighteen years after the Parinibbâna of the Sambuddha, Piyadarsana was anointed king." It moreover says (v. 110) that he reigned thirty-seven years.

and had vowed to sin no more. . . . At that time the lake had dried up, but Li-yul was uninhabited.—(Do., f. 428b.)

In the thirtieth year of Dharmâçoka's reign (f. 429b) his queen-consort brought forth a son. The soothsayers being summoned, declared that the child bore many marks of greatness, and that he would be king during his father's lifetime. Then the king, fearing that this child would dethrone him, gave orders that he should be abandoned; and the mother, apprehending that if the child were not abandoned the king would have him put to death, did as he had ordered. But when the child had been abandoned, there arose a breast on the earth from which he derived sustenance, so that he did not die. For this reason he was called Kusthana, or "breast of the earth." [1]—(F. 428b.)

Now at that time there lived a ruler of Rgya (China), a great Bôdhisattva. He had 999 sons, and had prayed to Vaiçravana that he might have one more to complete the thousand. Vaiçravana looked about, and perceiving that the little waif Kusthana was a promising person, he carried him off and made him the son of the ruler of Rgya. The ruler of Rgya brought him up, but one day while quarrelling with the children of (the king of) Rgya,

[1] Cf. *Huen Thsang*, xii. p. 224 *et seq.* His version of the story is easily made to agree with that of the text by suppressing the part which precedes Kusthana's arrival in China. In the *Goçrin.*, vy. f. 340, we read, "One hundred years after my nirvâṇa there will be a king of Rgya (China) called Tcha-yang, who will have a thousand sons, each one of which will go and seek a new country. Having heard of the Buddha's prediction about Li-yul and the Goçringa mountain in the west, he will implore of Vaiçravana another son to go settle in such a blessed land. He will give him a son of King Açoka of Jambudvipa, for whom a breast will have come out of the earth, for which reason he will be called 'Suckled from the earth' (*Sa-las nu-ma nu*), or Kusthana. When he shall have grown up, he will leave China with a great host, the great minister Hjang-cho, and others. He will come to this country (Li-yul), and will establish himself here, and the country will take its name of Kusthana from him. At that time a great many men will come here from Rgya-gar (India) desirous of becoming his subjects; they will be divided by a stream (?), and the great minister of China, Hjang-cho, and the others, will found many Chinese and Indian villages and towns, and there will King Kusthana become king over many families of men."

they said to Kusthana, "Thou art not the son of the sovereign of Rgya." He was distressed at that, and having ascertained from other men that this statement was borne out by the annals of Rgya, he asked the king to allow him to go seek his native land. The king answered, "Thou art my son; this is thy native land; be not thus distressed." Though he told him this many times, yet he hearkened not to him. Kusthana, the son of the ruler of Rgya, wanted a kingdom for himself; so he got together a host of 10,000 men, and with them went to seek a home in the west, and while thus employed he came to Me-skar of Li-yul.

Now Yaça[1] (Yâças), the minister of Râja Dharmâçoka from India, had so extended his family influence (?) that his relatives became obnoxious to the king; so he left the country with 7000 men, and sought a home to the west and to the east, and thus he came into the country below the river of U-then.[2]

Now it happened that two traders from among the followers of Kusthana ran away from Me-skar in their slippers (*ba-bu nang langs-nas*), and though there was no road, they came to To-la (*To-lar bros-pa-las*), and from the fact that they had walked (*hbrangs*) with slippers (*ba-beu*) on, this country received the name of *Ba-beu hbrangs-pai-sa* (or) *Hbru-so-lo-nya*. Then these men, seeing a goodly tract of uninhabited land, were pleased, and thought

[1] Yaças is also the name of the Buddhist who presided over the synod of Vaisâli (see p. 173). Açoka was also converted by a person of this name (see *Taranatha*, p. 25 *et seq.*) The personage of our text can hardly be the same as the latter.

[2] *U-then gyi shel-tchab.* This expression, *shel-tchab*, is of frequent occurrence in these works. Literally it means "crystal stream," but I am inclined to think it is a literal translation of a local term for river, particularly as it occurs in connection with streams which must have been distant from each other, and is also found under the form of *shel tchu.* This river may be the one alluded to by Huen Thsang (B. xii. p. 239) when he says, "About 100 li south-east of the capital there was a mighty river which ran to the north-west." This is apparently the Khoten-darya. Abel Remusat (*op. cit.*, p. 21) speaks of this same river as being 20 li from the city. It is called *Chu-tchi;* (p. 30) he gives its name as *Chu-pa.* The Tibetan word *U-then* corresponds very closely with the Mantchu name of Khoten, viz., *Ho-thian*, and with the Chinese, *Hu-tan.*

"This will do for a home for Prince Kusthana." After that they visited the encampment of the minister Yâças, which was south of where they were. Yâças having learned who was their chief, sent a message to Kusthana in Me-skar, saying, "Thou being of royal family and I a noble (lit. of ministerial family), let us here unite and establish ourselves in this district of U-then, and thou shalt be king and I minister." Then Kusthana came with all his followers and met Yâças in the country south (of the U-then river), which is called Hang-gu-jo.

The prince and the minister could not agree where to locate their home, and their hosts were divided, and so they commenced to quarrel; but Vaiçravana and Çrimahadevi having appeared to them, they built on that very spot a temple to each one of these gods, and from that day forth they honoured Vaiçravana and Çrimahadevi as the chief guardians of the realm.

So Kusthana and the minister Yâças were reconciled, and the first was made king (*rgyal-bu*) and the second minister. Then the Chinese (*Rgya*) followers of Prince Kusthana were established on the lower side of the U-then river, and in the upper part of Mdo me-skar and Skam-shed. The Indian followers of the minister Yâças were established on the upper bank of the river (*shel-tchu gong-ma*), and below Rgya and Kong-dzeng.[1] Between the two (? *shel-tchu dbus*) they settled, the Indians and Chinese indiscriminately. After that they built a fortress.

Li being a country half Chinese and half Indian, the dialect of the people (*hphral-skad*) is neither Indian nor Chinese (*i.e.*, a mixture of the two). The letters resemble closely those of India[2] (*Rgya*). The habits of the people are very similar to those of China. The religion and the sacred (*clerical*) language are very similar to those of India.—(Do., f. 429^{b}.)

[1] I am unable to give the modern names of any of these places.

[2] Cf. *Huen Thsang*, xii. p. 224. "The characters of their writing resemble those of India; their form has been slightly modified. . . . The spoken language differs from that of other kingdoms."

As to the early popular dialect of Li, it was taught to some cattle-herders of the Tsar-ma country by the Bôdhisattva Manjuçri, who had assumed human form and the name of Vairotchana, and from this place it spread over the rest of the country. The modern language was introduced by the Aryas (Buddhist missionaries).—(Lo-rgyus, f. 429[b].)

Kusthana was twelve years old when he gave up the princely estate of the ruler of Rgya and started out to seek his native land. He was aged nineteen when he founded (the kingdom) of Li-yul. Counting exactly from the nirvâṇa of the Buddha to the first king of Li-yul, 234 years had elapsed when Li-yul was founded.[1]—(Do., f. 430[a].)

One hundred and sixty-five years after the establishment of the kingdom of Li-yul, Vijayasambhava, son of Yeula, ascended the throne, and in the fifth year of his reign the Dharma was first introduced into Li-yul. This king was an incarnation of Maitreya and Manjuçri. Having assumed the form of a Bhikshu, the Arya Vairotchana, he came and dwelt in the Tsu-la grove, in the country of Tsar-ma. There he became the spiritual guide of the inhabitants of Li-yul, and taught the ignorant cattle-herders in the Li language, and invented (*bslabs*) the characters of Li. After this the Dharma appeared.—(Do., f. 430[a].) Then King Vijayasambhava built the great vihâra of Tsar-ma,[2] but he greatly longed for some relics of the body of the Tathâgata. So he asked the Arya how he could procure them, and he was told to build a tchaitya. When the vihâra was finished, Vairotchana told the king to sound the gaṇṭa and to invite the Aryas; but he replied,

[1] According to the *Dipawansa* (xv. p. 7), Mahinda introduced Buddhism into Ceylon 236 years after the nirvâṇa of the Buddha. The statement of our text does not agree with what is said (f. 428[b])—"234 years after the death of the Buddha lived Dharmâçoka," &c. (p. 233–234).

[2] Huen Thsang (xii. p. 227) says that this *vihâra* was about 10 li south of the capital. He adds that Vâirotchana came from Kachmere. Abel Remusat (*op. cit.*, pp. 20, 29) speaks of the Thsan-ma or Tsan-ma temple, evidently the same as the Tsar-ma of the text.

"May I never sound the gaṇṭa unless the Tathâgata comes here and gives me a gaṇṭa!" Immediately Vairotchana assumed the appearance of the Tathâgata, and after having taught like the Tathâgata sixty great çravakas at Tsar-ma, he gave King Vijayasambhava a gaṇṭa, and the king sounded it without ceasing for seven days.—(Do., f. 431[a].) After that Vairotchana invited the Nâga king Hu-lor[1] to bring from Kashmere a tchaitya which contained corporal relics of the seven Tathâgatas. It came through the air, and is at present at T'sar-ma. This tchaitya is in the Gandhakuta, and is surrounded by a halo.

During the seven following reigns no more vihâras were built, but after that (*i.e.*, his eighth successor) was King Vijayavirya, an incarnation of the Bôdhisattva Maitreya (f. 431[b]). One day while looking out of Srog-mkhar he perceived a light brilliant as gold and silver at the spot where now stands the Hgum-stir tchaitya. Then he learned that the Buddha had foretold that at that spot a vihâra would be built. Then the king called to his presence the Buddhist Buddhadhuta, and having made him his spiritual adviser, ordered him to direct the building of the Hgum-stir vihâra. Later on this king built on the Oxhead Mountain (*Goçircha*) the Hgen-to-shan vihâra.[2]—(Do., f. 432[a].) During the two following reigns no more vihâras were built. After that (*i.e.*, his third successor) reigned King Vijayajaya, who married the daughter of the ruler of Rgya (*China*), Princess Pu-nye-shar. Desiring to introduce silkworms[3] into Li-yul, she commenced raising some at Ma-dza; but the ministers (of China) having led the king to believe that these worms would become venomous snakes which would ravage the land, he

[1] In *Dul-va* (xi. f. 687[b]) we hear of this nâga as Hulunta, who was subdued by Madhyantika. See p. 167.

[2] This seems to be a corrupt form of the Sanskrit Goçircha or Goçringa.

[3] Huen Thsang (xii. p. 238) gives another version of this story. Remusat (*op. cit.*, p. 53) substantially reproduces it, but gives the Chinese princess's name as Lou-tche.

gave orders to have the snake-raising house (*sbrul gso-bai khar*) burnt down. The queen, however, managed to save some and reared them secretly. When after a time she had (thus) procured Ke-tcher silk and raw silk (*srin-bal*), she (had it made up and) put on silk and *men-dri*[1] (garments). Then she showed them to the king, and explained the whole thing to him, and he greatly regretted what he had done. He called from India the Bhikshu Sanghagosha and made him his spiritual adviser (*Kalyanamitra*), and to atone for his wickedness in having destroyed the greater part of the silkworms, he built the Po-ta-rya and Ma-dza tchaityas and a great vihâra (or, the tchaitya and the great vihâra of Ma-dza).[2]—(Lo-rgyur, f. 433[a].)

This king had three sons. The eldest entered the Buddhist order, took the name of Dharmânanda, and went to India. The second son became king under the name of Vijayadharma. When Dharmânanda returned to Li-yul, he introduced into the country the doctrines of the Mahâsanghika school, and was the spiritual adviser of the king. —(Do., f. 433[b].) Eight vihâras were occupied in Skamshid by sanghas of the Mahâsanghika school.

He was succeeded by his younger brother, Hdon-hdros, who called from India the venerable Mantasidhi (*sic*) to build a vihâra for him. He introduced into Li-yul the doctrine of the Sârvastivâdina school of the Hinayana.—(Do., f. 435[a].) He built the Sang-tir vihâra. This king had as his wife a princess from Rgya called Sho-rgya.—(F. 441[a].)

His successor was Vijayadharma's son, Vijayasimha, in whose reign the king of Ga-hjag waged war against

[1] Jäschke says that *men-hri*, or, as we have it, *men-dri*, is "a kind of fur (?)." I am inclined to think from the passage of the text that it may possibly have some connection with the *munga* silk of Assam (*Anthera Assama*). Perhaps it may be a local term for "satin."

[2] Huen Thsang (*op. cit.*, p. 237) says that this *vihâra* was 50 or 60 li south of the capital, and that it was called Lu-che-seng-kia-lan. Julien is unable to explain this term, but by referring to what Remusat says, "it means the *sanghârâma* of Lu-che."

Li-yul. He was defeated by Vijayasimha, and to save his life adopted Buddhism.—(F. 436[b].)

This king married a daughter of the king of Ga-hjag, the princess A-lyo-hjah, who helped to spread Buddhism in Shu-lik.[1]—(F. 443[a].)

Vijayasimha was succeeded by Vijayakirti, an incarnation of Manjuçri. This king, together with the king of Kanika,[2] the king of Gu-zan, &c., led his army into India, and having overthrown the city of So-kid, he obtained a great quantity of çariras, which he placed in the vihâra of Phro-nyo, which he had built.—(Do., f. 436[b].)

In the time of the fourteenth sovereign, Vijayakirti, foreign invaders overran and ruled the land, and greatly vexed the people. After this, A-no-shos of Drug-gu brought an army into Li-yul, and burnt down the greater part of the vihâras on the south side (lit. lower side) of the Hgen-to-shan (Goçircha).—(Do., 437[b].) The population decreased, and no new vihâras were built.

Fifteen hundred years after the death of the Blessed Çakyamuni, the king of Li-yul was an unbeliever who persecuted the clergy, and the people lost their faith in the Triratna, and no longer gave alms to the Bhikshus, who had to work in the fields and gardens.—(Sangh., vy. f. 413[b].)

Li-yul, Shu-lik, An-se,[3] &c., were consequently visited by all kinds of calamities. Each succeeding year was worse than the previous one; wars and diseases raged,

[1] Taranatha (p. 63) says that Shulik was this side (east) of Tukhara. May not this word have some connection with the Su-le (Kashgar) of the Chinese?

[2] Perhaps this is King Kanishka, who commenced to reign A.D. 75. His rule extended over Yarkand and Kokan. As to the king of Gu-zan, I am unable to identify this name. He was probably some petty monarch whose kingdom was near that of Khoten.

[3] These appear to be neighbouring countries to Li-yul, most likely to the west of it. An-se may possibly be the same as the Chinese An-hsi. The Chinese governor-general of Pohuan was styled Anhsi Tuhufu, and he ruled over Khoten (Yu-tien), Kashgar, (Su-le), and Siri-yeh. These four military governments were collectively called the four *chen*. See Bushell, *J. R. A. S.*, N.S., vol. xii. p. 529.

untimely winds and rains befell them. Unseasonable frosts, insects, birds, and mice devastated their fields, &c. Unbelieving ministers in Li-yul violently took possession of those abodes of the Bhikshus which former believing monarchs had erected. Then the Bhikshus assembled in the Ts'ar-ma vihâra, in which the Dharma had first been preached in this country, and after confession, on the evening of the fifteenth day of the last spring month, they there decided to leave the country.[1]—(Do., f. 414[b].) They resolved to turn their steps toward Bod-yul (Tibet), for they had heard that the Triratna was honoured in that land. So they got together during the season of vas provisions for their journey and means of transport (*khur-khal*). When vas was over, they departed, and having reached the vicinity of the Ye-shes-ri vihâra, they found in the ruins of an old tchaitya a great golden vase full of pearls.[2] They exchanged its contents for grain, which sufficed for their wants during the three winter months. Having crossed the river (*shel-tchu*)[3] they came to the highlands, where the inhabitants supplied them with food.—(Sang. vy., f. 415.) After leaving them behind, the lowlanders (*yul-mi smed-pa-rnams*) invited them to the Chang vihâra, and entertained them during seven days. While there, the Nâgas disclosed to them a golden vase full of gold-dust, which enabled the order to procure food for the spring months.

From the Ka-sar vihâra, where they spent seven days, they took the road to Me-skar. At the Stong-nya vihara, Vaiçravana and Çrimahâdevi transformed them-

[1] Sang. vy., f. 420[b], says that the Dharma vanished from Li-yul 120 years after the prediction had been made by Sanghavardana. Li-yul. vy., f. 420[b], says that he lived in the time of Vigayakirti, king of Li-yul, and as it is said that the Bhikshus arrived in Bod-yul in the reign of the seventh successor of Srong-btsan-sgam-po, we infer that this persecution of Buddhism in Li-yul occurred in the latter part of the ninth century A.D.

[2] The Li-yul. vy., f. 422[a], says that the king of the wind, who was a believer, threw down the cairn and disclosed its contents to them.

[3] Or, as we find it elsewhere, "the river of U-then (Khoten)."

selves into a man and woman of that country,[1] and entertained the clergy for a fortnight; and when they departed, Çrimahâdevi gave them a bag (*phur-rung*) full of gold pieces.—(Li-yul. vy., f. 422[a].)

Little by little they drew nigh to the country of the red-faced men (*Gdong-dmar-gyi-yul* = Tibet), but coming to a cross-road, they got into a lateral valley and lost their way. Then Vaiçravana assumed the appearance of a loaded white yak and the Bhikshus followed after it, thinking that it would take them to where men lived. He led them for four or five days, until they reached Ts'al-byi, in the red-faced men's country (Tibet), and then he vanished.—(Li-yul. vy., f. 422[a].) The inhabitants sent word to the king of Bod-yul that a great crowd of Bhikshus from Li-yul had arrived there, and they asked what was to be done.—(Sang. vy., f. 416[a].)

At that time reigned in Bod-yul the seventh successor of the king in whose reign Buddhism had been introduced into the country.[2] This king had taken as his wife a daughter of the sovereign of Rgya (China), and (this princess), Kong-cho by name, had come to the red-faced men's country (Tibet) with six hundred attendants. She was a fervent believer (in Buddhism), as was also the king of Tibet.—(Li-yul. vy., f. 421[b].)

When the queen heard of the presence of the Bhikshus of Li-yul at Ts'al-byi, she requested the king to allow her

[1] Of the steppe (*hbrog-mi-pho*), says the Sangh. vy., f. 415[b].

[2] This passage cannot be easily explained, for Ral-pa-chan, who is evidently the monarch alluded to, is always represented as a fervent Buddhist. The expulsion of the Bhikshus from Bod took place under his successor, Glang-dharma, whose short reign began A.D. 899. Sarat Chandra Das (*J. B. A. S.*, vol. l. p. 229) says that he ascended the throne between 908 and 914 A.D. What Sarat Chandra Das says, *loc. cit.*, about Glang-dharma reviling the first Chinese princess agrees very well with our text. Although it appears from Tibetan history that Ral-pa-chan introduced many Chinese customs into Tibet, I find it nowhere mentioned that he married a Chinese princess. The *Wei-thang-thu-chi* (Klaproth's trans., p 28) says that Khi-li-son-tsan (Khri-srong-lde-btsan) married the daughter of Li-jung, king of Yung. The word *kong-cho* is only a Chinese title for "royal princess." The full title of Khri-srong's wife was Kin-tching Kung-chu. Srong-btsan-sgam-po's wife is also called Kong-cho.

to get together riding-beasts (*bdzon*), clothing, &c., for the congregation, and to invite them (to their capital). The king consented, and when the Bhikshus arrived he had built for them seven vihâras.

Now the Bhikshus of An-tse, of Gus-tik, of Par-mkhan-pa and of Shu-lik were also greatly afflicted; so they set out for the Bru-sha country, and there also repaired the Bhikshus of Tokara and of Ka-tche (Kachmere), who were persecuted by unbelievers. When they had all come to Bru-sha,[1] they heard of the vihâras which were being built in Bod-yul, and that the king was a Bodhisattva who honoured the Triratna and made much of the images (*ri-mo tcher-byed-pa*); so they started out for Bod rejoicing, and they all lived there for three years in peace and plenty. At the expiration of this time there appeared a sore (*hbrum*) on the breast of the queen, and she, feeling that she was dying, besought the king to allow her to confer on the Triratna all her property; and to this the king consented. This epidemic of smallpox (*hbrum nad*) carried off the minister (*Dzang-blan-po*[2]) of Bod, his son, and a great multitude of people. Then the Dzang-blon of Bod-yul were angered and said to the king, "Before all these vagabonds came here our country was happy and prosperous, but now every kind of misfortune has come upon us. Kong-cho has died, so has the Dzang-blon-po, his son, &c. Let these Bhikshus be turned out of the country." So the king gave orders that not a single Bhikshu should remain in Bod-yul.—(Sang. vy., f. 417[a]; Li-yul. vy., f. 423[a].)

Then all the Bhikshus started out for Mahâgandhara[3] in the west, and it being then a time of war and trouble, the

[1] *Bru-dza* or *Bru-sha* is the name of a country west of Tibet, bordering on Persia. Jäschke, s. v.; E. Schlaginweit, *Könige von Tibet*, p. 55.

[2] "*Dzang-blon*" seems to be a kind of title given to a minister (or magistrate). Jaschke, s. v. I think it corresponds with the modern *Bkah-blon* (pr. Kalon).

[3] Gandhâra, the capital of which was Puruchapura, the modern Peshawar.

Bhikshus of India also started for Gandhara, so that down to the Ganges there was an end of following the Dharma.

Then the troops of Bod-yul hurried in pursuit of the Bhikshus, who came to a great lake. Then the Nâga king Elâpatra (*E-la-hdab*)[1] took the shape of an old man and went to the Bhikshus and asked them where they were going. "We have lost in an unbelieving land all means of subsistence," they replied, "and we are now on our way to Gandhara, where we hope to find the necessaries of life." Elâpatra asked them what provisions they had, and when they had accurately counted all that they had among them, they told him that they had provisions for fifteen days. "From here to Gandhara," replied the Nâga king, "requires forty-five days, and you must go around this lake; how can you manage with fifteen days' provisions? Moreover, the intervening country is very elevated, thickly wooded, infested with wild beasts, venomous serpents, and brigands." Then the Bhikshus, both male and female, gave way to grief, for they thought that their last hour was nigh.

But Elâpatra, kneeling down before them, said, "Weep not; for the sangha I will sacrifice my life; I will bridge this lake over with my body." Then he took the shape of an enormous serpent, and made a bridge wide enough for five waggons to pass abreast, with the fore part of his body encircling the top of a mountain in Bod, and with his tail wrapped around the top of a mountain in Gandhara. The fugitive Bhikshus passed the lake on this bridge, but the skin on the back of the Nâga king was torn off by the hoofs of the cattle and the men's feet, so that it made a great wound, from which flowed matter and blood, and any of the men or beasts who fell into (this wound) died from it. When every one had passed over, the Nâga king died, and the

[1] The Nâga had apparently changed his residence since days of old. When the Buddha was living he resided at Takchaçilâ. See the episode of the conversion of Katyayana. *Dulva*, xi. f. 118 *et seq.*, and p. 46.

lake drying up, his remains stayed there like unto a mountain. In days to come, the Buddha Maitreya will come that way with his 500 disciples. Elâpatra having finished his series of births, will then obtain the reward of Arhatship.—(Sang. vy., f. 418ᵃ.)

Now when the Bhikshus reached the land of Gandhara, they stayed there two years (in peace). In the third year the believing king of the country died, and his kingdom was divided between his two sons, one a believer, the other a follower of the Tirthikas, and they waged war against each other. Then a thousand brave, bold, resolute Çramaneras attacked the unbelieving king and his army, defeated him, and gave the throne to the believing prince.[1] After a reign of five months, this prince was murdered by the thousand Çramaneras, and one of the Bhikshus was made king, and he ruled for two years.—(Sang. vy., f. 418ᵇ.)

At the end of this time, the nobles and people of Gandhara took up arms, put the king to death, and killed all the Bhikshus living in Gandhara, and those who fled to Mid-India (Madhyadeça) alone were saved.—(Do., f. 418ᵇ.)[2]

At this time there lived three powerful monarchs, one in the west (the king of the Stag-gzig—Persians), one in the north (and one in the south ?).[3] These three kings

[1] The *Li-yul. vy.* does not mention this episode.

[2] The *Li-yul. vy.*, f. 424ᵃ, says, "All the Bhikshus fled, and the Dharma was extinct in Gandhara."

[3] The text of the *Sang. vy.*, f. 418ᵇ, is so obscure, and possibly corrupt, that I can make nothing out of it. That of the *Li-yul. vy.*, f. 424ᵃ, only mentions two kings, but in the next line it alludes to three. Wassilieff in *Taranatha*, p. 307, gives an account of this persecution, taken from the second Chinese version of Açôka's life. Speaking of these three kings, he says, "Dann werden drei böse Könige im S. Schi Kiue, im W. Po-lo, im Süden Jan-u-na erscheinen," &c. I think that "im S" is a mistake for "im W." As the passage of the *Sang. vy.* may prove intelligible to some of my readers, I reproduce it: "*Srig ni la-sogs-pa dzig-gis rgyal-po ni stag-gzig-gis rgyal-po byed-par-hygur. Drug-gu* (?) *rus ma-ts'ogs-du-mai rgyal-po ni drug-gus byed-par hgyur. Gdzan mang-po dzig-gis rgyal-po ni bod* (?) *ki-rgyal-pos byed par hgyur-te.*" May not *Stag-gzig* be the same as the Heiyi Tashih, "black-robed Arabs or Abassides" of the Chinese?

were allies, and they had a brave and valorous army of 300,000 men (200,000 says Li-yul vy.) with which they conquered every country (of India?) with the exception of Mid-India. They put to death many people, and laid waste the country. Then these three kings took council and led their armies to Madhyadeça (Mid-India) (or, as the Li-yul. vy. says, into Kauçambî). Now at that time there reigned over Kauçambî a king called Durdarça (*? Bzod-dkah*), at the time of whose birth there had fallen a rain of blood, and on whose breast was marked two hands red as if smeared with blood. This king had 500 ministers and an army of 200,000 men. And when the king of Stag-gzig (Persia) and the others turned their forces against him, Durdarça went towards them with his army, and after having fought them for three months, he put them to rout.—(Sang. vy., f. 419[a].)

Durdarça, wishing to atone for all his sins, invited from Paṭaliputra a Bhikshu called Çirçaka,[1] a man learned in the Tripitaka, and having confessed his sins, the Bhikshu told him that as a penance he must entertain all the Bhikshus of Jambudvîpa, and daily confess his sins before them. Then the king invited all the Bhikshus throughout India, and they, rejoicing, gathered together in Kauçambî to the number of 200,000. On the night of the fifteenth day of the month, the Bhikshus assembled together for confession, and they called upon the Bhikshu Çirçaka to repeat the Pratimoksha Sûtra. But he answered them, "What can the Pratimoksha do for you? (*khyed-rnams-la so-sor thar pas chi dzig bya*). What is the good of a looking-glass for a man whose nose and ears are cut off?" (*mi sna dang rna-ba bchad-pa-la me-long-gi chi-dzig bya*). Then an Arhat called Surata arose and cried with a lion's voice, "Bhikshu Çirçaka,

[1] Wassilieff, *loc. cit.*, calls the Bhikshu Tripitaka-Bahuçrutiya; the Arhat Sudhara, the disciple of Bahuçrutiya, he calls I-kia-tu (? Angada). He does not give the name of the disciple of Sudhara.

why speak you thus? I am whole as the Sugata ordained (that a Bhikshu must be)."

Then the Bhikshu Çirçaka was filled with shame; but Agnavi, the disciple of Çirçaka, said to the Arhat, "How dare you speak thus to such an exalted personage as my master?" and enraged, he seized a door-bar with both hands, and killed the Arhat. Karata, the Arhat's disciple, seeing his master killed, inflamed with anger, took a stick, and with it killed the Bhikshu Çirçaka. All the Bhikshus became enraged, and dividing into two camps, they killed each other.

And when it was dawn, the king saw all the Bhikshus lying dead, and his eyes were obscured with tears. Then he rushed to the vihâra, calling the names of the Arhat, and of the Bhikshu Tripitaka (Çirçaka). He pressed their corpses to his breast, crying, "Alas, Tripitaka! thou didst possess the treasure of the Dharma of the Sugata! Alas, Arhat! thou didst know the commandments of the Sugata, and here you lie dead!"—(Sang. vy., f. 420ᵃ.)

And as the shades of night were closing around the blessed law,[1] the Trayastrimcat Dêvas were defeated by the Asuras, and fled, and transmigrating, they passed among the Asandjasattva Dêvas (*Rtag-tu myos-po*).—(Do., f. 420ᵃ.)

We must not infer from the preceding narrative that Buddhism became extinct in Li-yul at the time of this persecution, for we learn from Remusat (*Hist. de la Ville de Khoten*, p. 80) that in the tenth century (940 A.D.) the people worshipped the spirits, but principally the Buddha.

In the fifth year, Khian-te (A.D. 967), Chen-ming

[1] This extinction of Buddhism in India occurred in the latter part of the ninth century (according to our text). Cf. with the above account of the extinction of Buddhism in Magadha, *Taranatha*, p. 193, (255 of the trans.), also *Manjuçri—mulatantra*, f. 462.

(Yâças ?) and Chen-fa (Saddharma ?), priests of Yu-thien, came to court (p. 85). These were evidently Buddhist Bhikshus.

In the time of the Yuen dynasty, however, Buddhism had been stamped out of the country by Islamism.[1]

[1] On the present state of Khoten, see W. H. Johnson's report of a journey to Ilichi, *J. R. G. S.*, vol. xxxvii. pp. 1–47.

APPENDIX.

I.

Extracts from Bhagavatî XV. on the Intercourse between Mahâvîra (*i.e.*, Nigantha Nataputta) and Gosâla Mankhaliputta.

By Dr. Ernst Leumann.

At the time when Gosâla Mankhaliputta had finished his twenty-fourth year of ascetism, he lived in the pottery bazar of the potter's wife Hâlâhalâ in Sâvatthî, and taught the âjîviya doctrines. Once the six Disâcarâs came to him, namely, Sâna, Kalanda, Kaṇiyâra, Attheda, Aggivesâyaṇa, Ajjaṇa Gomâyuputta. They had made extracts according to their own ideas from the ten (canonical) books, viz., from the eight parts [1] contained in the Pûvas, and from the two Mârgas,[2] and they confided themselves to Gosâla's guidance.

He himself took from the (above) eightfold Mahânimitta doctrine six principles :—(1.) Obtainment ; (2.) Non-obtainment ; (3.) Pleasure ; (4.) Pain ; (5.) Life ; (6.) Death.

Gosâla, in teaching this doctrine, believed himself to be a Jina. When this became known, the oldest pupil of Mahâvîra, named Indabhûti, came and asked his teacher about the origin and life of Gosâla.

[1] These are, according to the commentary Abhayadeva, *Divyam autpâtam ântarikshaṃ bhaumam ângaṃ svaraṃ lakshaṇaṃ vyañjanaṃ.* Since these eight mahâ-nimittas are also mentioned in the Bhadrabâhu inscription published by Mr. Lewis Rice (Ind. Ant. iii.), they probably also formed part of the original Jaina canon, although no trace of them can be found in the present one.

[2] *Gîtamârga - nṛttamârga - lakshaṇan.* Comment.

Mahâvîra said, "It is an error on the part of Gosâla if he believes himself to be a Jina; he is the son of a beggar (*mankha*) named Mankhali and of his wife Bhaddâ; he was born in a cow-stable (*go-sâlâ*), and was consequently called Gosâla. He himself became a beggar like his father.

"When, after having passed thirty years in my home up to the death of my parents,[1] I left it to begin a religious mendicant's life, I happened to come to Râjagriha in the second year, and to take upon me the vow of a half-month's fast in the Tantuvâya-sâlâ near the town. At that time Gosâla came also to the same place as a simple beggar.[2]

"When, later on, it happened that the citizen Vijaya, because I had taken my alms at his door, obtained great happiness, Gosâla reverently approached me with the desire to become my disciple; but I declined, and soon after I departed for Kollâga, where I took my alms at the door of the Brahman Bahula. Gosâla accidentally came also to that village, and having heard that I was there, he approached me again and renewed his request. I granted it, and we lived together during six years on the ground of the bazaar (*paṇiya-bhûmîe*), experiencing obtainment and non-obtainment, pleasure and pain, honour and dishonour.

"Once, at the beginning of a rather dry autumn, we went together from the town Siddha-thaggâma to the town Kummagâma. On our way we came across a large sesam shrub, which was covered with leaves and flowers and in a very flourishing condition. Gosâla asked me if it would perish or not, and where would the seven living beings of the flower[3] reappear after it had vanished. I answered that the shrub would perish, and that the seven living beings would all reappear in the same pericarp of the same sesam shrub. But he would not believe it, and, saying that I must be wrong, he approached the shrub, tore it out of the ground, and threw it away. (Shortly after we had left this spot) a sudden rain

[1] A corroboration of this statement is to be found in the Âcârânga (published by Professor Jacobi in the Pâli Text Soc.), ii. 15.

[2] If we accept Mahâvîra's statement as trustworthy, we are led to suppose that the Tantavâya hall was a place opened to all comers, and not reserved for only religious mendicants.

[3] *Satta tilapuppha-jîva, i.e.*, the seven senses, each representing a particular living object or "a life."

came on, so that the ground was moistened and the sesam shrub was able to take root again; so the seven lives really reappeared all in the same pericarp of the same shrub.

"When we came to the town Kummagâma, Gosâla saw the ascetic Vesibâyaṇa, and he went to (mock) him with the question, 'Art thou believed to be a sage, or merely the abode of lice?' The ascetic did not answer, but when Gosâla had repeated his question again and again, he became angry and shot forth his magical power to kill him. But through compassion for Gosâla I interceded, and paralysed the hot flash of the ascetic's power by a cool flash of mine. When the ascetic saw that his power had remained without effect through mine, he said to me (pacified), 'I see, I see.' Gosâla, wondering what that meant, asked me about it, and learnt from me that he had been saved through my mediation. He was somewhat terrified at the account, and wished to know how he could himself acquire that magical power. I explained to him the austere discipline which it required, and he thought of undergoing it.

"When we once[1] returned to the town Siddhatthagâma, we again passed the place where the sesam shrub was, and he reminded me that I had certainly been wrong in my statement. I answered that, on the contrary, a rain which had fallen in the meantime had made true all that I had foretold of the shrub, and I added that in this way plants in general can undergo the change of a reanimation. Gosâla again would not believe it; so he turned to the plant to split open the pericarp; when he had counted the seven living beings, he at once formed the idea that in this way (not only plants) but all living beings can undergo the change of a reanimation.

"That is his doctrine of the change through reanimation, and from that time Gosâla left me. After the lapse of six months he himself acquired magical power by means of the austere discipline, and now (recently) the six Disâcarâs have intrusted themselves to his guidance; but he is wrong in believing himself to be a Jina."

The rivalry of Mahâvîra and Gosâla became known in the

[1] *I.e.*, some days afterwards, for, as will be seen farther on, the flower had developed into a fruit.

town (*i.e.*, Sâvatthî), and also Mahâvîra's statement that Gosâla was wrong. When Gosâla heard of it, he began to bear a grudge against Mahâvîra, and once when a pupil of Mahâvîra's named Ânanda passed the settlement of the Âjîvakas in Hâlâhalâ's pottery bazar, Gosâla called him in, saying that he would tell him (of) a simile. Ânanda entered, and Gosâla said to him, "Once in days of old some merchants were passing through a forest with waggons and goods. After a while they exhausted their (supply of) water, and they could find no fresh supply; at last they discovered a large fourfold ant-hill:[1] opening the first part, they obtained an abundant supply of water; from the second part they got a quantity of silver; and from the third a heap of jewels. Before they had set about opening the fourth part, in which they expected to find some ivory, one of the men who was thoughtful, recommended not opening any more, and to let the three parts be enough, for the fourth might possibly bring them some evil. The others did not follow his advice, and on opening the fourth part they met with a huge serpent of a terrifying aspect, and through the fire of its eyes all the men were at once burnt up, with the exception of the one who had given the advice, who now, through the favour of the goddess (*i.e.*, the serpent), returned home safe and provided with riches. In like manner, O Ânanda, has thy teacher, the Samaṇa Nâyaputta (*i.e.*, Mahâvîra), obtained in a threefold manner (1) merit of ascetism, (2) great fame, and (3) many adherents among men as well as gods; but if he turns to me, then I will burn him up by means of my magical power, just as those who were burnt up by the serpent; but thou shalt be saved like the man who advised (them). Tell this to thy teacher, the Samaṇa Nâyaputta." Ânanda, who had been horrified at these words, imparted them all to Mahâvîra, who dwelt outside the town near the Koṭṭhaya ceiya, and he asked him if Gosâla really possessed the faculty of burning up anybody. Mahâvîra answered him in the affirmative; "only," he said, "Gosâla could not do any harm to one of the teachers of the faith (*arahantâ bhagavanto*), because their magical power would be still mightier than his, so they could easily withstand it;

[1] *Vammîya?* (*vālmīka*).

but none of our Niggantha ascetics," he continued, "shall hereafter hold any religious conversation with Gosâla, because he has turned out a heretic."

While Ânanda was still communicating this to the other Niggantha ascetics, Gosâla came out of the town with his Âjîvikas, and approaching Mahâvîra he said, "Thou, O venerable Kâsava,[1] hast been right in calling me thy pupil; but as this thy pupil has emaciated himself through austerity, he is dead and reborn in one of the worlds of the gods.[2] After having originally been Udâî Kuṇḍiyâyaṇiya, I left (in my last change) the body of Ajjuṇa Goyamaputta and entered that of Gosâla Mankhaliputta, and I still retain this seventh body of mine. According to my doctrine, O venerable Kâsava, all those who have reached or who will reach final beatitude[3] had or will have to pass (through) the eighty-four of hundred thousands of great kalpas, seven births as a deity, seven as a bulky (insensible) being, seven as a sensible being, seven with change of body by means of reanimation; and having by this time gradually expiated the five hundred thousand actions, and the sixty thousand, and the six hundred and the three particles of actions, they will reach final beatitude.

"The river Gangâ has the following dimensions:—500 yojanas in length, a half yojana in breadth, 500 dhanu in depth.

Seven Gangâ rivers of these dimensions make a *Mahâ-Gangâ*.
Seven Mahâ-Gangâs make a *Sâdîṇa-Gangâ*.
Seven Sâdîṇa-Gangâs make a *Maḍu-Gangâ*.
Seven Maḍu-Gângâs make a *Lohiya-Gangâ*.
Seven Lohiya-Gangâs make an *Avatî-Gangâ*.
Seven Âvatî-Gangâs make a *Paramâvatî-Gangâ*.

Which gives the last one an amount of 117,649[4] Gangâ rivers, according to my doctrine. If, now, it be supposed that

[1] *Âuso Kâsavâ* (*âyuchmaḥ Kaçyapa*).

[2] The argument is very obscure, but extremely ingenious. Gosâla consents to being called Mahâvîra's pupil, because he retains now, by accident, the body of that former pupil of Mahâvîra.

[3] The text from here on is: *Caurasīti mahâkappa-sayasahassâiṃ, satta divve, satta saṃjûhe, satta saṇṇigabbhe, satta pauṭṭaparihâre, pañca kammaṇi-sayasahassâiṃ saṭṭhiṃ ca sahassâiṃ chac-ca sac tiṇṇi ya kam-m'aṃse aṇupuvvenaṃ khavaittâ tas pacchâ sijjhanti bujjhanti jâva antaṃ karenti.*

[4] *I.e.*, 7 × 7 × 7 × 7 × 7 × 7 × 7; *Gangâ-sayasahassaṃ sattavasa ya sahassa chac-ca auṇapannam Gangâ sayâ blavantiti m'akkhâyâ.* All these statements about the different Gangâs

every century one single grain of sand is removed, then the time which would be required for the disappearance of the whole amount of those Gangâs would be one *Sara(s)*; three hundred thousand of such Sara(s) periods make one *Mahâkappa* period, and 84,000 of these make one *Mahâmâṇasa*.

"(Living beings, after having passed already through endless births, are successively reborn in the following order :)—

(1) As a deity in the upper Mâṇasa.
(2) As a sensible being for the first time.
(3) As a deity in the middle Mâṇasa.
(4) As a sensible being for the second time.
(5) As a deity in the lower Mâṇasa.
(6) As a sensible being for the third time.
(7) As a deity in the upper Mâṇasuttava.
(8) As a sensible being for the fourth time.
(9) As a deity in the middle Mâṇasuttava.
(10) As a sensible being for the fifth time.
(11) As a deity in the lower Mâṇasuttava.
(12) As a sensible being for the sixth time.
(13) As a deity in the Bambhaloga.
(14) As a sensible being for the seventh time.

"In this the last birth as a sensible being, I myself left my home early in youth for religious life, and then, after having obtained universal knowledge,[1] I underwent the seven changes of body by means of reanimation.

(1) With the first change, I left outside Râjagriha, near the ceiya Maṇḍikucchi, the body of *Udâî Kuṇḍiyâyaṇa*, and entered that of *Eṇejjaga* for the space of twenty-two years.
(2) With the second change, I left outside Uddaṇḍapura, near the ceiya Candoyarayaṇa, the body of Eṇejjaga, and entered that of *Mallarâma* for the space of twenty-one years.
(3) With the third change, I left outside Campâ, near the ceiya Angamandira, the body of Mallarâma, and entered that of *Maṇḍiya* for the space of twenty years.

are merely introduced as a simile to give an approximate idea of the immensity of time implied by the terms *Sara(s)*, *Mahâkappa*, and *Mahâmâṇasa*. As to Sara(s), a similar word is used by the Jains for the same purpose, viz., to denote one of those immense periods of time which could only suggest themselves to human fancy on Indian soil. It is the term *sâgarovama*, "a sea-like" period.

[1] *Saṃkhâṇaṃ*. This term seems to have had the same value with the Âjîvikas as *Kevali-nâṇa* with the Jains.

(4) With the fourth change, I left outside Vâṇârasî, near the ceiya Kâmahâvaṇa, the body of Maṇḍiya, and entered that of *Roha* for the space of nineteen years.

(5) With the fifth change, I left outside Âlabhiyâ, near the ceiya Pannakâlaga, the body of Roha, and entered that of *Bhâraddâi* for the space of eighteen years.

(6) With the sixth change, I left outside Vesâlî, near the ceiya Kaṇḍiyâya, the body of Bhâraddâi, and entered that of *Ajjuṇaga* for the space of seventeen years.

(7) With the seventh change, I left in Sâvatthî, in Hâlâhalâ's pottery bazar the body of Ajjuṇaga, and entered that of *Gosâla Mankhaliputta* for the space of sixteen years.

"So I have fulfilled the seven changes in the course of 133 years, according to my doctrine.[1] In this respect thou hast been right in calling me thy pupil."

The story goes on to relate subsequent events, the death of Gosâla, and his punishments in a long series of subsequent births; but there is no further mention of any of his doctrines.

II.

The Doctrines of the Six Heretical Teachers according to Two Chinese Versions of the Samana-phala Sûtra.

By Bunyiu Nanjio, Esq.

No. 545. Chin. Bud. Tripit., kh. 17, f. 1 (A.D. 412–413).

The Buddha said to the king, "Have you ever asked this question to any çrâmana or brâhmana?"

The king said to the Buddha, "I have formerly been to a place where was a çrâmana or brâhmana, and have asked him a similar question. I remember having once gone to Fu-ran-ka-shio (Pûrna Kâçyapa), and hav-

No. 593. Chin. Bud. Tripit. (A.D. 381–395).

The Buddha said, "Mahârâja, have you ever asked such a question to any heretic?"

The king said to the Buddha, "I once upon a time went to the place where Fu-ran ka-shio (Pûrna Kâçyapa) was, and I asked him (about the reward of the çrâmana).

"He answered me, 'There is no such thing as this, nor (such

[1] . . . *Bhavantîti m'akkhâyâ.*

ing asked him (about the reward of the çrâmana).

"That Pûrna Kâçyapa answered me, 'If the king himself or another kills or injures beings who cry and grieve on account of it, or if he steals, or commits adultery, or lies, or robs others by entering their house' (lit. jumping over the fence of their house), 'or if he sets anything on fire, or does evil by cutting a path; to do even these things, Mahârâja, is not to do evil.

"'Mahârâja, if any one cuts all beings into pieces, and makes a heap which will fill the world, it is not an evil deed, nor is there any requital for this crime. There is no requital for the evil-doer who cuts beings to pieces on the south (bank) of the Gangâ, nor is there a reward for the righteous doer who makes a great assembly for distributing (alms), and who gives to all equally.'"

. . . Again (the king) said to the Buddha, "I once went to Matsu-ka-ri ku-sha-ri (Makkhali Gosâla) and asked him (the same question).

"He answered me, 'Mahârâja, there is no (such thing as) distributing, nor giving, nor law of sacrifice, nor good and evil, nor reward and punishment for good and evil deeds, nor present world, nor world to come, nor father, nor mother, nor dêva, nor fairy (?), nor world of beings, nor çrâmana and brâhmana who practise equally, nor this world and a world to come, for which one can show others any proof. All

a thing as) the world honoured, nor reward for righteousness and favour, nor (is there) sin and happiness, father and mother, nor Ra-kan (arhat) who has acquired the path (mârga), nor happiness in worship, nor the present world and the world to come, nor one who walks with his whole heart and mind in the path.

"'Therefore, though they (*i.e.*, beings) have body and life, yet after death the four elements are scattered about and destroyed, their heart (or soul) comes to nought, and is never born again. They are buried under the ground, they rot, and nothing is left of them.'"

. . . King A-ga-se (Ajâtasatru) said to the Buddha, "Moreover, I went to Maku-ka-ri Ku-ga-ru (Maskarin Gosâlîputra) and asked him (the same question).

"He answered me, 'There is no present world, nor world to come, nor power and powerlessness, nor energy. All men have obtained their pleasure and pain (?).'"

who say that these things are, are all liars.' "

. . . Again he said to the Buddha, "I once went to A-i-da Shi-sha-kin-ba-ra (Ajita Kesakambara), and asked him (the same question).

"He answered me, 'When a man who is composed of the four elements dies, the earth element goes back to the earth, the water to water, the fire to fire, the wind to wind. Thus all become destroyed, and all one's organs go back to nought.

"'When a man dies, and his body is put in a cemetery, where it has been carried on a bed, the bones become pigeon-coloured if the body has been burnt, or all are changed into ashes and earth.

"'Whether one be wise or foolish, when he dies, all is destroyed, because (all is subject to) the law of destruction.' "

. . . Again I went to A-i-tan (Ajita), and asked him (the same question).

He answered me, "Yes, Mahârâja." When others went to him and questioned him, he also made this reply: "There is a world to come in which we shall be born again." When I asked him, he also said, "There is a world to come." "But if there is a world to come in which we shall be born, is there a world or not according to my conception and idea? Is there a world to come or not?" If any one asks hin. (these questions) whether there is a world to come or not, (&c.), (he answers), "There is," or "There is not."

. . . Again he said to the Buddha, "I once went to Hi-fuda Ka-sen-zen (Kakuda Kâtyânana), and asked him (the same question).

"He answered me, 'Mahârâja, there is no power, no energetic man, no power, no means, no cause, no reason (for) the attachment of beings, no cause, no reason (for the) purity of beings. No power in all living beings who are unable to obtain freedom, no enemy.

"'All are fixed in certain numbers, and in these six different conditions of existence they experience either pain or pleasure.

. . . Again I went to Ha-ku Ka-sen-zen, and asked him (the same question).

He answered me, "Yes, Mahârâja, if there is a man who has received a body, there is no cause or reason (for it), nor idea, nor pride and accumulated injuries. He has obtained a dwelling-place; there he lives and stands. Therefore if he has obtained a body, he does not lose it. What is thought (by him), what he knows and thinks prevail within him, (are) called sin and virtue, good and evil. If there is a man who has been cut off, and who sees with his eyes, there is no dispute (about the question). If the life of the body comes to an end, there is nothing to grieve about in the death of life.

"Others do not speak of this desire. . . . As to these desires and supports (?), there are five theories and sixty-two different sorts or species. These sixty-two different kinds are spoken of by those who have no nature (?), as sixty-two matters or things which accompany nature, without any thought or idea. When they enter into eight difficulties they will throw them away, and being benefited thereby, they will be at ease. Being at ease, they are constantly in heaven. When they are in heaven, there are eighty-four great remembrances (or intense thoughts) which are accompanied by magical arts and miracles. Then they can remove the pain of old age and disease. There are neither men acquainted with the way nor brahmachâris. Thus do I say; my precepts are pure and free from love and desire (or the desire of love). When desire comes to an end, that state of being which always follows is as the going out of a burning lamp.

"Thus it is, and there is no brahmachâri who has found the way or path."

. . . Again he said to the Buddha, "Once upon a time I went to San-niya Bi-ra-ri's son (Sanjayin Vairattiputra), and asked him (the same question).

"He answered me, 'Mahârâja, there is a visible reward of the çramana.' I asked, '(Is it) thus?'

. . . Again I went to Sen-hi-ro-ji, and asked him (the same question).

He answered me, "Yes, Mahârâja, what a man does himself or lets another do, to cut, rob, see or not to see, to dislike what is sought after, to lament, to break

He replied, 'It is so; the truth is so; it is different (from that), it is not different, it is not not different. Mahârâja, there is no visible reward of the çramana.' I asked, '(Is it) thus?' He replied, 'It is so,' (&c., as above). 'Mahârâja, there is a visible no-reward of the çramana.' I asked, '(Is it) thus?' He replied, 'It is so,' (&c., as above). 'Mahârâja, there is, and there is not a visible reward of the çramana.' I asked, '(Is it) thus?' He replied, 'It is so,' (&c., as above).

vases, to be devoid of covetousness, to break (down) and destroy castles of the country, to injure people, to kill, to steal, to commit adultery, to lie, to be double-tongued, to drink intoxicating liquors; though one commits these deeds there is no crime nor demerit.

"One who is charitable does not receive any reward for his virtue. For one who does injury (to others), who acts unrighteously, and who commits all kinds of evil, there is neither sin nor virtue, nothing to be lost or made, no cause nor reason, no truth, no honesty.

"Even the man who practises what is right and lawful, there is nothing in it which corresponds with right or wrong."

. . . Again he said to the Buddha, "Once upon a time I went to Ni-ken's son (Nirgrantha Djnâtiputra), and asked him (the same question).

"He answered me, 'Mahârâja, I am an all-knowing and all-seeing man, I know everything that is. While walking or standing still, sitting or lying down, I am always enlightened, and my wisdom is ever manifest.'"

. . . Again I went to Ni-ken's son, and asked him the same question.

He answered me, "Yes, Mahârâja, whether it be evil or good which is here given to all sentient creatures, it is the *karma* of their former existences. They were born through the cause and by reason of love and desire. Through cause and reason (*pratityasamudpada*) are old age and disease. Then there are the ideas of cause and reason in their learning the path, in the way their children and grandchildren are born to them, and after that they obtain the path (?).

N.B.—The Chinese characters for proper names are given with their Japanese sounds.

GENERAL INDEX.

INDEX OF TIBETAN WORDS WHICH OCCUR IN THIS VOLUME, WITH THEIR SANSKRIT EQUIVALENTS.

Amrai-grong—Amrâgama.
Amra skyong-ma—Amrapâlî.

Ba-lang bdag—Gavampati.
Bal-glang ltar-gyi-grong — Hasthigâma.
Bchom-brlag—Mathura.
Bchom-ldan-hdas—Bhagavan.
Bkra-shis—Svastika.
Bla-ma—Uttara.
Bre-bo—Drona.
Bre-bo-ma—Ḋroṇâ.
Bre-bo-zas—Droṇodana.
Btang-bzung—Mutchilinda.
Btsun-po—Bhadanta.
Byang-tchub-sems-pa—Bodhisattva.
Byang-tchub-kyi-snying-po—Bodhimanda.
Bya-gag-rkang—Kukutupada.
Bu-ram shing-pa—Ikshvaku.
Bu-mang-po—Bahuputra.
Bzang-ldan—Bhadrika.
Bzang-len—Sulabha.
Bzang-po—Bhallika.
Bzod-dkah—Durdarça (?).

Çakya-hphel or spel — Çakyavardana.
Çakya-thub-pa—Çakyamuni.
Chod-pan-htching-pai-mchod-rten—Makuta bandhana tchaitya.

De-bdzin-gshegs-pa—Tathâgata.
Dbang-phyug-tchen-poi-sde — Mahesvarasena.
Dbyar-ts'ul-ma or Dbyar-byed—Varshikâ and Varshakara.
Dgah-bo—Nanda.
Dgah-mo—Nandâ.
Dgah-stobs—Nandâbâla.
Dgra-bchom-pa—Arahan or Arhan.
Dge-ba—Kalyana.
Dge-bai-snying-po—Kalyanagarbha.
Dge-hdun hphel—Sanghavardana.
Dge-hphel—Kalyanavardana.
Dge-mtchog—Varakalyana.
Dkar-mo—Çuklâ.
Dmag-brgya-ba—Çatanika.
Dmar-bu-chan—Pâṭali.
Dmar-bu-chan grong—Pâṭaligâma.
Dmar-bu-chan grong-khyer—Pâṭaliputra.
Don-ka—Karnika.
Dpe-med—Anupama.
Dpe-chan—Upâvana.
Dril-bu-sgra—Kinkinisvara.
Dri-med—Vimala.
Dum-bu—Sakala.
Dus-legs—Kâlika.
Dza-lu-kai-ts'al-mang-pa — Jalûkâ mahâvana.

Elai-mdab—Elapatra.

Ga-gon—Trapusha.
Gang-po—Purṇa.
Gdju-brtan—Dhanvadurga.
Glang-po-tche-hdul—Hastinâjaka.
Gnas-len-kyi-bu—Mâthara.
Gnas-hjug—Vasishta.
Gnod-pa-chan—Naçi or Varaṇa.
Gos-chan—Vâsavî.
Grags-pa—Yâças.
Grags-hdzin-ma—Yaçôdhâra.
Gro-dzin—Çroṇa.
Grong-khyer spyil-po-chan—Kotigâma.
Grong-khyer sgra-chan—Nâdika.
Grong-khyer rtsa-chan—Kusinârâ.
Gru-hdjin—Potala.
Gser-gyi-mdog—Kanakavarna.
Gser-od — Suvarnaprabhasa and Kanakavati (?).
Gso-sbyong-hphags—Utposhada.
Gtang-ba tchen-po—Mahâtyâga.
Gtsang-ma—Çuddhâ.

Gyo-ldan—Sâlha.
Gyung-pa—Pushkasa.

Hdod-pa-na spyod-pai lha—Kâmâvatcharas devas.
Hdun-pa—Tchandaka.
Hdzam-bui grong—Jambugâma.
Hphags skyes-po—Virudhaka.
Hts'o-byed gdzon-nus gsos—Jivaka Kumarabhanda.

Ka-tii khyu mtchog—Kaṭissabha.
Khyab-hjug gling—Vethadvipa.
Kun-dgah-bo—Ananda.
Kun-hdzin—Sarvadhâra.
Kunjikai-gnas—Gunjaka.
Kun mongs med — Asita (lit. Akleça).
Kun-tu hts'o nyer-hgro—Ajivaka.
Kus-tü grong—Kusinagara.

Lag-bzangs—Subahu.
Lag-na dbyug-chan—Daṇḍapaṇi.
Lag-rna—Karakarna.
Legs-mthong—Sudarçana.
Legs-mthong tchen-po—Mahâsudarçana.
Legs-ongs—Suratha (?).
Legs-par rab sad—Suprabuddha.
Lha-yis bstan—Devadaha.
Lhan-chig skyes—Sahadsha.
Lhar bchas—Sahadeva.
Lhas sbyin—Devadatta.
Lnga sde—Panchavarga.
Long-spyod grong—Bhoga nagara.

Ma-he ldan—Mahismati.
Ma-la gnod—Ambharisha.
Ma-pham-pa—Adjita.
Ma-hgags-pa—Aniruddha.
Ma-skyes-dgra—Adjatasatru.
Ma sdug—Appriya (?).
Mchod-rten—Tchaitya.
Mdjes-pa—Kâru and Tushti.
Mdjes-dgah-bo—Sundarânanda.
Mdjes-ldan—Kârumant.
Mdog-nag—Krichnavama.
Mig-dmar—Raktâksha.
Ming-tchen—Mahânâman.

Nag-po—Kala.
Nam-gru—Revata.
Nam-mkah-lding—Garuda.
Nga-las-nu—Mandhatar.
Nor-chan—Çonaka and Vâsabhagâmi.
Nye-ba—Nikata.
Nye-bar-hkhov—Upali.
Nye-gos-chan—Upavâsavî.
Nye-mdjes-pa—Upakâru and Santushti.
Nye-mdjes-ldan—Upakârumant.
Nyer-rgyal—Upatishya.
Nyer sbas-pa—Upagupta.
Nyi-mai-gung—Madhyanika.

Od-ma-chan-gyi grong—Beluva.
Od-mai dbyug-pa chan—Ambalatthika.
Od-mdjes—Rokha.

Padma snying-po—Pushkarasarin.
Phreng-ba chan—Mallika.
Phreng-chan—Mallikâ.

Rab-bzang—Subhadra.
Rab-dgah—Abhinanda.
Rab-snang—Pradyota.
Ras-bal chan—Karvasika.
Rangs-byed-kyi-bu lhag-spyod—Rudraka Ramaputra.
Rdo-rje phag-moi-gnas—Vadjravarahi.
Rgyal-byed—Jeta.
Rgyal-srid dgah—Râjyananda.
Rgyu-stsal shes-kyi bu ring-du hphur—Arâta Kâlâma.
Rgyun shes-kyi-bu—Atraya.
Ri-dags skyes—Mrigadjâ.
Ri-dags hdzin—Mrigadhara.
Rjo (rje ?) grong—Bhaṇḍagâma.
Rkang-gdub chan—Nûpara.
Rna-ba-chan—Karnika.
Rnam-thos-kyi-bu—Vaiçravana.
Rtag-tu smyos-pa—Asandjasattva.

Sa-ga—Visâkha.
Sa-pai-grong—Pa-vai-grong ? See Sdig-pa-chan—Pâvâ.
Sai-snying-po—Kshitigarbha.
Sa-skyong—Gopâla.
Sa-hts'o-ma—Gôpâ.
Sa-las-nu—Kusthana.
Sbas-pa—Gupta.
Sbos-kyis ngad-ldan—Gandhamadana.
Sde—Sena.
Sde-chan—Senani.
Sde-dpon—Nayaka.
Sdig-pa-chan—Pâvâ.
Seng-ge hgram—Sinhahanu.
Seng-ge sgra—Sinhanâda.

Ser-skya—Kapila.
Sgra sgrogs—Roruka.
Sgra-gchan-zin—Rahûla.
Sha-nai-gos-chan—Çânâvasika.
Sho-shum-pa—Susroni.
Skal-ldan shing-rta—Bhagirathi.
Skar-mdah gdong—Ulkâmukha.
Skar-rgyal—Tishya.
Skul-byed tchen-po—Tchunandana.
Skya-nar-gyi-bu—Pâtaliputra.
Skya-bseng-kyi-bu—Paṇḍava.
Skye-dguhi bdag tchen-mo—Mahâpradjapati gautamî.
Sna tchen-po-la-gtogs—Mahâmatra.
Snags-ldan—Kanthaka.
Sprin-bu go-tcha—Kauçika.
Spong-byed—Vriji.
Spu-tchen-po—Mahâloma.
Spyod-pai-bu ring-po or Rgyu-bai-bu ring-po—Dirghâtchârâyana.
Stogs-rings—Koshthila.
Stobs-kyi bshes-gnyen—Balamitra.

TCHAR-BYED—Udayana.
Tchu-dbus—Madhyantika.
Tchu-bo-dbyig chan—Hiranyavati.
Thams-chad grub-pa—Sarvârthasiddha.
Thams-chad hdod-pa—Sarvakâma.
Ts'ad-med-ma—Amritâ.
Ts'ad-med zas—Amritodana.

YAN-LAG skyes—Angirasas.
Yang-dag skyes—Sambhûta.
Yang-dag rgyal-ba-chan—Sanjaya.
Yid bstan-da—Sthiramati.
Yid-ong ldan—Anumana.

ZAS dkar—Çuklodana.
Zas gtsang—Çuddhodana.
Zla-sgrur—Kuyyasobhito.

THE END.